PrimeFaces Blueprints

Create your very own portfolio of customized web applications with PrimeFaces

Sudheer Jonna

Ramkumar Pillai

BIRMINGHAM - MUMBAI

PrimeFaces Blueprints

Copyright © 2014 Packt Publishing

All rights reserved. No part of this book may be reproduced, stored in a retrieval system, or transmitted in any form or by any means, without the prior written permission of the publisher, except in the case of brief quotations embedded in critical articles or reviews.

Every effort has been made in the preparation of this book to ensure the accuracy of the information presented. However, the information contained in this book is sold without warranty, either express or implied. Neither the authors, nor Packt Publishing, and its dealers and distributors will be held liable for any damages caused or alleged to be caused directly or indirectly by this book.

Packt Publishing has endeavored to provide trademark information about all of the companies and products mentioned in this book by the appropriate use of capitals. However, Packt Publishing cannot guarantee the accuracy of this information.

First published: August 2014

Production reference: 1190814

Published by Packt Publishing Ltd.
Livery Place
35 Livery Street
Birmingham B3 2PB, UK.

ISBN 978-1-78398-322-3

www.packtpub.com

Cover image by Benoit Benedetti (benoit.benedetti@gmail.com)

Credits

Authors
Sudheer Jonna
Ramkumar Pillai

Reviewers
Ramanath Chandramohan Bhongale
Aristides Villarreal Bravo
Vineet Jain
S V Narayana
Enrique Enolva Tan

Commissioning Editor
Akram Hussain

Acquisition Editor
Richard Harvey

Content Development Editor
Sankalp Pawar

Technical Editor
Tanvi Bhatt

Copy Editors
Dipti Kapadia
Gladson Monteiro
Insiya Morbiwala
Aditya Nair
Alfida Paiva

Project Coordinator
Harshal Ved

Proofreaders
Simran Bhogal
Maria Gould
Ameesha Green
Paul Hindle

Indexers
Mariammal Chettiyar
Rekha Nair
Tejal Soni

Graphics
Valentina D'silva

Production Coordinator
Adonia Jones

Cover Work
Adonia Jones

About the Authors

Sudheer Jonna was born in Andhra Pradesh, India, in 1987. Currently, he works as a senior software engineer in Chennai, India. He completed his Master's degree in Computer Applications from JNTU. In the past 3-4 years, he has worked on providing architectural designs and building various web applications based on Struts, JSF, Spring, jQuery, and JPA.

He is a JSF and PrimeFaces expert. He has been working with the PrimeFaces component library since 2011. He is a committer / project member of PrimeFaces and PrimeFaces Extensions open source projects. He has been a well-known, recognized member of the PrimeFaces community for the past few years. He is also the author of *Learning PrimeFaces Extensions Development*, *Packt Publishing*.

Besides working with the mentioned technologies, he also writes technical articles, provides online training, designs and develops web application architecture, writes books and reviews, and provides suggestions through online forums and blogs. He is interested in the research and development of various popular Java EE frameworks and many other latest technologies.

He shares his knowledge through GitHub (`https://github.com/sudheerj`); you can also follow him on Twitter (`@SudheerJonna`) or contact him on Gmail at `sudheer.jonna@gmail.com`.

> I would like to thank my friend, Çağatay Çivici, the book reviewers, and the team at Packt Publishing for their support and great teamwork for the past few years.
>
> Also, a very big thanks to my parents, brother, sister, colleagues, roommates, and friends for their support in helping me complete this book very quickly.

Ramkumar Pillai is the leading authority on latest global technical trends and a proficient technical architect of the Java J2EE technology. He has been employed by major software companies across the globe, and he currently works as a senior consultant in advanced web technology.

He can be described as a smart professional with significant IT experience in technical architecture and project management on leading Java technology stacks. He has received acclaim for his contributions to PrimeFaces, Grails and Groovy, and Play Frameworks all through his career in the form of deliverables, documentation, or presentations. He was also a co-speaker at the conference on the latest trends in the web technology stack at Dallas, Texas, in September 2012.

When he is not working, he creates web designs and illustrations for retail marketing portals and blogs about almost anything, be it Big Data or his favorite Bonsai culture.

He has also been a lead consultant for companies such as Triadic Technologies and Smarterscart. He is the kind of person who believes "good is the enemy of great", and he is currently working on a few research and development projects that are not related to his favorite subject, Java.

> I would like to thank all who have supported me with the production of this book, and also Packt Publishing for providing me with this opportunity.

About the Reviewers

Ramanath Chandramohan Bhongale completed his engineering degree in Information Science from KVGCE Sullia (affiliated to VTU) in 2005 and is currently working at KPIT Technologies Ltd. as a technical lead on Java, J2EE, and various development projects. He is passionate about sharing knowledge by conducting corporate seminars and writing technical blogs. His major work experience is in creating and managing automated systems for workflow and testing, developing, and deploying flows.

> I would like to express my special gratitude to my wife, Raksha, who gave me the support that I needed in carrying out this assignment. Additionally, I would like to thank my friend, Pankaj Patel, who helped me in re-reviewing difficult sections. Finally, I would like to thank the team at Packt Publishing who gave me an opportunity to contribute to the successful publication of this book.

Aristides Villarreal Bravo is a Java developer, a member of the NetBeans Dream Team, and the leader of a Java User Group. He is also the CEO of Javscaz Software Developers.

Aristides has organized and participated in various conferences and seminars related to Java, Java EE, the NetBeans platform, free software, and mobile devices, both nationally and internationally. He writes tutorials and blogs about Java, NetBeans, and web development too.

He has given several interviews on sites such as NetBeans, NetBeans Dzone, and javaHispano and developed various plugins for NetBeans. He specializes in JSE, JEE, JPA, Agile, and Continuous Integration.

You can visit him at `http://avbravo.blogspot.com`.

> I would like to thank my grandfather for his lighting over time.

Vineet Jain is currently working as a project lead in a leading software company. He has a total of over 6 years of experience, during which time he has worked for a number of projects in Java and other technologies. He has a rich experience in building applications using PrimeFaces and PrimeFaces extensions.

S V Narayana was born in Andhra Pradesh, India, in 1981. Currently, he is working as a project lead in Chennai, India. He has completed his professional degree (BTech) in Electrical and Electronic Engineering from S.V. University (NBKRIST, Vidyanagar, Nellore, Andhra Pradesh). For the past eight years (since 2006), he has been architecting, designing, and developing software professionally and has been using Java as his primary programming language. He is a Java, Java EE, and PrimeFaces expert. He has been working with the healthcare and BFS domains.

You can contact him at `svnari@gmail.com`.

Enrique Enolva Tan currently works as senior Java web developer at STM Philippines, a division of Duke Manufacturing based in St. Louis, Missouri, United States, with more than 7 years of experience in Java EE and related frameworks, and 16 years of overall experience in both IT infrastructure and application development engineering.

He has developed and deployed various types of application websites, which range from retail and fast food to online gaming casinos. He has also held several managerial positions in information technology in the online gaming casino industry.

He aspires to be a successful technopreneur — he is working on several concepts for patents in Mobile Name System (MNS), Mobile Certificate Authority (MCA), and Subscriber Identity Module Search and Trust Platform (SIM-STP).

He devotes his free time to develop his own website (`www.hanapsim.com`) for SIM Search and Trust Platform using the Java, JSF, and PrimeFaces technologies.

> I would like to thank Rechil Lentejas Artizo and my kids, Aerozekiel, Aerikezedek, and Aerika Faith for bearing with me even though I sacrificed some of our family time to review this book.

www.PacktPub.com

Support files, eBooks, discount offers, and more

You might want to visit www.PacktPub.com for support files and downloads related to your book.

Did you know that Packt offers eBook versions of every book published, with PDF and ePub files available? You can upgrade to the eBook version at www.PacktPub.com and as a print book customer, you are entitled to a discount on the eBook copy. Get in touch with us at service@packtpub.com for more details.

At www.PacktPub.com, you can also read a collection of free technical articles, sign up for a range of free newsletters and receive exclusive discounts and offers on Packt books and eBooks.

http://PacktLib.PacktPub.com

Do you need instant solutions to your IT questions? PacktLib is Packt's online digital book library. Here, you can access, read and search across Packt's entire library of books.

Why subscribe?

- Fully searchable across every book published by Packt
- Copy and paste, print and bookmark content
- On demand and accessible via web browser

Free access for Packt account holders

If you have an account with Packt at www.PacktPub.com, you can use this to access PacktLib today and view nine entirely free books. Simply use your login credentials for immediate access.

Table of Contents

Preface	**1**
Chapter 1: Creating a "Hello World" Application	**7**
An introduction to JavaServer Faces and PrimeFaces	8
Setting up and configuring PrimeFaces	9
Setting up and configuring using Maven	9
Setting up and configuring for non-Maven (or Ant) users	11
Application-level configuration	11
Checking the JSF runtime compatibility	13
Developing your first PrimeFaces application	14
Change the old trend of development with Ajaxified components	15
Learning Partial Processing	15
Partial Page Rendering	17
Partial submit	17
PrimeFaces polling	18
PrimeFaces code completion, NetBeans bundles PrimeFaces, and the code generation tool	18
Eclipse code completion	19
NetBeans code completion	21
NetBeans bundles PrimeFaces	21
The code generation tool	22
Generating a CRUD application	23
Adding entities and generating PrimeFaces pages	23
Summary	27
Chapter 2: Creating an Employee Registration Application	**29**
Introduction to the employee registration project	30
The employee registration application	30
Application use cases	30
The UML use case diagram	31

The architectural design	31
Creating a project and implementing the application screens	**32**
The project structure	33
Understanding the application template design	34
Implementing the application screens using the form components	34
Creating the login screen using the input components	35
Exploring the employee registration form	40
The Client Side Validation framework in form validations	44
Exploring the change password functionality	53
Tracking the list of job posts	55
Managing the application through an admin role	56
Working with the employee registration project code	57
Summary	**57**
Chapter 3: Creating a Simple Restaurant Point of Sale Application	**59**
A quick start	**59**
Application use cases	**60**
The architectural design	**60**
The application architecture diagram	61
The entity diagram	62
Implementing the application	**62**
Template tags	63
The UI composition tag	63
The layout component	66
The grouping components	70
Supporting tags in the login screen	73
The dataGrid component	74
The dataTable component and its usage	76
The accordion component and its usage	77
Integrating the restaurant's menu card model	78
Updating the component on a click	79
Working with sample code	85
Summary	**85**
Chapter 4: Global Mutual Funds Tracking	**87**
An introduction to the global mutual funds tracking project	**88**
The global mutual funds tracking application	88
Application use cases	88
Sketching the UML use case diagram	89
The architectural design	89
Creating a project and implementing the application screens	**91**
The project structure	91
Understanding the application template design	92
Database configurations	92

Implementing the application screens using data iteration components	93
Implementing the login screen	93
Login credentials	97
Exploring the mutual funds screens	98
Working with the project code of the global mutual funds tracking application	**119**
Summary	**119**
Chapter 5: Investor Information Analysis and Reporting	**121**
Understanding the investor information analysis and reporting project	122
About the application	122
Application use cases	123
The UML use case diagram	124
The architectural design	124
Creating the project and implementing the application screens	**126**
The project structure	126
The application template design	127
Database configurations	127
Implementing application screens using analysis and reporting components	128
Implementing the login screen	128
The login credentials	131
Exploring the summary tables	131
Implementing the export functionality in summary screens	143
Implementing the charts functionality in summary screens	153
Working with investor information analysis and reporting the application project code	**163**
Summary	**163**
Chapter 6: Creating a Simple Online Shopping Cart Application	**165**
Understanding the application	**165**
The application use case	166
Functional requirements	166
The architecture	167
The ER diagram	168
The implementation	**168**
The persistence layer	169
The administration / back office module	171
The menubar component	173
Store management	173
The category page	175
The flow diagram	176
The storefront	177
Implementing the cart mechanism	177
Code walk-through	182

Working with the sample code	183
Summary	**183**
Chapter 7: Creating an Online Video Portal Application	**185**
A quick overview	185
Understanding our requirements	186
The system architecture	187
Implementations	187
The ER diagram	188
Working on the application persistence layer	189
Possible errors in hibernate DML	189
Working on the presentation layer	190
The home page	190
Enabling registration and login	193
The user dashboard page	197
Scheduling the application components	199
Implementing the location page	202
Integration	202
Working with the sample code	206
Summary	**206**
Chapter 8: Creating an Online Printing Station Application	**207**
Understanding the need of this application	207
Requirement analysis	208
Functional requirements	208
The architecture	209
Fulfilling our application requirements using PrimeFaces	209
The ER diagram	209
Implementing our landing page	210
The TagCloud component	211
The scrollPanel component	213
The chart component	214
The contentFlow component	215
Supporting components	216
The login page	216
The registration page	218
The user dashboard page	220
Placing the print job order	223
The slider component	224
Code walk-through	225
The fileUpload component	226
The file download component	229
Working with the sample code	230
Summary	**230**

Chapter 9: Creating an Online Chat Application — 231

- The application use case — 232
- Requirement analysis — 232
  - A flow diagram — 232
- The architecture — 233
- Implementing the requirements — 233
  - The ER diagram — 233
  - Implementing, deploying, and running the application — 234
    - The editor component — 235
    - The selectOneButton component — 235
    - The password component — 236
    - Code walk-through – the landing page before login — 236
    - The landing page after login — 239
    - Supporting components — 241
    - The User Profile page — 242
  - The Push technology — 243
    - Implementing the chat module using PrimePush — 244
  - Working with the sample code — 249
- Summary — 250

Chapter 10: Creating a Healthcare Products Application — 251

- Introducing our healthcare products application — 252
  - Application use cases — 252
    - The UML use case diagram — 252
  - The architectural design — 253
- Creating a project and implementing the application screens — 254
  - Laying out our application structure — 255
  - Designing the application template — 255
  - Database configurations — 256
  - Implementing application screens using data hierarchy, data display, and utility components — 256
    - Implementing the login screen — 256
    - Login credentials — 258
    - Implementing the HealthKart screen — 259
    - Implementing the admin screen — 262
    - Implementing the view-expired message using idleMonitor — 265
- Applying themes in your PrimeFaces applications — 266
  - Applying existing themes — 266
  - Creating a new theme from scratch — 267
    - Font settings — 268
    - Corners — 269
    - Header/Toolbar — 270
    - Content — 271
    - Clickable states – default, hover, and active state — 272
    - Cues – highlight and error — 273

Overlays and shadows	274
Theme Converters	**277**
PrimeFaces Theme Converter	277
ThemeRoller to PrimeFaces Themes Converter	278
Changing themes on the fly using ThemeSwitcher	280
Working with the project code of the healthcare products application	**280**
Summary	**281**
Index	**283**

Preface

PrimeFaces is a leading lightweight open source user interface component library for JSF-based web applications. It provides a rich set of 100+ UI components with a single JAR, zero configuration, and no prerequisites. PrimeFaces aims to create built-in Ajax components that are based on standard JSF 2.0 Ajax APIs with a rich look and feel, with the help of a theming mechanism.

The initial development of PrimeFaces was started in 2008 by a Turkish JSF expert, Çağatay Çivici. Prior to developing PrimeFaces, he had been working on the YUI4JSF library. This experience of working with the YUI4JSF library allowed him to start developing PrimeFaces, which was initially based on the YUI JavaScript library. A few days later, the PrimeFaces team decided to replace this library with the powerful jQuery framework in order to create the component widgets.

This book will guide you through the process of creating a wide range of rich UI web applications based on successful, real-world business models. Each chapter comes with a custom web project, which you can build with a detailed, step-by-step procedure. This is accompanied by explanations of the key features used. By the end of each chapter, you will learn how to build specific, customized web applications using the PrimeFaces components. The projects inside this book make use of the latest versions of PrimeFaces (Version 5.0) and JSF (Version 2.2).

What this book covers

Chapter 1, Creating a "Hello World" Application, discusses how to create a simple "Hello World" PrimeFaces application in a step-by-step procedure and how to create the recommended PrimeFaces - supported environment (required software, browsers, IDE, tools, and so forth) that is required for real-world application development. A brief introduction to PrimeFaces and its role in UI applications will also be covered at the beginning of the chapter.

Chapter 2, Creating an Employee Registration Application, shows you how to create an employee registration application, which is an example of how to form components and their validations. The big set of PrimeFaces form components will be divided into two main categories, which are input components and select components, to create the registration type of the form filling application. These components and their validations that are used will also be explained in detail.

Chapter 3, Creating a Simple Restaurant Point of Sale Application, explains how to create a restaurant POS application with the help of the PrimeFaces layout and grouping components. These topics provide the templating mechanism needed for a fancy application, and each concept will be explained in detail.

Chapter 4, Global Mutual Funds Tracking, directs you on how to create a global mutual funds tracking application with the help of a data container and dialog components. This project emphasizes the usage of the data container and dialog components in order to maintain the big datasets in investment/financial schemes. The master-client and hierarchical data relationships (which are linked to these components) will also be well explained.

Chapter 5, Investor Information Analysis and Reporting, shows you how to create an investor information analysis application, which is useful because it is an example of data visualization and reporting components. Big datasets for reporting data will be analyzed in the form of charts and various formats of export features. The data visualization and reporting components used within this application will also be explained.

Chapter 6, Creating a Simple Online Shopping Cart Application, shows you how to create an online shopping cart application using the major menu variations and drag-and-drop components in PrimeFaces. This shopping cart application can be used to cover various products, such as electrical goods or household products.

Chapter 7, Creating an Online Video Portal Application, directs you on how to create an online movie portal application, which makes use of PrimeFaces multimedia, maps, and schedule components. This application can be used in the entertainment world and to book events that vary seasonally, such as special events in the summer or winter. Customers can pick the events that interest them and book them accordingly.

Chapter 8, Creating an Online Printing Station Application, guides you through how to build an online printing station application. This application handles all types of files using the PrimeFaces file upload and download components. This application will showcase a new concept that provides a platform to track, submit, and process printing jobs from multiple users across different locations.

Chapter 9, *Creating an Online Chat Application*, shows you how to create an online chat room application using the PrimePUSH. The PrimePUSH API deals with the asynchronous communication between the server and client using this chat room application. This chapter uses the simple social network application as our sample project.

Chapter 10, *Creating a Healthcare Products Application*, shows you how to create an online healthcare products application using common utility components and theming concepts (such as using built-in themes, customizing these, and creating new ones).

What you need for this book

As a reader of this book, you will need Java 5 or above and Maven installed on your machine, along with the JSF and PrimeFaces libraries. Optionally, you can use software and tools such as the Eclipse IDE, MySQL DB, and any browser tools to debug the application. You should also have a basic knowledge of JSF, PrimeFaces, and jQuery.

In order to run the customized web projects in this book, you need to store them on GitHub. This means that you can pull the source code at any time in order to have an efficient practical experience.

The software libraries or tools used in all of the customized projects of this book are listed as follows:

- JDK 1.5+ from Oracle's official site. You can download this at http://www.oracle.com/technetwork/java/javase/downloads/index.html.
- The Mojarra Java Server Faces implementation's latest version. This can be downloaded at https://javaserverfaces.java.net/download.html.
- The latest version of PrimeFaces from the PrimeFaces official site, which can be downloaded at http://www.PrimeFaces.org/downloads.html.
- The latest version of PrimeFaces Extensions, which can be downloaded at http://PrimeFaces-extensions.github.io/.
- MySQL from its official site (http://www.mysql.com/), or any other relational database based on the JDBC driver.
- Eclipse from the official site (http://www.eclipse.org), or any other Java IDE.
- The Apache Maven build tool from the official site (http://maven.apache.org/) to work with customized projects.

Preface

- PrimeFaces components result in a rich UI application with lots of CSS, JS, and HTML markup resources; it would be very helpful to use browser tools such as the Firebug plugin for Firefox, FirebugLite for the Chrome browser, Developer Tools (*F12*) for Internet Explorer, and Developers Tools (which you can access using *Ctrl + Shift + I*) for the Chrome browser.
- To work with the Blueprint projects, you need to check out the source code using a Git client or using IDE Git repositories. The step-by-step instructions to run the customized web projects are covered in GitHub (https://github.com/sudheerj/PrimeFaces-blueprints).

Who this book is for

This book is for anyone who wants to learn how to create customized PrimeFaces web applications. If you want to create a different set of categories for customized applications using PrimeFaces components, then this book is for you.

Conventions

In this book, you will find a number of styles of text that distinguish between different kinds of information. Here are some examples of these styles, and an explanation of their meaning.

Code words in text, database table names, folder names, filenames, file extensions, pathnames, dummy URLs, user input, and Twitter handles are shown as follows: "These managed beans interact between XHTML/Facelets and the POJO class with the @ManagedBean annotation."

A block of code is set as follows:

```
<div id="header">
<ui:insert name="header">
  <ui:includesrc="/templates/common/header.xhtml" />
</ui:insert>
</div>
```

Any command-line input or output is written as follows:

```
mvn clean package
```

New terms and **important words** are shown in bold. Words that you see on the screen, in menus or dialog boxes for example, appear in the text like this: "Select the PrimeFaces component suite from the **Components** tab."

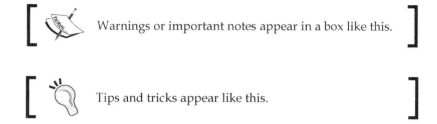

Warnings or important notes appear in a box like this.

Tips and tricks appear like this.

Reader feedback

Feedback from our readers is always welcome. Let us know what you think about this book—what you liked or may have disliked. Reader feedback is important for us to develop titles that you really get the most out of.

To send us general feedback, simply send an e-mail to feedback@packtpub.com, and mention the book title through the subject of your message.

If there is a book that you need and would like to see us publish, please send us a note in the **SUGGEST A TITLE** form on www.packtpub.com or e-mail suggest@packtpub.com.

If there is a topic that you have expertise in and you are interested in either writing or contributing to a book, see our author guide on www.packtpub.com/authors.

Customer support

Now that you are the proud owner of a Packt book, we have a number of things to help you to get the most from your purchase.

Downloading the example code

You can download the example code files for all Packt books you have purchased from your account at http://www.packtpub.com. If you purchased this book elsewhere, you can visit http://www.packtpub.com/support and register to have the files e-mailed directly to you.

Errata

Although we have taken every care to ensure the accuracy of our content, mistakes do happen. If you find a mistake in one of our books—maybe a mistake in the text or the code—we would be grateful if you would report this to us. By doing so, you can save other readers from frustration and help us improve subsequent versions of this book. If you find any errata, please report them by visiting http://www.packtpub.com/support, selecting your book, clicking on the **errata submission form** link, and entering the details of your errata. Once your errata are verified, your submission will be accepted and the errata will be uploaded to our website, or added to any list of existing errata, under the Errata section of that title.

Piracy

Piracy of copyright material on the Internet is an ongoing problem across all media. At Packt, we take the protection of our copyright and licenses very seriously. If you come across any illegal copies of our works, in any form, on the Internet, please provide us with the location address or website name immediately so that we can pursue a remedy.

Please contact us at copyright@packtpub.com with a link to the suspected pirated material.

We appreciate your help in protecting our authors, and our ability to bring you valuable content.

Questions

You can contact us at questions@packtpub.com if you are having a problem with any aspect of the book, and we will do our best to address it.

1
Creating a "Hello World" Application

This chapter will show you how to create your own "Hello World" application in order to give you a head start with the application development for PrimeFaces. This chapter will provide you with a brief introduction to its features and its role in web applications, with a step-by-step setup and configuration. Most importantly, it will give you an insight into how Ajaxified components change the old development trend. We will also learn how to make application development easier with code completion, IDE support, and the code generator tool used for creating the **CRUD** web application. The specific topics that will be covered in this chapter are as follows:

- An introduction to **PrimeFaces**, its features, and its role in customized application development
- PrimeFaces setup and configuration for development
- How to quickly develop a project: a "Hello World" application, in this case
- How to change the old trend of development using Ajaxified components
- How to use code completion, NetBeans bundles PrimeFaces, and the code generator tool

An introduction to JavaServer Faces and PrimeFaces

JavaServer Faces (JSF) is a component-based MVC framework used for building rich **User Interface (UI)** Java web applications. JSF is a powerful framework with a six-phase lifecycle, and it will automate the common web application tasks such as decoding the user input, processing the input validations and conversions, and rendering or updating the output in the form of generated HTML. Page authors can easily build a customized UI by just dragging-and-dropping the reusable components on the page that provide a rich look and feel to modern UI applications. JSF has built-in support for input conversions and validations, and Ajax support for the components.

Going by the growing popularity of JSF technology, many open source and proprietary UI component frameworks were created to have user interfaces with a fancier look and feel. These component suites were created by introducing their own new components and extending the standard JSF components with additional features. Among all these component suites, PrimeFaces is the best and most popular component suite considering its features, quick releases with more new components and bug fixes, ease of development, extensive documentation, and support from its community.

PrimeFaces is a leading, lightweight, open source user interface component library for JSF-based web applications. In the JSF world, it is miles ahead of the other existing component sets because of the many features it has at its disposal:

- Over 100 sets of components
- Built-in Ajax-supported components
- Ease of development, as there are no configurations required
- A single jar install without the need for any mandatory third-party libraries
- More than 30 predefined themes and custom themes by using the ThemeRoller support
- Multibrowser support

It is so well designed that it is important to consider its importance when developing web applications. Page authors and application developers can easily develop web pages by simply dragging-and-dropping the components of the webpage and then adding the required features in a step-by-step fashion: customizing the CSS style classes, extending the component widgets, and rendering according to the custom requirements.

Setting up and configuring PrimeFaces

PrimeFaces is a lightweight single library with minimal external libraries. The only external libraries required are those with component-specific features. Apart from these component-specific features, projects only require JSF runtime implementations such as **Oracle Mojarra** or **Apache MyFaces**.

The setup and configuration for Maven and non-Maven users is explained in the following two sections.

Setting up and configuring using Maven

In this section, we will define the various Maven configuration steps required to run a PrimeFaces-based application. Perform the following steps:

1. Configure the PrimeFaces library dependency or Maven coordinates in your project `pom.xml` file as shown here:

   ```
   <dependency>
           <groupId>org.primefaces</groupId>
           <artifactId>primefaces</artifactId>
           <version>5.0</version>
   </dependency>
   ```

2. Add the PrimeFaces repository to the repositories list of your project `pom.xml` file as follows:

   ```
   <repository>
           <id>prime-repo</id>
           <name>Prime Repo</name>
           <url>http://repository.primefaces.org</url>
   </repository>
   ```

    Note that this step is not required for releases after PrimeFaces 4.0. The team started adding its library in the Maven central repository.

3. Configure either of the JSF runtime implementations, Oracle Mojarra or Apache MyFaces. Choose either of the following two blocks of code:

   - This is the runtime implementation for Oracle Mojarra:

   ```
   <dependency>
       <groupId>com.sun.faces</groupId>
       <artifactId>jsf-impl</artifactId>
       <version>2.2.6</version>6
   </dependency>
   ```

○ This is the runtime implementation for Apache MyFaces:

```
<dependency>
    <groupId>org.apache.myfaces.core</groupId>
    <artifactId>myfaces-impl</artifactId>
    <version>2.2</version>
</dependency>
```

> **Downloading the example code**
> You can download the example code files for all Packt books you have purchased from your account at http://www.packtpub.com. If you purchased this book elsewhere, you can visit http://www.packtpub.com/support and register to have the files e-mailed directly to you.

Depending on the component-specific features, you can use the following mandatory and optional dependencies. Here is a list of dependencies categorized into mandatory and optional. The following are the mandatory dependencies:

Dependencies	Version	Description
JSF runtime	2.0, 2.1, and 2.2	Oracle's Mojarra or Apache MyFaces implementation
PrimeFaces	5.0	The PrimeFaces UI component library

The following are the optional dependencies:

Dependencies	Version	Description
iText	2.7	To use the DataExporter component for PDF format
POI	3.7	To use the DataExporter component for Excel format
Rome	1.0	To use the Feed reader component
commons-fileupload	1.3	To use the fileupload component (when web server / application server doesn't support servlet 3.0)
commons-io	2.2	To use the fileupload component

Setting up and configuring for non-Maven (or Ant) users

In this section, we will define the various non-Maven (or Ant) configurations required to run a PrimeFaces-based application. Perform the following steps:

1. Download the PrimeFaces library from the official download section of PrimeFaces at http://www.primefaces.org/downloads.html.
2. Following this, add the PrimeFaces JAR library to the classpath.
3. You should then download either the JSF library runtimes from Oracle's Mojarra or those from Apache MyFaces from their official sites and add them to the classpath. You can access the JSF library at Oracle by going to https://javaserverfaces.java.net/2.2/download.html or alternatively access it at Apache by going to http://myfaces.apache.org/download.html.
4. After this, you should download the component-specific third-party libraries from their official site and add them to the classpath.

Application-level configuration

As you know, PrimeFaces is a JSF-based component suite. Therefore, the first thing you have to do is configure the JSF Faces Servlet in your project deployment descriptor file (web.xml). The following is a mandatory configuration for any JSF-based application:

```
<servlet>
  <servlet-name>Faces Servlet</servlet-name>
  <servlet-class>javax.faces.webapp.FacesServlet
  </servlet-class>
  <load-on-startup>1</load-on-startup>
</servlet>
<servlet-mapping>
  <servlet-name>Faces Servlet</servlet-name>
  <url-pattern>/faces/*</url-pattern>
</servlet-mapping>
<servlet-mapping>
  <servlet-name>Faces Servlet</servlet-name>
  <url-pattern>*.jsf</url-pattern>
</servlet-mapping>
```

```xml
<servlet-mapping>
  <servlet-name>Faces Servlet</servlet-name>
  <url-pattern>*.faces</url-pattern>
</servlet-mapping>
<servlet-mapping>
  <servlet-name>Faces Servlet</servlet-name>
  <url-pattern>*.xhtml</url-pattern>
</servlet-mapping>
```

It is not mandatory to use all of the JSF extensions or servlet mappings. Any of the preceding servlet mappings is enough to configure Faces Servlet to your project.

There are other configurations that can be made to your project. These are shown in the following table:

Context parameter name	Default value	Description
THEME	Aristo	Used to apply a specific theme to your application. All theme names are valid values.
SUBMIT	Full	Enables the Ajax submit mode. The valid values are `full` and `partial`.
DIR	Ltr	Defines the component content orientation. The valid values are `ltr` and `rtl`.
RESET_VALUES	False	When this is enabled, any Ajax-updated inputs are reset first. The valid values are `true` and `false`.
SECRET	PrimeFaces	Defines the secret key to encrypt-decrypt the value of the expressions that are exposed in rendering `StreamedContents`.
CLIENT_SIDE_VALIDATION	False	Controls client-side validations to the form components.
UPLOADER	Auto	Defines the `fileuploader` mode. The valid values are `auto`, `native`, and `commons`.

As an example, the following code snippet configures a theme with `context-param`:

```
<context-param>
        <param-name>primefaces.THEME</param-name>
        <param-value>delta</param-value>
</context-param>
```

Checking the JSF runtime compatibility

PrimeFaces 5.0 supports all the JSF runtime versions: 2.0, 2.1, and 2.2 at the same time using feature detection without having to compile a dependency to any specific version. In other words, some of the features that are available are based on the runtime version used. The newly released JSF 2.2 version supports more popular HTML5.

The runtime detection policy for PrimeFaces is quite useful for the newly added features in JSF library. The **JSF 2.2** `passthrough` attribute's feature is a good example of the runtime detection policy. That is, the passthrough attribute only gets rendered if the runtime is JSF 2.2.

An introduction to the `autofocus` and `pattern` HTML5 attributes' integration with PrimeFaces can be seen in the following example:

```
<!DOCTYPE html>
<html xmlns="http://www.w3c.org/1999/xhtml"
xmlns:h="http://java.sun.com/jsf/html"
xmlns:p="http://primefaces.org/ui"
xmlns:pt="http://xmlns.jcp.org/jsf/passthrough">
    <h:head>
    </h:head>
      <h:body>
        <h:form>
           <p:inputText value="#{bean.value}" pt:autofocus="autofocus"
             pt:pattern= "[A-Za-z]"/>
        </h:form>
      </h:body>
</html>
```

Developing your first PrimeFaces application

In the previous section, you have learned how to set up and configure PrimeFaces for JSF-based web applications. To start using its components in your web project, you have to add the following namespace at the top of the namespace section:

```
xmlns:p="http://primefaces.org/ui"
```

Once you have successfully completed the setup and configuration for PrimeFaces, you will be shown how to develop a simple "Hello World" application by simply following these steps:

1. The first step is to create a simple `helloworld.xhtml` page. This will display the "Hello World" message from the PrimeFaces Panel component. You will be able to display this message using the following section of code:

   ```
   <!DOCTYPE html>
   <html xmlns="http://www.w3.org/1999/xhtml"
     xmlns:h="http://java.sun.com/jsf/html"
     xmlns:f="http://java.sun.com/jsf/core"
     xmlns:p="http://primefaces.org/ui">
   <f:view contentType="text/html" >
     <h:head>
       <title>Primefaces Hello World page</title>
     </h:head>
     <h:body>
       <h:form>
           <p:panel  header="Hello" footer="Blueprints world"
             style="width:300px;margin-left:40%;margin-top:15%">
             Welcome to Primefaces
           </p:panel>
       </h:form>
     </h:body>
   </f:view>
   </html>
   ```

2. Following this, package the application somewhere in the target directory (by default) and then run the application with the help of the following Maven commands:

   ```
   mvn clean package
   ```
   ```
   mvn jetty:run
   ```
   or:
   ```
   mvn tomcat:run
   ```

3. After this, go to the browser address bar and access the "Hello World" application by navigating to http://localhost:8080/chapter01/views/helloworld.jsf.

4. You should now be able to see the **Hello World** message with the help of the panel component in the web page. This can be seen in the following screenshot:

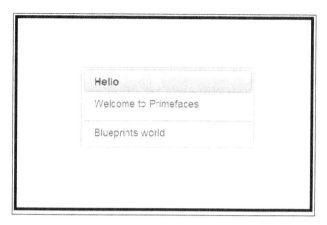

Change the old trend of development with Ajaxified components

One of the design goals of the PrimeFaces component suite is to simplify the web development by using Ajaxified components. The Partial Processing and Partial Page Rendering features play a major role in creating a powerful AJAX framework.

Learning Partial Processing

PrimeFaces provides the **Partial Processing** feature in order to execute the JSF lifecycle phases required for the specified components with the help of a process attribute. Here, you can only process the required components instead of the entire web page, which are called *lightweight* requests. This occurs quite commonly, such as when creating the PrimeFaces web pages. This is done with the help of registration form fields, which include a certain group of validation results that validate the different components depending on the executed action. However, you can avoid unnecessary validations for other components and prevent validation errors on the submission of the form. The process attribute is not only used to process the specific components but also to process the specific regions with the help of the @this, @form, @parent, @none, and @all expressions. You can also combine the components with these simple expressions at the same time using a comma separator (,).

Creating a "Hello World" Application

The most common scenario is the dependent drop-down input values along with the other required components of the same page. This feature can be explained with an example.

In the case of submitting the order details, you can see one or more dependent relationships. In this example, a list of products depends on the selected category and the list of orders depends on the selected product. Firstly, you have to select the category and then based on this category, select the product. After choosing the product, you then select one order from the list of populated orders. You should also assume that this registration form contains other required form fields such as a `calendar` and the `inputText` components. The preceding use case scenario is represented in the following code snippet:

```
<h:outputText value="Category: " />
<p:selectOneMenu id="categories" value="#{ppController.category}">
<f:selectItems value="#{ppController.categories}" />
<p:ajax listener="#{ppController.updateProducts}" event="change"
  update="products" process="@this"/>
</p:selectOneMenu>

<h:outputText value="Product: " />
<p:selectOneMenu id="products" value="#{ppController.product}">
<f:selectItems value="#{ppController.products}" />
<p:ajax listener="#{ppController.updateOrders}" event="change"
  update="orders" process="@this"/>
</p:selectOneMenu>

<h:outputText value="Order: " />
<p:selectOneMenu id="orders" value="#{ppController.order}">
<f:selectItems value="#{ppController.orders}" />
</p:selectOneMenu>

<h:outputText value="Number of Orders: " />
<p:inputText value="#{ppController.ordersCount}" id="ordercount" />
  required="true" />

<h:outputText value="Date of Order: " />
<p:calendar value="#{ppController.selectdate}" id="selectdate" />
  required="true" />
```

You can clearly see that without using the Partial Processing feature, validation errors might occur on the number of orders of the input field and the date of the order calendar components.

Partial Page Rendering

PrimeFaces provides the **Partial Page Rendering** (PPR) feature to update certain specified components instead of the whole page with the help of the `update` attribute. You will be able to see the updated output without refreshing the page. The update attribute accepts both components and simple expressions such as `@this`, `@form`, `@parent`, `@none`, and `@all`. As before, you can use the comma-separated list of components and expressions at the same time to update the value.

The following code updates the welcome message from one container to another container:

```
<h:form id="loginform">
    <h:outputText value="Enter username"/>
    <p:inputText value="#{pprController.username}"
      action="#{pprController.updateOutput}" value="Update" >
    <p:ajax event="change" update=":welcomeform:message"  />
    </p:inputText>
</h:form>
<h:form id="welcomeform">
    <h:outputText id="message" value="#{pprController.message}"/>
</h:form>
public String updateOutput() {
    message = "Hello!!! welcome to PrimeFaces BluePrints";
    return null;
}
```

Remember that you have to include the full absolute client path when the target component resides in a different container.

Partial submit

Even though the Partial Processing feature creates lightweight requests, the entire form's data is sent to the server during the Ajax post requests, just like any other non-Ajax request. The JSF core implementation, with PrimeFaces, serializes all of the form fields instead of the partially-processed components. This becomes a drawback for the larger views, which contain a large number of components.

The **Partial submit** feature can be used to reduce the network traffic for larger views; this posts only the partially-processed form data to the server. Before introducing the Partial submit feature, all of the form data was sent to the server, but this meant that any information of the unprocessed components was ignored on the server-side.

By default, the Partial submit feature is disabled, but you can enable it to make it global using the following configuration:

```
<context-param>
    <param-name>primefaces.SUBMIT</param-name>
    <param-value>partial</param-value>
</context-param>
```

The command action components such as `commandButton` and `commandLink`, and `ajaxbehavior` components such as `p:ajax` equipped with the `partialsubmit` property which overrides the global configuration for each component base:

```
<p:commandButton value="Submit" partialSubmit="true" />
<p:commandLink  partialSubmit="true" />
<p:ajax partialSubmit="true" />
```

PrimeFaces polling

PrimeFaces introduced one more Ajax component that makes periodical Ajax requests to the servers. This component is quite useful when you need to populate server information on the frontend at regular intervals, and the most common example is updating the server time at regular intervals for the frontend web pages. The following code snippet shows how to update the system time at a regular period of time:

```
<h:form id="form">
    <p:poll interval="2" listener="#{pollingController.updateTime}"
      update="servertime" />
    <h:outputText id="servertime"
      value="#{pollingController.systemTime}" />
</h:form>
```

The poll component behavior is handled with the help of the `interval`, `autoStart`, and `stop` attributes along with the client-side API functions.

PrimeFaces code completion, NetBeans bundles PrimeFaces, and the code generation tool

You can use any of your favorite **Integrated Development Environment (IDE)** tools for the development of web pages. Popular IDEs such as Eclipse and NetBeans support code completion for quick UI development.

Eclipse code completion

Firstly, you need to have the JSF facet enabled in order to work with IDE code completion. The following steps will need to be performed in order for the PrimeFaces code completion to be used with the Eclipse IDE:

1. The first thing you need to do is enable the JSF facet by checking the **JavaServer Faces** facet under **Project Facets**.

2. Go to **Properties** | **Project** | **Facets** and select the **JavaServer Faces** checkbox. This can be seen in the following screenshot:

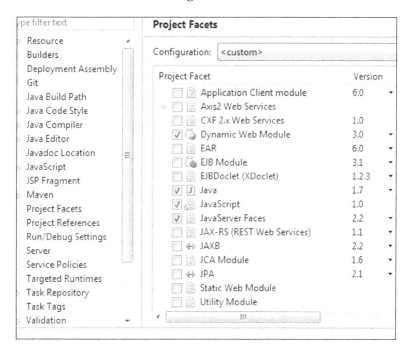

3. If the wizard tells you that further configurations are required, then you have to download or manage the JSF libraries in order to support the code completion feature.

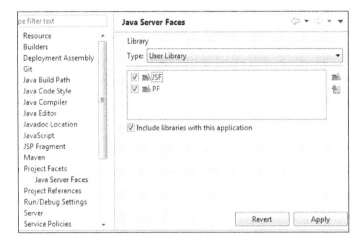

4. Otherwise, the final step in order for the code completion to work with JSF and PrimeFaces tags is just using *Ctrl* + spacebar on your keyboard. What you should now see is presented in the following screenshot:

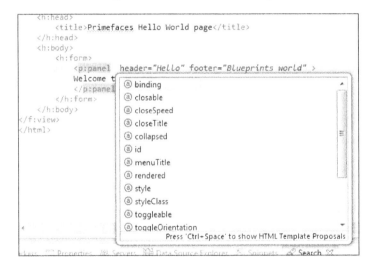

NetBeans code completion

NetBeans versions 6.9 and above support the PrimeFaces code completion feature without requiring any configuration. The following screenshot represents all the available properties of the `accordionPanel` component using the code completion feature:

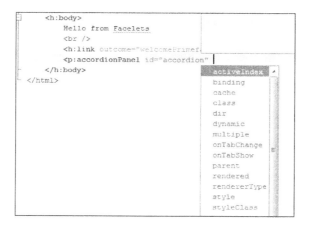

NetBeans bundles PrimeFaces

NetBeans versions 7.0 and above provide built-in support for the PrimeFaces component suite. When creating a new project, you have to select the JSF framework from the list of all **Frameworks** and then select the **PrimeFaces** component suite from the **Components** tab, as shown in the following screenshot:

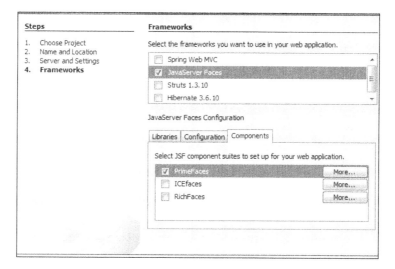

The code generation tool

The NetBeans IDE provides a developer-friendly environment for Java developers, especially for JSF development, which has many cool features. This tool is a forked version of the JSF pages from the entity class wizard, but the difference is that it creates PrimeFaces pages with a page layout, menus, and dialog boxes. You can easily generate the entire CRUD web application just by selecting the entity classes.

Remember that NetBeans 8.0 provides the code generation tool within the IDE itself. It is not necessary to install the plugin in this version.

You should follow these steps in order to work with the PrimeFaces code generation tool:

1. Firstly, download the latest version of the nbpfcrudgen-x.x-y.y.yimpl.zip plugin file and unzip the package that contains the .nbm file. You can access this by visiting http://sourceforge.net/projects/nbpfcrudgen/files/.

2. Then launch your latest NetBeans IDE and install any updates by navigating to **Help | CheckUpdates** from the menu.

3. Following this step, go to **Tools | Plugins**. Click on the **Downloaded** tab and then click on the **Add Plugins** button.

4. Browse to the location where you downloaded the NBM file and select the file that makes the module appear in the list of downloaded modules.

5. Click on the **Install** button. The NetBeans IDE Installer will now display the summary of the modules that are ready to be installed. Click on **Next** and accept the license agreement.

> At the time of this writing, there were no licenses attached to the module, but the tool is released under both CDDL and GPL licenses.

6. At the time of writing this, the tool is not signed and NetBeans warns you about the security. Click on the **Continue** button to proceed with the installation steps. If you are not ready to use the unsigned code, then click on the **Cancel** button as you can choose to wait for a signed, updated version.

7. NetBeans will complete the installation process. If the IDE version doesn't match the module implementation, then the installation process will be aborted.

8. Finally, the module is installed and it will display the module name under the **Installation** tab as **PrimeFaces CRUD generator**.

Generating a CRUD application

The following steps are used to create any PrimeFaces project in the NetBeans IDE:

1. If you are using the latest version of NetBeans, then please make sure you add the latest version of PrimeFaces instead of an older, bundled version. You can add the latest version of PrimeFaces (PrimeFaces 5.0 at the time of writing this) by navigating to **Tools | Ant | Libraries.**
2. Navigate to **File | New | Project**. Choose the **Java Web** option from **Categories** and the **Web application** option from **Projects**.
3. Then create a new project, name it, and choose the project location.
4. After this, configure the server settings that require J2EE version and frameworks.
5. Finally, you should choose the **Component** tab to select the latest PrimeFaces version and click on **Finish** to create the project.

Adding entities and generating PrimeFaces pages

In this section, we will provide a step-by-step approach to generate the PrimeFaces pages from the added entities:

1. Navigate to **File | New File** from the menu. Choose the **Persistence** option from **Categories** and the **Entity Classes from Database** option from **File Types**.
2. Then you can configure the database tables, entity classes, and mapping options to generate the corresponding entities for the database.
3. Following this, navigate to **File | New File** from the menu. Choose the **PrimeFaces CRUD Generator** option from **Categories** and the **PrimeFaces Pages from Entity Classes** option from **File Types**.
4. Finally, you can configure it to generate the PrimeFaces pages and class files. Click on **Finish** to complete the code generation process.

If you have followed all the preceding steps correctly, then you are ready to run the application with a built-in Glassfish server. Click on the **Run** button in order to check the generated pages. You can have a look at some sample pages generated using the code generation tool in the following subsections.

Display page layout, dataTable list, and menu features

You can see that the page layout, dataTable list, and menu features are created by default:

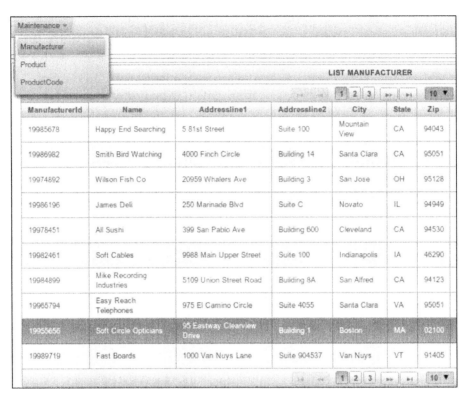

Chapter 1

The dataTable create operation using the dialog component

You can create the dataTable record from the dialog component by providing the details as follows. This is shown in the following screenshot:

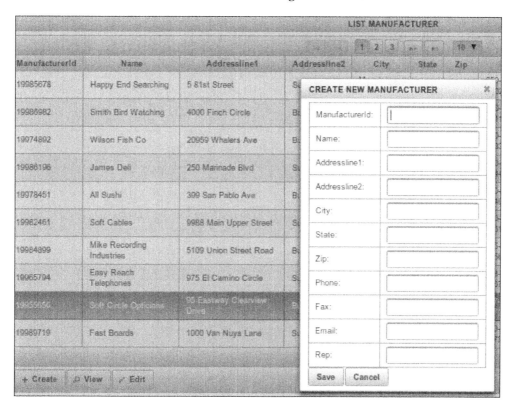

The dataTable update operation using the dialog component

You can update the dataTable record details using the dialog component as follows:

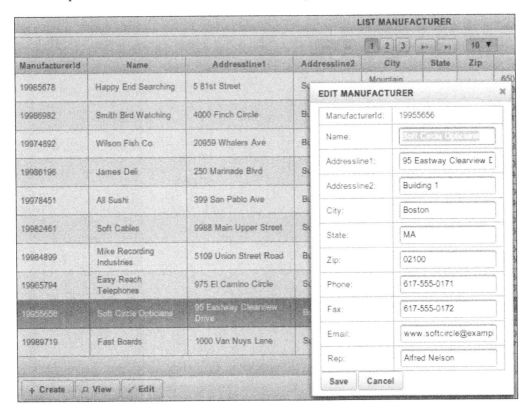

The dataTable read or view operation using the dialog component

You can view a particular dataTable record's details using the dialog component as follows:

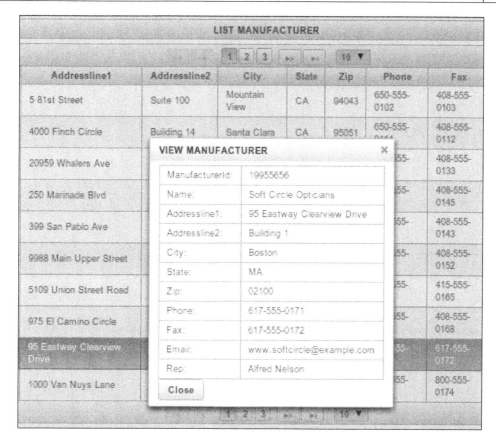

Summary

In this chapter, you have been introduced to the PrimeFaces component suite, its features, and its role in developing custom applications. You have also learned about the setup and configuration for the PrimeFaces library by creating a simple "Hello World" application by using the panel components, changing the old development trend with Ajaxified components, using the PrimeFaces code completion technique, making use of NetBeans support, and using the code generator tool.

In the next chapter, you will be shown the form components of the PrimeFaces library along with how to create a customized web application that allows you to make an employee registration form.

2
Creating an Employee Registration Application

This chapter teaches you how to create a simple employee registration application. The PrimeFaces library provides you with a huge variety of form components to develop registration form-based applications effectively. An important goal of this project is to demonstrate the basic input components that you can enter directly into text boxes, the select components that allow you to choose the right value from all possible options, and many other advanced components, including the editor components. To explain all these components, you will be developing an employee registration application where a jobseeker registers themselves so that they can apply to the jobs in the job portal, while the admin controls and configures the application details. The jobseeker can also view the job details and change the password when required. The specific topics that will be covered are as follows:

- A brief introduction to the employee registration application, use cases, and the architectural design
- The project creation and application screen implementation using form components
- Understanding how to build your own employee registration project and exploring its components

Introduction to the employee registration project

Form filling tasks are common in any online web application where a web user enters the required new entry details or modifies the existing details. In the real world, the data entered in applications will be stored in the database, meaning that you can read or write the data any time. These form filling activities are quite common, especially with registration forms. Typical examples include registrations for online tickets, hotel bookings, college seats, births and marriages, vehicle ownership, employees, and many others.

The employee registration application

In this section, you will see how to create an employee registration application using the PrimeFaces library. An employee registration application is a single form or a collection of forms where an individual seeks employment. The applicant must fill out all the required details such as personal information, skills, and salary. Based on the details provided, the employer can offer employment to the applicant.

You will make use of the form elements to create the user friendly interactive components in order to give your application a fancy look and feel. The library provides a huge set of more controlled form components that include input, select, and advanced. Based on the ease of use and functional requirements, you can start with any component and apply it in this application.

Before you implement the various form components using the PrimeFaces library, you should take a brief look at the project requirements and architectural designs in the following sections.

Application use cases

The purpose of this application is to provide employment to the applicant who is able to view all of the jobs posted by an employer and apply for those that interest him or her. A first-time visitor to the job site might need to register before they can log in to the application and seek employment. The jobseeker has to provide all the required details, such as personal information, which includes address details, education details, and professional experience, as well as information about relevant skills to complete the registration process.

Once registered, an applicant is ready to log in to the application. Please note that the change password functionality allows you to change your password from the first-time generated password. Apart from a jobseeker, an administrator can also log in to the application in order to change the application configuration details as well as view all of the registered employees.

The UML use case diagram

The following use case diagram is used to represent the various functionalities occurring in the entire application process. These functionalities, such as the registration, change password functionality, login, viewing the list of jobs, modifying the application configurations, and viewing the list of registered employees, are treated as individual use cases, which is exactly how they will be adopted in this application.

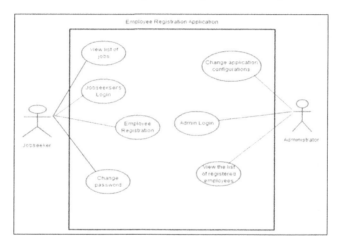

The two roles that perform these functionalities in this application are the **jobseeker/applicant** and the **administrator**. Based on the login user, these roles will have unique functionalities.

The architectural design

The architecture of this application can be presented as follows:

- The presentation layer will be composed of standard JSF and PrimeFaces components.
- The **Facelets** or **XHTML** is used as the view technology in order to render the UI components.
- You will use PrimeFaces's built-in **sunny** theme to skin or style the web pages. (Please refer to *Chapter 10, Creating a Healthcare Products Application*, for a detailed themes configuration.)

- The managed beans will be used to hold session tracking and events handling as well as to execute the business logic. These managed beans interact between XHTML/Facelets and the `POJO` class with the `@ManagedBean` annotation.
- The **data access** layer is used to interact with the MySQL database using **Datasource** and plain **JDBC** concepts.
- The Apache Maven build tool will be used to build the project and for dependency management.

The following architecture diagram represents the three major layers of the web application and their interaction with the MySQL database. The flow from the presentation layer to the other layer components and database is represented by straight lines:

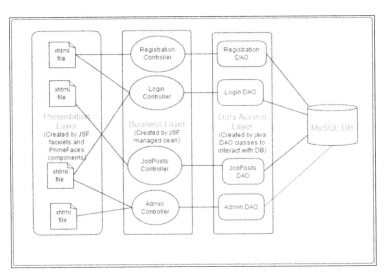

Creating a project and implementing the application screens

This section will show you how to implement an employee registration application using the PrimeFaces form components. The first step to is to start the project by creating the template structure using standard JSF Facelets and then to apply all the possible form components for the creation of the login screen, the change of password functionality, and the registration and application configuration screens. We can also use a few of the supported components to complete the fully fledged registration application.

Before the actual implementation, you should create the project structure with all the folder structures.

> Remember to run all the SQL commands of mysqlquery.txt (which exist under the query folder) before proceeding with the front end application design.

The project structure

The structure of the application should consider presentation, business, and data access as the layers in order to make a proper web application. After you have properly implemented these sections, the project structure in the navigator view of the Eclipse IDE should look as shown in the following screenshot (remember that the project structure will vary a little bit based on the other popular IDEs used, such as NetBeans):

After this, you should make sure that you have configured all of them using the step-by-step configurations detailed in *Chapter 1, Creating a "Hello World" Application*.

Understanding the application template design

You are going to use single main templates formed with the combination of three smaller template files. The `masterTemplate.xhtml` file uses Facelets' `ui:insert`, `ui:include` tags for the header, content, and footer sections, as shown in the following code (please refer to the source code for the complete runnable file):

```
<div id="header">
<ui:insert name="header">
  <ui:includesrc="/templates/common/header.xhtml" />
</ui:insert>
</div>
<div id="content">
<ui:insert name="content">
  <ui:includesrc="/templates/common/content.xhtml" />
</ui:insert>
</div>
<div id="footer">
<ui:insert name="footer">
  <ui:includesrc="/templates/common/footer.xhtml" />
</ui:insert>
</div>
```

The `header` section deals with the website logo, advertisements, and logout functionalities. On the other hand, the `footer` section deals with the application information through the command links. Finally, the content section or template is just provided for the default content.

Implementing the application screens using the form components

Throughout the application, all of the major UI components are created by the form components. This basically means that they are categorized into the input and select components.

Creating the login screen using the input components

Here, you will create the login screen where either the applicant or administrator can log on to the application. Before navigating to the other screens of this application, you will first have to validate whether the login user has been authenticated or not. Also, you should make sure that the user authentication is related to the roles of the applicant or administrator. This page also provides the registration and change password links to proceed with the new employee registration as well as replace the old password with a new one.

You can create the login form containing the username and password fields with the help of the inputText and keyboard components of PrimeFaces, as shown in the following code:

```
<h:form id="loginform">
  <p:panel style="width:30%;height:30%;margin-left:35%">
  <p:messages id="login"></p:messages>
  <h:panelGrid columns="3" cellpadding="5">
  <h:outputLabel for="username" value="Username:" />
  <p:inputText value="#{loginController.username}" id="username"
    required="true" requiredMessage="Username cannot be empty"
    validatorMessage="The length of the username should be between
    3 and 8 chapters"
    label="username">
    <f:validateLength minimum="3" maximum="8" />
  </p:inputText>
  <p:watermark for="username" value="Enter username" />

  <h:outputLabel for="password" value="Password:" />
  <p:keyboard value="#{loginController.password}" id="password"
    required="true" requiredMessage="Password cannot be empty"
    password="true" />
  <p:watermark for="password" value="Enter password" />

  <h:outputText></h:outputText>
  <p:commandButton id="loginButton" value="#{msg['login.login']}"
    update="login" style="float:right"
    action="#{loginController.validateUser}" ajax="false" />
  <f:facet name="footer">
    <h:panelGrid columns="3" style="margin-left:30%">
    <p:outputPanel id="register">
    <p:commandLink value="#{msg['login.register']}" ajax="false"
      immediate="true"
      action="registrationform?faces-redirect=true"></p:commandLink>
```

```
      </p:outputPanel>
      <p:spacer width="10" />
        <p:commandLink value="#{msg['login.changpasswd']}"
           onclick="PF('$changepwd').show();"></p:commandLink>
      </h:panelGrid>
    </f:facet>
    </h:panelGrid>
    </p:panel>
  </h:form>
```

In the preceding code snippet, you wrapped the form components with the `panelGrid` and `panel` components. The `username` field is created by the `inputText` component that has the attached JSF validator and secured password entry with the help of the `keyboard` component. Both the `username` and `password` fields have been attached with a placeholder text known as the `watermark` component to provide the notification messages. You can also add the validations to this login form by using the `p:messages` component, which displays all the messages at the top of the panel. The customized messages will be displayed with the help of the `requiredMessage` and `validatorMessage` properties when the user doesn't enter the input or when length validation fails.

After adding the input components, you can see the login command button that is used to navigate either the jobs list page or the admin page based on the user roles. Below this button, you can see the register and change password links to work with the new applicant's registration and change password functionality.

The backing managed bean is defined with the `username` and `passwords` fields along with the `validateUser()` method. This method validates both the jobseeker and admin roles' authentication by accessing the data access layer, as follows:

```
public String validateUser() throws SQLException {
  FacesMessagemsg = null;
  booleanisValidUser = false;
  if (username.equalsIgnoreCase("admin")
      &&password.equalsIgnoreCase("admin")) {
    return "/views/admin?faces-redirect=true";
  }
  LoginDAOdao = new LoginDAO();
  isValidUser = dao.validateUser(username, password);

  if (isValidUser) {
    return "/views/jobposts?faces-redirect=true";
```

```
      } else {
        msg = new FacesMessage(FacesMessage.SEVERITY_WARN, "Login Error",
             "Invalid credentials");
        FacesContext.getCurrentInstance().addMessage(null, msg);
        return null;
      }
    }
```

You should now configure the MySQL Datasource details, such as the Datasource name, URL, user, and password information for the Jetty web server, as shown in the following code:

```
<Configure class="org.eclipse.jetty.webapp.WebAppContext">
<New id="DSTest" class="org.eclipse.jetty.plus.jndi.Resource">
<Arg>jdbc/blueprintsdb</Arg>
<Arg>
<New class="com.mysql.jdbc.jdbc2.optional.
MysqlConnectionPoolDataSource">
<Set name="Url">jdbc:mysql://localhost:3306/blueprintsdb</Set>
<Set name="User">root</Set>
<Set name="Password">mysql</Set>
</New>
</Arg>
</New>
</Configure>
```

In the data access layer (in this case, `LoginDAO.java`), you can access the Datasource and establish the DB connection as follows:

```
Private DataSource ds;
Connection con;
Public LoginDAO() throws SQLException {
try {
   Context ctx = new InitialContext();
   ds = (DataSource) ctx.lookup("java:comp/env/jdbc/blueprintsdb");
   if (ds == null){
    throw new SQLException("Can't get data source");
    }
   // get database connection
   con = ds.getConnection();
   if (con == null){
      throw new SQLException("Can't get database connection");
```

```
        } catch (NamingException e) {
          e.printStackTrace();
        }
      }
}
```

To validate the user, you just need to make a MySQL query with the username and password details provided. If the count variable is greater than one, then it means that the logged in user is valid. The variable does this by returning a true Boolean value. Otherwise, the application can't be accessed as it returns a false Boolean value. The following code snippet validates the user with the given username and password credentials:

```
public boolean validateUser(String userid, String password) {
  try {
    // Check whether the logged jobseeker is valid user or not
    PreparedStatement ps = con.prepareStatement
    ("select * FROM blueprintsdb.employee WHERE
    userid='" + userid + "' and password='" + password + "'");
    ResultSet resultSet = ps.executeQuery();
    if (resultSet.next()) {
      return true;
    } else {
      return false;
    }

  } catch (SQLException e) {
    e.printStackTrace();

  } catch (Exception e) {
    e.printStackTrace();

  }
  return false;
}
```

You should now find the login screen with the required functionalities, as shown in the following screenshot:

Chapter 2

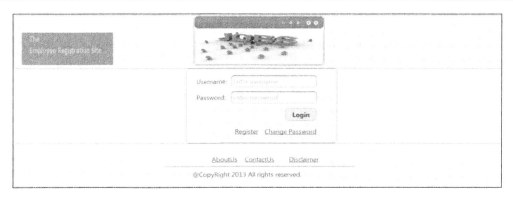

The library also provides validation messages through the p:messages and p:message components. The p:messages component is used to group all the messages at the top, whereas the p:message component has been attached to each form component in order to display the message next to the component, as shown in the following screenshot:

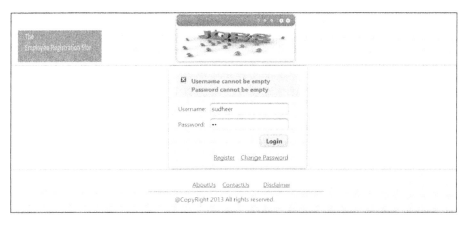

The preceding screenshot generates the validation or required messages for the username and password fields at the top of panelGrid with the help of the p:messages component.

Exploring the employee registration form

A new visitor to the website must register before they can log in to the application. They will need to enter their personal details as well as their professional background and education. Before submitting their registration details, they will also have to confirm these and edit them if required. The entire registration process can be developed by using the PrimeFaces form components in a step-by-step procedure.

The personal details that are displayed in this entire registration process include the `userid`, first and last names, date of birth, gender, and marital status fields in a panel container with the appropriate styles. The input and select components, such as `inputText`, `calendar`, `selectOneRadio`, `selectManyButton`, and `selectOneCheckbox`, are used for these details' fields as shown in the following code:

```
<p:panel header="Personal Details">
  <h:messageserrorClass="error" />
  <h:panelGrid columns="2" columnClasses="label,
    value" styleClass="grid">
  <p:outputLabel for="userid" value="UserID: " />
  <p:inputText id="userid" required="true"
    requiredMessage="UserID shouldn't be empty"
    value="#{registrationController.employee.userid}" />
    value="#{registrationController.employee.userid}" />

  <p:outputLabel for="firstname" value="Firstname: " />
  <p:inputText id="firstname" required="true"
    requiredMessage="Firstname shouldn't be empty"
    value="#{registrationController.employee.firstname}" />

  <h:outputText value="Lastname:" />
  <p:inputText label="Lastname"
    value="#{registrationController.employee.lastname}" />

  < p:outputLabel for="dob"value="Date of birth: " />
  <p:calendar id="dob" value="#{registrationController.employee.dob}"
    required="true" pattern="dd/MM/yyyy" effect="slideDown"
    navigator="true" showButtonPanel="true"yearRange="c-50:c+50" />

  <h:outputText value="Gender: " />
  <p:selectOneRadio id="gender"
    value="#{registrationController.employee.gender}">
    <f:selectItemitemLabel="Male" itemValue="M" />
    <f:selectItemitemLabel="Female" itemValue="F" />
  </p:selectOneRadio>
```

```
    <h:outputText value="Marital Status: " />
    <p:selectOneButton
      value="#{registrationController.employee.maritalStatus}">
      <f:selectItem itemLabel="Single" itemValue=" Single" />
      <f:selectItem itemLabel="Married" itemValue="Married" />
      <f:selectItem itemLabel="Divorced" itemValue="Divorced" />
    </p:selectOneButton>
    <h:outputText value="Skip to last step: " />
    <p:selectBooleanCheckbox value="#{registrationController.skip}" />
  </h:panelGrid>
</p:panel>
```

From the preceding code section, the default pop-up calendar component is used as the select component with more user controls such as the navigator, showButtonPanel, and yearRange properties, all the way up to the date of birth field. On the other hand, the selectOneRadio, selectBooleanCheckbox, and selectManyButton components are used to select a single option in a variety of different approaches.

By following these steps, you should end up with a web page as shown in the following screenshot:

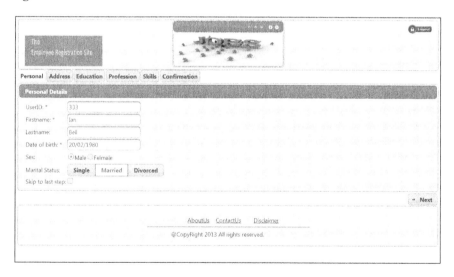

After you click on the **Next** button, you will be navigated to the address details.

Creating an Employee Registration Application

The **Address** tab covers details of the address, phone, postal code, and e-mail fields with the help of the `inputText` area as well as the `selectOneMenu`, `inputMask`, and `inputText` components, as shown in the following code:

```
<p:panel header="Address Details">
<p:growl id="error"  showDetail="true"/>
<h:panelGrid columns="3" columnClasses="label, value,label">
  <h:outputText value="Address: " />
  <p:inputTextarea id="textarea"
    value="#{registrationController.employee.address}" rows="5"
    cols="30" counter="counter" maxlength="150"
    validatorMessage="Length should not be less than 5 characters"
    counterTemplate="{0} more characters remaining.">
    <f:validateLength minimum="5" />
  <p:clientValidator />
  </p:inputTextarea>
  <p:message for="textarea" />
  <h:outputText></h:outputText>
  <h:outputText id="counter"></h:outputText>
  <h:outputText></h:outputText>

  <h:outputText value="Country: " />
  <p:selectOneMenu value="#{registrationController.employee.country}"
    effect="fold"
  var="countryvar" editable="true"
  valueChangeListener="#{registrationController.handleCountryChange}">
    <f:selectItemitemLabel="Select One" itemValue="" />
    <f:selectItems value="#{registrationController.countries}" />
      <p:ajax event="change" update="city" />
  </p:selectOneMenu>
  <h:outputText></h:outputText>

  <h:outputText value="City: " />
  <p:selectOneMenu id="city"
    value="#{registrationController.employee.city}"
    effect="fold" editable="true">
    <f:selectItemitemLabel="Select One" itemValue="" />
    <f:selectItems value="#{registrationController.cities}" />
  </p:selectOneMenu>
  <h:outputText></h:outputText>

  <h:outputText value="Phone: " />
  <p:inputMask value="#{registrationController.employee.phone}"
    mask="(999) 999-9999? x99999" />
  <h:outputText></h:outputText>
```

[42]

```
        <h:outputText value="Postal Code: " />
        <p:inputMask
          value="#{registrationController.employee.postalCode}"
          mask="999-99-9999" />
        <h:outputText></h:outputText>

        <h:outputText value="Email: " />
        <p:inputText id="email"
          value="#{registrationController.employee.email}">
          <f:validator validatorId="custom.emailValidator" />
        </p:inputText>
        <h:outputText></h:outputText>

        <h:outputText value="Skip to last step: " />
        <p:selectBooleanCheckbox value="#{registrationController.skip}" />
        <h:outputText></h:outputText>
    </h:panelGrid>
</p:panel>
```

From the preceding section of code, the `inputText` area is used to represent the address field with the user defined rows, columns, and a JSF validator; the dependent `selectOneMenu` components between the country and city fields are used to select one option. On the other hand, the `inputMask` components are used to enter input data in a customized pattern in the postal code and phone number fields.

By adding all the address fields, you should end up with a web page like the one shown in the following screenshot:

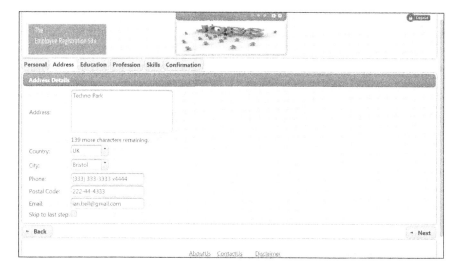

After completing the address details, click on **Next** to navigate to the education details.

The Client Side Validation framework in form validations

The PrimeFaces library introduced a more advanced **Client Side Validation (CSV)** framework to JSF applications via a smooth integration of CSV on JSF's lifecycle. You can enable the CSV framework in your application in the following ways:

- The first method is to configure the global parameter in a `web.xml` file. By default, this parameter is disabled. The configuration to enable the CSV framework in the web application is given as follows:

```
<context-param>
      <param-name>primefaces.CLIENT_SIDE_VALIDATION</param-name>
      <param-value>true</param-value>
</context-param>
```

- Another method is via the page level configuration where `validateClient` is set to a true value. This property can be applied on the `commandButton` and `commandLink` components. For example:

```
<p:commandButton value="Save" ajax="false" icon="ui-icon-
  check" validateClient="true"/>
```

With the help of the `p:clientValidator` CSV component, you can validate the address field without triggering the `commandButton` or `commandLink` components. In comparison, the custom JSF validator is applied to the e-mail field in order to accept the value in a suggested pattern. The custom e-mail validator, called `JSFEmailValidator.java`, is available in the GitHub source code, if you require more details.

To generate messages on the client side, you will have to validate the entered value with the given e-mail pattern in JavaScript, as follows:

```
PrimeFaces.validator['custom.emailValidator'] = {

pattern : /\S+@\S+/,

validate : function(element, value) {
   //use element.data() to access validation metadata,
   //in this case there is none.
   if (!this.pattern.test(value)) {
     throw {
       summary : 'Validation Error',
```

```
            detail : value + ' is not a valid email.'
          }
        }
    }
}
```

You have to add the preceding script to the `<script type="text/javascript">` script tag.

The **Address Details** tab with the CSV validations will now look like the following screenshot:

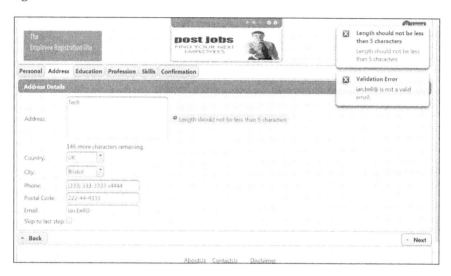

By entering the lowest number of characters in the address field value, the blur event fires the validation next to the address component along with the message display for PrimeFaces' `growl` component. In comparison, an improper e-mail ID will result in a validation message with the help of the `growl` component.

The **Education** tab that covers details such as your university name, qualifications, or most recent degree grade can be created using the `inputText`, `selectManyButton` and `slider` components as follows:

```
<p:panel header="Education">
<h:messages errorClass="error" />
<h:panelGrid columns="2" cellspacing="10" columnClasses="label,
  value">
  <p:outputLabel for="university" value="University: " />
  <p:inputText id=" university" required="true"
    requiredMessage="University cannot be empty"
    value="#{registrationController.employee.university}" />
```

Creating an Employee Registration Application

```
    <h:outputText value="Qualification: " />
    <p:selectManyButton
      value="#{registrationController.employee.qualification}">
      <f:selectItemitemLabel="BTech" itemValue="1" />
      <f:selectItemitemLabel="MTech" itemValue="2" />
      <f:selectItemitemLabel="MS" itemValue="3" />
    </p:selectManyButton>

    <h:outputText id="output" value="Last degree percentage
      %#{registrationController.employee.percentage}" />
    <p:slider for="txt2" display="output" style="width:200px"
      displayTemplate="Last degree percentage %{value}" />
    <h:inputHidden id="txt2"
      value="#{registrationController.employee.percentage}" />
    <h:outputText></h:outputText>
    <h:outputText value="Skip to last step: " />
    <p:selectBooleanCheckbox value="#{registrationController.skip}" />
  </h:panelGrid>
</p:panel>
```

From the preceding code, `selectManyButton` is used to select multiple options from all the available options such as the `BTech`, `MTech`, and `MS` values. However, the slider component can be used to select your last year degree percentage by just sliding the button.

By adding the latest degree details, you should end up with a web page like the one shown in the following screenshot:

After you have entered the education details, click on **Next** and you will be navigated to the **Profession** details tab.

The **Profession** tab covers details such as professional experience, current company name, current and expected packages, and joining date using the `inputText`, `spinner`, `autocomplete`, and `calendar` components, as shown in the following code:

```
<p:panel header="Profession">
  <h:messageserrorClass="error" />
  <h:panelGrid columns="2" columnClasses="label, value">
  <p:outputLabel for="profession"value="Profession: " />
  <p:inputText id="profession" required="true"
     requiredMessage="Profession can't be empty"
     value="#{registrationController.employee.profession}" />

  <p:outputLabel for="experience" value="Experience: " />
  <p:spinner id="experience" required="true"
     requiredMessage="Experience can't be empty"
     min="2" value="#{registrationController.employee.experience}" />

  <h:outputText value="Company: " />
  <p:autoComplete id="acMinLength" minQueryLength="3"
     value="#{registrationController.employee.company}" effect="fade"
     completeMethod="#{registrationController.complete}" />

  <p:outputLabel for="current" value="Current Package: " />
  <p:spinner id="current" required="true"
     requiredMessage="Current package can't be
     empty"prefix="$"   min="3"
     value="#{registrationController.employee.currentPack}" />

  <p:outputLabel for="expected" value="Expected Package: *" />
  <p:spinner id="expected" required="true"
  requiredMessage="Expected package can't be empty"prefix="$"   min="3"
  max="20" value="#{registrationController.employee.expectedPack}" />

  <p:outputLabel for="jod" value="Joined Date: *" />
  <p:calendar id="jod"
     value="#{registrationController.employee.joinedDate}"
     required="true" requiredMessage="Joined date can't be empty"
     showOn="button" mode="popup" pattern="dd/MM/yyyy" />

  <h:outputText value="Skip to last step: " />
  <p:selectBooleanCheckbox value="#{registrationController.skip}" />
  </h:panelGrid>
</p:panel>
```

From the preceding code, the `autoComplete` component is used to select the company name with the autocompletion feature. On the other hand, the `spinner` component is used to select the experience, current package, and expected package details by incrementing or decrementing one step at a time.

By adding the profession details, you should end up with a web page like the one shown in the following screenshot:

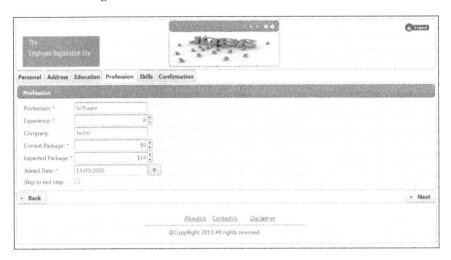

After completing the **Profession** details, click on the **Next** button and you will be navigated to the **Skills** tab.

The **Skills** tab will cover details such as frameworks, databases, servers, and IDE expertise using the `selectCheckboxMenu`, `selectManyCheckbox`, `multiSelectListbox`, and `selectOneListbox` components as shown in the following code:

```
<p:panel header="Skills">
  <h:messageserrorClass="error" />
  <h:panelGrid columns="2" columnClasses="label, value">
  <p:outputLabel id="frameworks" value="Frameworks: " />
  <p:selectCheckboxMenu id="frameworks"
     value="#{registrationController.employee.selectedFrameworks}"
     label="Frameworks" filter="true" filterMatchMode="startsWith">
     <f:selectItems value="#{registrationController.allFrameworks}" />
  </p:selectCheckboxMenu>

  <h:outputText value="Databases: " />
  <p:selectManyCheckbox id="database"
     value="#{registrationController.employee.selectedDBs}">
```

```
    <f:selectItems value="#{registrationController.allDBs}" />
  </p:selectManyCheckbox>

  <h:outputText value="Server Expertise:" />
  <p:multiSelectListbox id="servers"
    value="#{registrationController.employee.selectedServer}">
    <f:selectItems value="#{registrationController.allServers}" />
  </p:multiSelectListbox>

  <h:outputText value="IDE Expertise: " />
  <p:selectOneListbox
    value="#{registrationController.employee.selectedIDE}"
    <f:selectItems value="#{registrationController.allIDEs}" />
  </p:selectOneListbox>

  <h:outputText value="Skip to last step: " />
  <p:selectBooleanCheckbox value="#{registrationController.skip}" />
</h:panelGrid>
</p:panel>
```

From the preceding code, `selectCheckboxMenu` and `selectManyCheckbox` are used to select multiple options from all the available options, while `multiSelectListbox` and `selectOneListbox` are used to select single input values with different approaches.

By adding the previously mentioned skills, you should end up with a web page like the one shown in the following screenshot:

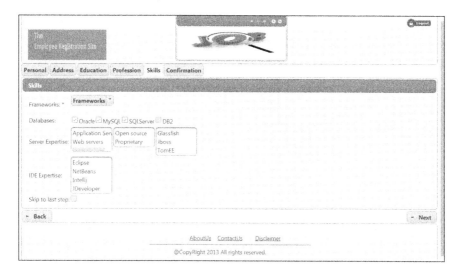

After filling in all the skill details and clicking on the **Next** button, navigate to the **Confirmation** tab.

The **Confirmation** tab will prompt you before submitting or saving the registration details. Here, you can change your personal and address detail, instead of repeating the same steps. You can enable the edit mode of the registration fields by wrapping the `inplace` components as shown in the following code:

```
<p:panel header="Confirmation">
<h:panelGrid id="confirmation" columns="6">
<h:outputText value="Firstname: " />
<p:inplace id="firstnameinplace" editor="true">
<p:inputText value="#{registrationController.employee.firstname}" />
</p:inplace>

<h:outputText value="Lastname: " />
<p:inplace id="lastnameinplace" editor="true">
  <p:inputText value="#{registrationController.employee.lastname}" />
</p:inplace>

<h:outputText value="DOB: " />
<p:inplace id="dobinplace" editor="true">
  <p:calendar pattern="dd/MM/yyyy"
    value="#{registrationController.employee.dob}" />
</p:inplace>

<h:outputText value="Country: " />
<p:inplace id="countryinplace" editor="true">
  <p:inputText value="#{registrationController.employee.country}" />
</p:inplace>

<h:outputText value="City: " />
<p:inplace id="cityinplace" editor="true">
  <p:inputText value="#{registrationController.employee.city}" />
</p:inplace>

<h:outputText value="Postal Code: " />
<p:inplace id="postalinplace" editor="true">
  <p:inputText value="#{registrationController.employee.postalCode}"
  />
</p:inplace>

<h:outputText value="Email: " />
<p:inplace id="emailinplace" editor="true">
```

```
    <p:inputText value="#{registrationController.employee.email}" />
  </p:inplace>

  <h:outputText value="Phone " />
  <p:inplace id="phoneinplace" editor="true">
    <p:inputText value="#{registrationController.employee.phone}" />
  </p:inplace>
</h:panelGrid>
<p:commandButton value="Submit" update="growl"
    actionListener="#{registrationController.saveEmployee}" />
</p:panel>
```

From the preceding code, you can edit the important registration field values before you submit the registration by wrapping the form components using the `inplace` component.

By following the previously mentioned steps, you should end up with a web page like the one shown in the following screenshot:

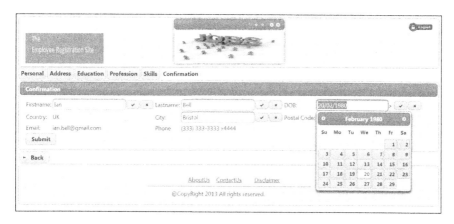

The preceding screenshot shows you the **Confirmation** tab before the registration has been submitted. You can change the field values where required.

In the data access layer (represented by `EmployeeDAO.java`), you can save the newly registered jobseeker details. Based on the Boolean flag value, a success or failure message will appear in the employee registration web page. The following code snippet is used to save newly registered jobseeker details:

```
Public boolean saveEmployee(Employee employee,StringuniqueID) throws
Exception{
  try{
      String pattern = "yyyy-MM-dd";
```

```java
      SimpleDateFormat formatter = new SimpleDateFormat(pattern);
         // Register employee
      PreparedStatement ps = con.prepareStatement("INSERT INTO
      blueprintsdb.employee (userid,firstname,lastname,dob,gender,
      maritalstatus,address,country,city,phone,postalcode,email,
      university,qualification,percentage,profession,experience,
      company,currentpack,expectedpack,joineddate,frameworks,dbs,
      servers,ides,password)VALUES('"+employee.getUserid()+"','"
      +employee.getFirstname()+"','"+employee.getLastname()+"','"
      +formatter.format(employee.getDob())+"','"
      +employee.getGender()+"','"+employee.getMaritalStatus()
      +"','"+employee.getAddress()+"','"
      +employee.getCountry()+"','"+employee.getCity()+"','"
      +employee.getPhone()+"','"+employee.getPostalCode()+"','"
      +employee.getEmail()+"','"+employee.getUniversity()+"','"
      +employee.getQualification()+"','"+employee.getPercentage()
      +"','"+employee.getProfession()+"',"
      +employee.getExperience()+","'"+employee.getCompany()
      +"',"+employee.getCurrentPack()+","+employee.getExpectedPack()
      +",'"+formatter.format(employee.getJoinedDate())+"','"
      +employee.getSelectedFrameworks()+"','"
      +employee.getSelectedDBs()+"','"+employee.getSelectedServer()
      +"','"+employee.getSelectedIDE()+"','"+uniqueID+"')");

      int count=ps.executeUpdate();
      if(count>0){
        return true;
         }

        }
    catch(SQLException e){
    e.printStackTrace();

    }catch(Exception e){
    e.printStackTrace();

        }
    return false;
  }
```

Here, you can clearly see that a prepared statement allows you to insert all the registration fields in the MySQL database.

After you click on the **Submit** button, you should end up with a web page like the one shown in the following screenshot:

Also, you might receive either a success or a failure message, as shown in the preceding screenshot.

Exploring the change password functionality

A jobseeker will use the change password functionality to change a previously generated password with their own. This password can be changed any time and as often as they like.

In this section, you can use the input and password components with the required validations. The new password and confirm password fields are linked and are matched via the `match` attribute. The dialog component with the change password functionality is displayed as follows by simply clicking on the **Change Password** link:

```
<p:dialog id="changepwd" header="Change Password"
widgetVar="$changepwd" modal="true" resizable="false">
<h:form id="changepwdform">
  <p:messages id="changepass"/>
  <h:panelGrid columns="3" cellpadding="5">
  <h:outputLabel for="userid" value="Username:" />
  <p:inputText value="#{loginController.username}" id="userid"
    required="true" requiredMessage="Username cannot be empty"
    validatorMessage="The length of the username should
    exist between 3 and 8 chapters" label="username">
      <f:validateLength minimum="3" maximum="8" />
  </p:inputText>
  <p:watermark for="userid" value="Enter username" />
```

```
    <h:outputLabel for="oldpassword" value="Old password:" />
    <p:password value="#{loginController.password}" id="oldpassword"
      required="true" requiredMessage="Password cannot be empty"
      label="password" />
    <p:watermark for="oldpassword" value="Enter old password" />

    <h:outputLabel for="newpassword" value="New password:" />
    <p:password value="#{loginController.newpassword}"
    match="confirmpassword" id="newpassword"
      required="true" requiredMessage="New password cannot be empty"
      label="newpassword" />
    <p:watermark for="newpassword" value="Enter new password" />

    <h:outputLabel for="confirmpassword" value="Confirm password:" />
    <p:password value="#{loginController.newpassword}"
      id="confirmpassword" required="true"
      requiredMessage="Confirm password cannot be empty"
      label="confirmpassword" />
    <p:watermark for="confirmpassword" value="Enter confirm password" />

    <f:facet name="footer">
      <p:commandButton id="changepassword" value="Submit"
      update="changepass"
        actionListener="#{loginController.changepassword}" />
    </f:facet>
    </h:panelGrid>
  </h:form>
</p:dialog>
```

In the data access layer (represented by `LoginDAO.java`), you have to make a MySQL query to update the old password with a new one when the given credentials already exist in the database. Refer to the following code for it:

```
publicbooleanchangePassword(String userid,
String oldpassword,String newpassword) {
try {
    // Change password functionality
PreparedStatement ps = con
        .prepareStatement("UPDATE blueprintsdb.employee SET
password='"+ newpassword+ "' WHERE userid='"
+ userid + "'  and password='" + oldpassword + "'");
  int count = ps.executeUpdate();
  return (count > 0);

    }
```

```
      catch (SQLException e) {
      e.printStackTrace();
      }
      catch (Exception e) {
      e.printStackTrace();
      }
   return false;
   }
```

The **Change Password** screen will now appear as shown in the following screenshot:

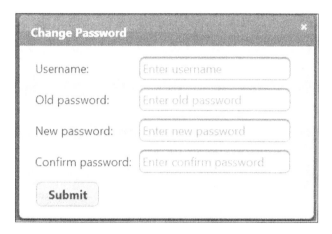

After providing the jobseeker login details along with the new password, the old password will be updated with the new one. On submitting the request to change the password, the change password status will be updated with a success or failure message.

Tracking the list of job posts

In this section, you can view the list of jobs posted by an employer. They will post details such as the company name, technology domain, necessary experience, job position, and location. If the profile matches yours, then you can apply for these jobs.

You can see how the usage of `dataTable` acts as a supported component to populate the list of all jobs, as shown in the following screenshot:

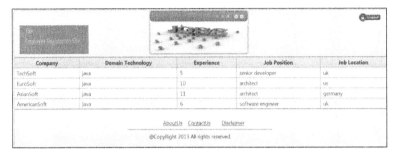

From the list of all the jobs posted by employers, you can apply for the jobs that match your requirements.

Managing the application through an admin role

The administrator is responsible for controlling and managing the entire registration application, while the admin can change the application configurations and view the list of registered employees.

The application configurations, such as the **AboutUs** and **ContactUs** sections, can be viewed and modified by the admin using the `editor` component. By toggling between the **Edit** or **Save** button, you can enable or disable the changes.

By following these actions, you should end up with a web page like the one shown in the following screenshot:

The administrator can also view the list of registered employees through `dataTable` or a helper component as shown in the following screenshot:

The administrator can also view and analyze employee traffic from time to time.

Working with the employee registration project code

If you wish to work on the sample code, all you need to do is download it from the git repository at https://github.com/sudheerj/primefaces-blueprints, where you can use your preferred IDE. From there, you can start playing with the code. You can run it by using the `mvn jetty:run` command in the Maven console and then navigate your browser to `http://localhost:8080/web` using the registered employee credentials while using admin/admin as the administrator credentials to log in to the application.

Summary

In this chapter, you learned how to develop your own employee registration application. The topics covered in this chapter showed you how to create your own login and registration screens, how to change the password, and how to create the jobs list page of the admin screens with the help of a variety of input, select, and advanced editor components from the PrimeFaces library.

In the next chapter, you will learn the procedure to create your own real-time business model called a restaurant application, which will also show you how the layout and grouping components of PrimeFaces work.

3
Creating a Simple Restaurant Point of Sale Application

In this chapter, you will learn how to create a simple restaurant **Point of Sale** (**POS**) application. An important goal of this chapter is to also demonstrate the PrimeFaces layout component, the grouping component, and some additional supporting JSF components used in this application. To understand these components, we'll look at a real-world restaurant business model (POS), which is commonly used in restaurants to take orders and control general activities within the restaurant. This chapter will also demonstrate the restaurant's menu card module, which allows the ordering of menu items. You will be provided with a high-level architecture and screen mocks of the menu card system to make the explanation simpler and easier.

A quick start

If you remember, in *Chapter 1, Creating a "Hello World" Application*, we learned about the procedure to create a JSF 2 Project with PrimeFaces enabled. The same procedure can be used to start with this application.

In this section, you will get things started quickly by introducing the sample web project that will be implemented using PrimeFaces. Imagine this: your client has a great idea for a web application. They want to build a website called *Restaurant POS* that aims to change their paper menu card to a digital online menu. The user can explore the available restaurant menu items within their category of choice and order them online. The user can also save their favorite menu item in a favorites list, potentially allowing them to order the menu item with a single click. This project will give you the opportunity to use the full spectrum of the PrimeFaces layout and grouping component as well as the templating feature from JSF Facelets. The internal employees of the restaurant will use this POS application. Most of the restaurants will use different layouts, with a different look and feel, depending on the season (as a way of increasing the mental productivity of their employees).

The advantage of using PrimeFaces here is that it allows you to enable a rich UI. PrimeFaces provides you with over a hundred components that are ready to use in some simple steps. Also, it is a lightweight framework compared to other available frameworks.

However, the first step is to review a user case, the project requirements, architecture, and design before you can implement JSF pages in this application.

Application use cases

The restaurant's internal user will log in to the system; once done, the menu card system will appear and will be ready to take orders. This system will have a list of categories on the left-hand side, where each category will have a list of menu items. The customers will be invited to take their seats; the waiter will then approach the table and collect their orders manually. They will then use the digital menu card system to enter their respective orders by first selecting a category and then selecting the desired food item from the available menu. The user (waiter) can also add as many menu items as they would like to in order to serve multiple customers. The order will then be printed via the kitchen printer for the chef to prepare the food. The food will be ready to be served once the chef completes processing the order.

The architectural design

The architecture of this application can be presented as follows:

- The presentation layer will be composed of PrimeFaces components
- The **XHTML** files are used as the view technology to render the UI components
- You will use the theme that comes with PrimeFaces

- You will use the JSF 2 project to demonstrate the layout components
- The Support-Pac module project contains all the models used in this project; this enables the reusability of those models for various projects
- The managed beans will be used to hold session tracking and transactions
- Maven's `pom` file will be used to build and provide a dependency resolution

The application architecture diagram

This simple architecture diagram shows you the full stack of technology and how it is inter-related:

The CDI architecture

The preceding diagram describes the high-level architecture used in this sample web application. The presentation tier will be implemented using a mixture of JSF 2 and PrimeFaces components. The application tier will be based on JSF 2's Facelet APIs and will make use of the Java Facelet application; also, JPA can be used to communicate with the database. The application will then be deployed as a WAR file in the Tomcat server.

> For convenience, this project will use the jetty Maven plugin to run the application. You can use the following Maven command to run the application:
> `mvn jetty:run`
> If you prefer to run the application from IDE, you can install Maven plugin, for example, m2e for Eclipse,

The entity diagram

The following is what you will see in the **entity diagram** of the model used in the POS menu card:

- The category entity has a unique ID, with the parent ID set as 0 by default. If the parent ID has not been set to 0, then it will be one of the available category IDs. This means that we can refer the unique ID to the same column with different values on our own.
- The `enabled` flag indicates whether to display the category or not.
- The image path holds the location of the image icon in order to show the category.

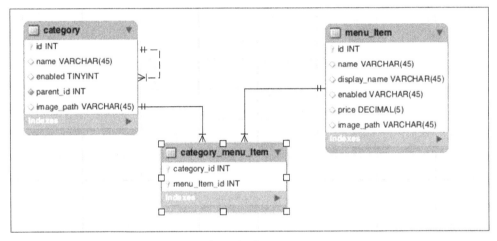

An entity diagram

Implementing the application

This section will show you how to implement the restaurant menu card system and its requirements using the PrimeFaces components. The JSF Facelet provides some tags that will help you to make the web application's layout dynamic, using the view and composition tags called template tags. It also has many supporting tags associated with templating, a detailed explanation of which will be shown in the following subsections.

Template tags

Templating is an important concept in the web technology; it is used to make the application dynamic in nature. It is also helpful to maintain and reuse the code along with reducing code complexity.

When describing templating within Facelets, we have two roles: defining the template and using the template client. The following diagram will show you how the template is defined and included:

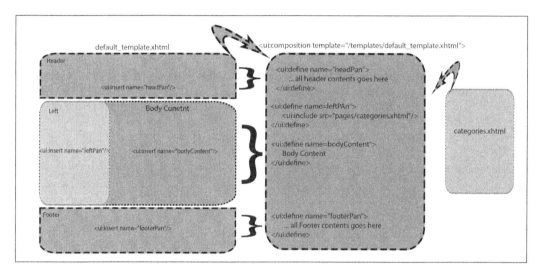

Any document can act as a template, but what makes a document a template? It just simply uses one or more `<ui:insert/>` tags to inject content from another Facelet page. The other half of the equation is the template's client. This includes the documents that use the `<ui:composition/>`, `<ui:define>`, or `<ui:decorate/>` tags.

The UI composition tag

The UI composition tag is a templating tag provided by JSF Facelets that wraps the content to be included in another Facelet page. The idea behind ui:composition is that a UI component tree can be defined in multiple Facelet pages and executed in a part or whole. The content outside the UI composition tag will be ignored by the Facelets' view handler. Any content inside the UI composition tag will apply the specified template when another Facelet's page includes the page that contains this UI composition tag.

If the template attribute is specified with a template page URL, the JSF page that contains the composition tag will display the content with the help of associated template. If the composition tag contains `ui:define` tags, the content of these tags will be inserted into the template where the matching `ui:insert` tags can be found. The template page can use a nameless `ui:insert` tag to insert all of the content within the composition tag.

Using the JSF Facelet tags in an XHTML file allows you to design a single screen layout that must be used consistently throughout the application. Furthermore, you must consistently specify the placeholders to render the actual content at the appropriate place from various pages. Note that JSF 2.2 strictly uses the XHTML standard to define the tags in the XHTML file.

The following code snippet is what you will use in your sample, which demonstrates how you can create your default template:

```
<!DOCTYPE html>
<html xmlns="http://www.w3.org/1999/xhtml"
xmlns:f="http://java.sun.com/jsf/core"
xmlns:h="http://java.sun.com/jsf/html"
xmlns:ui="http://java.sun.com/jsf/facelets"
xmlns:p="http://primefaces.org/ui">
<h:head>
<f:facet name="first">
<meta http-equiv="Content-Type" content="text/html; charset=UTF-8"/>
<meta http-equiv="pragma" content="no-cache"/>
<meta http-equiv="cache-control" content="no-cache"/>
<meta http-equiv="expires" content="0"/>
</f:facet>
<h:outputStylesheet library="css" name="styles.css"/>
   <ui:insert name="headPan"/>
</h:head>
<h:body>
<p:layoutfullPage="true">
<p:ajax event="resize"/>
<p:layoutUnit position="north">
   <p:panel header="PrimeFaces">
   </p:panel>
</p:layoutUnit>
<p:layoutUnit position="west" collapsible="true" gutter="1">
   <ui:insert name="leftPan"/>
</p:layoutUnit>
```

```
<p:layoutUnit position="center">
  <ui:insert name="bodyContent"/>
</p:layoutUnit>
<p:layoutUnit position="east" collapsible="true" gutter="1">
  <ui:insert name="rightPan"/>
</p:layoutUnit>
</p:layout>

</h:body>
</f:view>
</html>
```

> The associated filename within the template directory is default_template.xhtml.

This code snippet can show you how to design the template file with placeholders. Pay attention to the `ui:insert` tag; it is used in the template file in order to place the placeholder for its content.

Have a look at how you can define the placeholders using the `ui:composition` and `ui:define` tags in the following code:

```
<ui:composition template="/templates/default_template.xhtml">
<ui:define name="headPan">
<!-- Test contents Comment Head-->
</ui:define>

<ui:define name="leftPan">
  <ui:includesrc="pages/categories.xhtml"/>
</ui:define>

<ui:define name="bodyContent">
  ….
</ui:define>
<ui:define name="rightPan">
  …
</ui:define>
…
</ui:composition>
```

As previously discussed, the ui:composition tag is specified with the template attribute. It is set to your default template file, default_template.xhtml. Your template file has four ui:insert placeholders with the names headPan, leftPan, bodyContent, and rightPan. In your main page, you will define each name and its content. Facelet's view resolver will substitute the content at runtime. Notice that the content of leftPan is defined in a separate file, including the ui:include tag in the leftPan content, such that you can reuse and maintain the same code anywhere in the application.

 An advantage of using the include-file approach is that developers only need to focus on looking at a particular part of the code.

The layout component

The layout component is based on a border layout model that consists of five different layout units (or regions): top (north), left (west), center, right (east), and bottom (south). The main purpose of the layout component is that it is used to arrange the UI elements in the desired order using the layout units.

Layout has two different modes: you can either use it for a full-page layout or for a specific region in your page. This setting is controlled with the fullPage attribute, which is set to false by default. The regions in a layout component are defined by layoutUnits. The following code is for a simple full-page layout with all the possible units. Note that you can place any of the content in each layout unit. The following code snippet is used to render the layout component in full page with all the regions:

```
<h:form>
<p:layout fullPage="true">
<p:layoutUnit position="north" size="50">
<h:outputText value="Banner or Header content." />
</p:layoutUnit>
  <p:layoutUnit position="south" size="100">
<h:outputText value="Footer content." />
</p:layoutUnit>
  <p:layoutUnit position="west" size="300">
<h:outputText value="Navigation content" />
</p:layoutUnit>
  <p:layoutUnit position="east" size="200">
<h:outputText value="Advertisement Content" />
</p:layoutUnit>
  <p:layoutUnit position="center">
```

```
    <h:outputText value="Actual Workspace Content" />
    </p:layoutUnit>
    </p:layout>
    </h:form>
```

The following image depicts the output of the preceidng code:

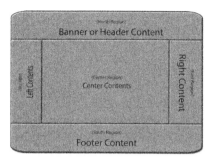

The border of a full-page layout

Forms in a full-page layout

When working with forms and a full-page layout, you will have a problem while using a form that contains `layoutunit`. This is because the generated form may not be the same. Therefore, the following code snippet is invalid:

```
<p:layout fullPage="true">
<h:form>
    <p:layoutUnit position="west" size="100">
            <h:outputText value="Left Pane" />
    </p:layoutUnit>
    <p:layoutUnit position="center">
        <h:outputText value="Right Pane" />
    </p:layoutUnit>
</h:form>
</p:layout>
```

Each layout unit must have its own form instead.

> You should avoid trying to update the layout units because of the same reason. You should update its content instead.

Implementation

First, you should take a look at how the layout components in the region that contains `Layoutunits` are designed in the `default_template.xhtml` file.

The layout component is designed as a full page with a `true` value; this enables the content to span the fullscreen mode. You have designed each region using `LayoutUnits` with a `ui:insert` tag, where the `insert` tag is used as a template to make a placeholder for its contents. Apart from the `center` layout unit, other layout units can have their dimensions defined via the `size` option used to specify the initial size. If we don't specify the dimension, it will be defined during the runtime based on the content's size. The center region occupies the remaining available space. If you try to specify the size of other regions to fit the fullscreen mode, the center region will always be present.

A possible error

The center region is mandatory when using the layout component. If you miss the center region layout, you will encounter the following error while starting up the application. This error will not be there in the server log:

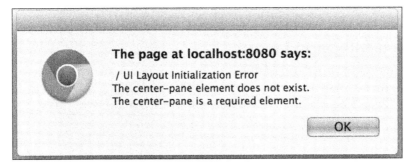

A screenshot displaying the error message

Events and methods in the layout component

The layout component supports three events called **close**, **resize**, and **toggle**. It also supports three JavaScript APIs called **toggle**, **show**, and **hide**. In this restaurant application, you will use the Ajax tag in order to capture the specified event. For example, resize event is triggered whenever the layout unit size changes

Using the `ui:define` tag, you can define the appropriate content. Each region is identified with the specified name attribute, with the content inside the `define` tag placed in the appropriate placeholder.

You have another good feature: the layout component has the ability to control the component using JavaScript. The `default_template.xhtml` file you are provided with has an option through which you can toggle between the center panel and the fullscreen mode upon pressing the button.

The icon to toggle to fullscreen mode

When the user clicks on the **Toggle Full Screen** button, the screen toggles to the fullscreen mode by closing all the side and top panels. The following is the JavaScript code that helps you do this:

```
<h:outputScript>
var hiddenFlag = false;
function hideShow() {hiddenFlag;;
var varswitherId = $("#switherId");
if (hiddenFlag) {
  layoutit.hide('north');
  layoutit.hide('west');
  layoutit.hide('east');
  layoutit.hide('south');
  switherId.attr("title", "Restore Window");
} else {
  layoutit.show('north');
  layoutit.show('west');
  layoutit.show('east');
  layoutit.show('south');
  switherId.attr("title","Maximize Window");
}
}
</h:outputScript>
```

In the preceding code snippet, `layoutit` is the name that is assigned for the layout component, and the `widgetVar` attribute is used to specify a name for the component. This helps to refer to the name outside the JSF context. That is how you can get a reference for the `layoutit` name in JavaScript. This code snippet contains the JavaScript API calls to show and hide the regions. Since the center region automatically occupies the remaining available space, you just need to toggle the other regions north, south, east, and west; then, the center region will immediately resize to the remaining available space.

You will be using a `p:commandLink` tag inside the center region with the ID as `switherId`. The JavaScript API will be called from the click event of `switcherId`. The JavaScript methods `show` and `hide` accept only one name parameter that is automatically assigned by the PrimeFaces engine, namely, north, south, east, or west, while rendering the layout and its regions.

Ajax's behavior events

The layout provides custom Ajax behavior events for each change that takes place in the layout's state. In this application, you will use the Ajax tag to catch the resize event. The following table shows

Event	Fired
toggle	When a unit is expanded or collapsed
close	When a unit is closed
resize	When a unit is resized

The grouping components

The grouping components are used to arrange the items in a grid fashion. PrimeFaces includes a wide range of components in order to support grouping UI elements: a data grid, panel grid, row, column, dataTable, dataList, and many more. In this chapter, you will use the `panelGrid` component, the `dataGrid` component, the `column` tag, and a row tag.

The panelGrid component

PrimeFaces' `panelGrid` is an extension of the standard JSF's core `panelGrid` component with additional features such as theming and column span and row span.

You will now see how to arrange the login page's content using the `panelGrid` component:

```
<h:form id="login" prependId="false">
<p:growl id="msg" rendered="#{param.error}">
<h:outputText value="#{userController.loginStatus}"/>
</p:growl>
<p:dialog header="User Login"
id="dialog"
modal="true"
closable="false"
position="center"
widgetVar="modalLogin"
```

```
showEffect="slide"
draggable="false"
resizable="false"
visible="true">
<p:panelGrid id="loginBox" columns="2"  cellpadding="3"
style="margin: 0 auto; border: 0px;
padding-top: 20px;">
<h:outputLabel for="j_username"  value="Username "/>
<h:outputLabel for="j_password" value="Password "/>
          <p:keyboard id="j_username" required="true"
widgetVar="usernameKeyBoard"
value="#{userController.userName}"
onfocus="$('#keypad-div').css( 'z-index', 9999 );"/>
<p:keyboard id="j_password" required="true"
password="true" value="#{userController.password}"
onblur="$('#keypad-div').css( 'z-index', 9999 );"/>
<p:commandButton id="loginBtn" value="Login"
ajax="false" action="#{userController.loginMeIn()}"/>
<p:defaultCommand target="loginBtn"/>
</p:panelGrid>
</p:dialog>
</h:form>
```

In the preceding snippet of the login page, you used the dialog panel to show the login box on top of everything, forcing the user to log in. Also, you used the panelGrid component with its basic usage to align the username and password fields, with the buttons in a table row fashion. You can now see how the screen and generated code look after the page is rendered:

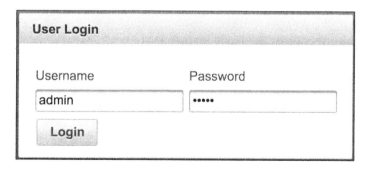

Creating a Simple Restaurant Point of Sale Application

This following HTML code is generated at runtime by a JSF page resolver when you view the source of the preceding login screen:

```
<table id="loginBox" cellpadding="3" style="margin: 0 auto; border: 0px; padding-top: 20px;">
<tbody>
<tr>
<td><label for="j_username">Username </label></td>
<td><label for="j_password">Password </label></td>
</tr>
<tr>
<td><input id="j_username" name="j_username" type="text"
onfocus="$('#keypad-div').css( 'z-index', 9999 );" class="ui-
inputfieldui-keyboard-input ui-widget ui-state-default ui-corner-all
hasKeypad" role="textbox" aria-disabled="false" aria-readonly="false"
aria-multiline="false"></td>
<td><input id="j_password" name="j_password" type="password"
onblur="$('#keypad-div').css( 'z-index', 9999 );" class="ui-
inputfieldui-keyboard-input ui-widget ui-state-default ui-corner-all
hasKeypad" role="textbox" aria-disabled="false" aria-readonly="false"
aria-multiline="false"></td>
</tr>
<tr>
<td><button id="loginBtn" name="loginBtn" class="ui-button ui-widget
ui-state-default ui-corner-all ui-button-text-only" type="submit"
role="button" aria-disabled="false"><span class="ui-button-text ui-
c">Login</span></button></td>
<td></td>
</tr>
</tbody>
</table>
```

The generated output code of the basic PrimeFaces `panelGrid` component is actually nothing but a normal HTML `table` tag with `<tr><td>`, where the Columns attribute of `panelGrid` is the one that decides the number of columns that should appear in the table.

The additional feature of the `panelGrid` component is the row span and the column span. In order to achieve the HTML row and column span using the `panelGrid` component, take a look at the following sample snippet that demonstrates this:

```
<p:panelGrid>
<p:row>
<p:columnrowspan="3">1R1C</p:column>
<p:columncolspan="4">1R2C</p:column>
</p:row>
```

[72]

```
<p:row>
<p:columncolspan="2">CCC</p:column>
<p:columncolspan="2">DDD</p:column>
</p:row>
<p:row>
<p:column>EEE</p:column>
<p:column>FFF</p:column>
<p:column>GGG</p:column>
<p:column>HHH</p:column>
</p:row>
</p:panelGrid>
```

The output for the preceding code snippet produces the HTML table as show in the following screenshot:

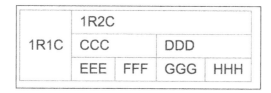

The advantage of using this component is that the PrimeFaces view resolver will never allow the developer to miss the columns, and it also acts as a guide to define the table's format.

Supporting tags in the login screen

You will be using two extra components, dialog and keyboard, from PrimeFaces in order to satisfy user-specific needs.

A requirement of the login page is that it needs a virtual keyboard as an input source, the reason for this being that the application could then be used in touch screens.

The `dialog` tag is used to render the login form because it has a nice functionality to render it all over the application with an overlay, and it will always be displayed in the center screen. In order to achieve this feature, you may need to write more code without this dialog component. It becomes challenging when you use the keyboard component on the dialog component. In general the PrimeFaces dialog component will always render on top of other components with an overlay to block all the other components. The keyboard component will be rendered below the dialog component and it becomes inaccessible. In order to overcome this situation, you can use a CSS trick to change the z-index CSS property of the keyboard component shown at the top of the dialog component.

Here is the snippet that does the job for us:

```
<p:keyboard id="j_username" required="true" widgetVar="usernameKeyBo
ard"value="#{userController.userName}"onfocus="$('#keypad-div').css(
'z-index', 9999 );"/>
<p:keyboard id="j_password" required="true" password="true"
value="#{userController.password}"onblur="$('#keypad-div').css(
'z-index', 9999 );"/>
```

If you look at the preceding snippet, you can see that both the keyboard components have the `onblur` event set to some CSS fix. This will just update the z-index for that component whenever it gets activated or focused.

The dataGrid component

The `dataGrid` component does a similar job as that of `panelGrid` apart from the fact that `dataGrid` displays a collection of data in a grid layout. You can use a column specification by using a `column` attribute. On top of this, the `dataGrid` component supports good pagination. This means that you can just set the rows and define the columns with pagination enabled, not to mention there are many other advantages available in `panelGrid`.

Please refer to the list of attributes and their usage that is listed for the `dataGrid` component. In the PrimeFaces user guide, you will get information on how you used the `dataGrid` component in the example.

The dataGrid component's attributes

The following code snippet is used in your center form to render the menu items. You will be using a `dataGrid` component to render the menu items in the center container.

```
<h:form id="centerForm">
<p:panel header="Menu Card" style="width: 99%; border: none;"
id="menuItemContiner">
<p:dataGrid value="#{menuItemController.menuItems}" var="menus"
style="border: none;" columns="4" >
<p:panelstyleClass="order-box">
<p:panelGrid columns="1" columnClasses="aligns">
<p:columnGroup>
<h:outputText value="#{menus.id}"/>
<h:outputText value="#{menus.name}"/>
<h:outputText value="#{menus.categoryId}"/>
</p:columnGroup>
<p:columnGroup>
```

```
<p:commandButton value="Favorite"
update=":leftPanForm:accord:favorites"
actionListener="#{menuItemController.addToFavorite(menus.id)}"/>
<p:commandButton value="Add" update=":rightPanForm"
actionListener="#{menuItemController.addLineItem(menus.id, menus.
displayName, menus.price)}"/>
<p:spacer/>
</p:columnGroup>
</p:panelGrid>
</p:panel>
</p:dataGrid>
</p:panel>
</h:form>
```

As you can see from the preceding snippet, you have used the `dataGrid` and `panelGrid` components together. This is a unique situation where you will need to combine both. This is explained better in the following screenshot:

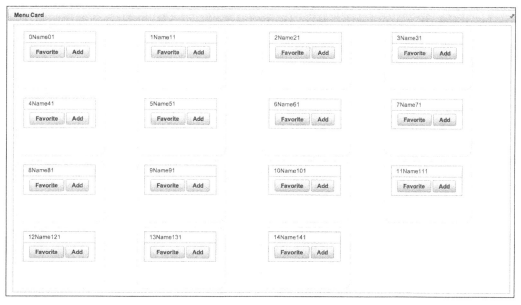

A screenshot of the menu item view

In the preceding screenshot, you should notice that each menu item has five attributes. The `dataGrid` component is meant to iterate the collection object, and the `panelGrid` component is used to group the five object elements by specifying the `columns` attribute as 3. Note that by default, the `panelGrid` and `dataGrid` components use three columns. In this case, you will have specified the `dataGrid` component's `columns` attribute to 4.

The dataTable component and its usage

In this restaurant application, you are using the `dataTable` component to render the ticket in a tabular fashion. You may be asking yourself why we are using the `dataTable` component instead of `dataGrid`. The `dataTable` component renders the collection of data in a tabular format without any extra work. The column groupings show the total number of fields as well. You can still use the `dataGrid` component in its place, but you will need to add in some extra lines to achieve this functionality. From a developer's point of view, however, you would need to reduce the line of code for better maintenance and to leverage the use of PrimeFaces' components. The `rowIndexVar` attribute is used as a row number in the first column, and it is used as *X+1* because the index starts from zero. The following is the code snippet used to achieve this:

```
<h:form id="rightPanForm">
  <p:dataTable value="#{menuItemController.lineItems}" var="cats"
style="border: none;" rowIndexVar="x">
    <p:column>
     #{x+1}
    </p:column>
    <p:column>
#{cats.displayName}
</p:column>
<p:column>
#{cats.quantity}
</p:column>
<p:column>
#{cats.price}
</p:column>
<p:columnGroup type="footer">
<p:row>
<p:columncolspan="3" footerText="Totals:"
style="text-align:right"   />
<p:columnfooterText="#{menuItemController.lineTotal}$" />
</p:row>
</p:columnGroup>
</p:dataTable>
</h:form>
```

The following is a screenshot of an open ticket:

Ticket			
1	Name9_4	2	8.0
2	Name7_4	1	18.0
3	Name10_4	1	0.0
4	Name4_4	1	11.0
5	Name11_4	1	12.0
		Totals:	57.0$

The accordion component and its usage

The **accordion component** is used in this application to separate the left panel in order to show the categories and favorite items. Based on the client requirement the left panel should have either one of category list or favorite list in order to display more items in the panel. This will benefit the user during the ordering phase by easy navigation to more items. The **favorite list** is used to collect the frequently ordered menu items from the menu item list to reduce the number of clicks. The user can add their favorite item to the list and populate the center panel with these favorites. The menu item can be from any category. The following screenshot shows the left panel with the category and favorites list:

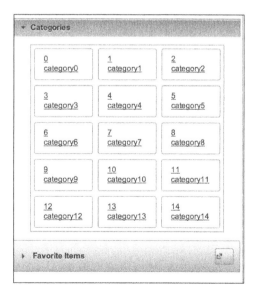

Integrating the restaurant's menu card model

This section explains the business model of the restaurant's menu card system and ordering. The following screenshot shows the full menu card system:

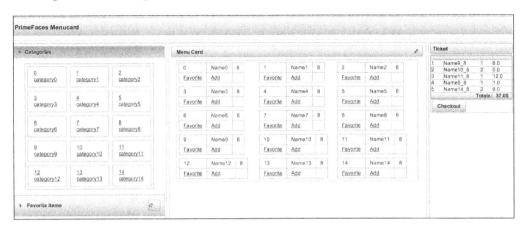

As you can see, the full restaurant menu card system is shown with an ordering platform. On the left-hand side, there are the **Categories** and **Favorite** menus. The center contains the menu items for the selected category, so if they choose from the favorites list, it will also display the same center panel. Finally, on the right panel, there is a ticket where you can add any number of menu items and check for payment.

Looking back at the left panel, the `accordionPanel` component is used because the advantage of this component is that you can render many tab-styled areas to show the elements. In this case, you are using both the category and favorite lists. Have a look at the code in detail:

```
<h:form id="leftPanForm">
<p:accordionPanel id="accord">
<p:tab title="Categories">
<p:dataGrid value="#{menuItemController.categories}" var="cats"
style="border: none;">
<p:commandLink style="a:link { text-decoration:none; }"
update=":centerForm:menuItemContiner"
actionListener="#{menuItemController.findAllMenuItemsForCategory(cats.id)}">
<p:panel>
<h:outputText value="#{cats.id}"/><br/>
```

```
<h:outputText value="#{cats.name}"/>
</p:panel>
</p:commandLink>
</p:dataGrid>
</p:tab>
<p:tab>
<f:facet name="title">
<h:panelGrid columns="2" width="100%">
<h:outputText value="Favorite Items"/>
<p:commandButton icon="ui-icon-extlink" iconPos="center"
update=":centerForm:menuItemContiner"
actionListener="#{menuItemController.loadFavorites}"
style="float: right;"/>
</h:panelGrid>
</f:facet>
<p:outputPanel id="favorites">
<p:dataGrid value="#{menuItemController.favoriteItems}" var="mens"
id="favoriteFormContiner">
<p:panel>
<h:outputText value="#{mens.id}"/><br/>
<h:outputText value="#{mens.name}"/>
</p:panel>
</p:dataGrid>
</p:outputPanel>
</p:tab>
</p:accordionPanel>
</h:form>
```

From the preceding code, you can see how the left panel is designed using the accordion component. The important part to note here is how the click event is integrated. When the user clicks on the category, the center panel gets updated with the appropriate content. The next section will explain this procedure.

Updating the component on a click

When the user selects a category, the appropriate menu items are populated in the center panel. In the preceding code snippet, you will notice that the commandLink and commandButton components are specified with the action listener set to a method. This means that each time the user clicks on the component, the listener method will be executed, and based on the method parameter, the menu items will be populated in the member variable on the controller. You will also notice that the update attribute of the commandLink and commandButton components are specified to target the DOM element's ID. Also, you specified the center panel ID with a full path reference.

Whenever the event is triggered, the listener method populates the menu item list with the appropriate menu items for the specified category. Upon its completion, the target component will get updated, and it will be refreshed with the latest data from the populated list. This renders the screen with updated values. Because all of these things are happening via AJAX requests, the user may not realize the update is happening.

Similarly, you will perform the same kind of update in the ticket items, favorites, and other things. PrimeFaces helped this page to behave as an AJAX-interactive page.

A problem encountered during implementation

The important part of this process is to understand how to specify the target DOM element's ID. If you are not specifying an ID for the PrimeFaces components, then the PrimeFaces view resolver will assign a dynamic ID for each component. It is difficult to take the reference of a particular target DOM element. In order to get the correct DOM element ID, please perform the following steps:

1. Firstly, you need to specify the target element with a meaningful name in the ID attribute. In this case, you can use menuItemContainer.

2. After this, specify a meaningful name in the ID attribute of the target elements that enclose the Form tag. In this case, you can use centerForm.

3. Following this, you should use the browser's debugging facilities to inspect the element in order to find the exact name, which is generated at runtime for our desired target. In this case, it is generated as centerForm:menuItemContainer. The following screenshot shows exactly what to expect:

    ```
    ▼<div id="centerForm:menuItemContiner" class="ui-panel ui-widget ui-widget-content
    none;" data-widget="widget_centerForm_menuItemContiner">
        ►<div id="centerForm:menuItemContiner_header" class="ui-panel-titlebar ui-widget-
        …</div>
    ```

4. Finally, you can specify the same ID by suffixing : with the generated ID. In this case, this is :centerForm:menuItemContainer.

The following is another example to make it clear how to get the DOM element ID to be used as an update target. Looking at the following screenshot of the Chrome inspect element, you can see leftPanForm:accord:favorites. For div to be used as a target, have a look at the following screenshot to see how you can achieve this by just specifying the right name in the JSF's page:

```
▼<div id="leftPanForm:accord:j_idt22" class="ui-accordion-content ui-helper-reset ui-widget-
   "tabpanel" aria-hidden="false" style="display: block;">
   ▶<div id="leftPanForm:accord:favoriteFormContiner" class="ui-datagrid ui-widget">…</div>
```

The following code is used to render a command button with a specified target component name to update:

```
<p:commandButton value="Favorite" update=":leftPanForm:accord:favorit
es" actionListener="#{menuItemController.addToFavorite(menus.id)}"/>
```

In the preceding snippet, note how the update target name is used in the command button. Now you know how to achieve this using the Chrome inspect element. For more information on the Chrome inspect element, visit https://developer.chrome.com/devtools/docs/shortcuts. Here, the following XHTML code shows the hierarchy of how the components are defined:

```
<h:form id="leftPanForm">
<p:accordionPanel id="accord">
<p:tab title="Categories">
<p:dataGrid …..
   <p:outputPanel id="favorites">
```

You can find the preceding code snippet in the categories.xhtml file.

If you specify the wrong DOM ID, which is not present on this page, then you will receive an error saying that the DOM element is missing for the given ID. Otherwise, you won't receive any indication of an error.

> The naming format is formName:parentcomponentID:componentId.

The preceding naming format should help you understand how to define the component for reference. The categories.xhtml file is a single file that is included on the left-hand side category that contains an h:form tag with the leftPanForm ID; the form contains an accordion panel with the accord ID. Inside this accordion panel, we have two tabs: one for category and another for the favorite list with the ID as favorites. In order to specify this as a target, you have to use leftForm:accord:favorites.

Similarly, you need to be careful about the action listener. You may have already specified the right method with the right parameter, but one thing to remember is when you click on the button or link, it will process the request as an HTTP GET method. Therefore, the bean has to be view scoped in order to retain the previously populated values. The following code snippet is used in our menu page, this is how you populate the menu items on each click of category:

```
<p:commandLink style="a:link { text-decoration:none; }"update=":center
Form:menuItemContiner" actionListener="#{menuItemController.findAllMen
uItemsForCategory(cats.id)}">

public void findAllMenuItemsForCategory(intcategoryId) {
        Random rand = new Random(50);
        //instead we can populate from Database.
menuItems = new ArrayList<>();
for (inti = 0; i< 15; i++) {
menuItems.add(new MenuItem(i, "Name" + i, "Name" + i+"_"+categoryId,
rand.nextInt(20), true, categoryId));
        }
    }
```

When an action listener is specified for a command link or a command button, the specified method will be processed when the button is clicked. In your restaurant application, whenever the category is clicked, the method `findAllMenuItemsForCategory` will be processed; this contains the logic to retrieve the menu items for the specific category ID.

You will be using the same kind of process method to populate and update the components in this application, which as a reminder are the favorites list, the center menu card, and the ticket panel. You can use either the `commandLink` or `commandButton` components to perform this action.

Controllers in use

Your restaurant application has two different controllers (or managed beans): `UserController.java` and `MenuItemController.java`. They are explained here:

- `UserController` is used to track the user profile that is defined as the session-scoped bean in order to hold the session that contains the login credentials for validation.
- `MenuItemController` has all the functionalities related to the menu card system. This can be used by the view scope because this expires for every view.

`UserController` makes use of the session scope because it has to retain the value for the entire session. With `MenuItemController` in the view scope, this will retain the value for the whole request.

The following are the methods used to handle the transaction of the menu card system:

- `public void init()`: The `init` method is used to initialize the bean with necessary information. In your case, this method is called only once whenever the bean is initialized. The annotation, `@PostConstruct`, will enable this feature for this method. In this application, you will use this method to populate the category types. In real time, you can call DAO instead of hardcoded values.
- `private void populateCategory()`: This method is responsible for populating the category list.
- `public void findAllMenuItemsForCategory(intcategoryId)`: This method will be executed when the user clicks on this category, and it is called with the category ID as the parameter. This method is also responsible for populating the menu items associated with the category ID.
- `public void addLineItem(int id, String displayName, double price)`: This method is responsible for adding the selected menu item to the ticket, and this can be executed from any of the menu items.
- `public void loadFavorites()`: This method is executed when the user wishes to load all of their favorite items in the display of the center panel. The button near the favorite panel at the top is responsible for this event.
- `private void updateTotal()`: This private method is used to update the total whenever the user adds a new item to the ticket.
- `public void addToFavorite(int id)`: This is another method that can be executed from all the menu items using the favorite link. This will add the selected menu item to the favorites list to make it available for easy navigation.

The following is the transaction variable that holds the values during runtime:

```
private Category category;
privateMenuItemmenuItem;
private double lineTotal = 0.0;
private List<Category> categories = new ArrayList<>();
private List<MenuItem>menuItems = new ArrayList<>();
private List<LineItem>lineItems = new ArrayList<>();
private List<MenuItem>favoriteItems = new ArrayList<>();
```

The preceding transaction variables are used to hold the runtime values respectively during the process of ordering. The associated getter and setter methods are also defined in the same bean controller. These variables are used in the JSF page to get the data from the controller. The `menuItems` variable is used in the center panel's `dataGrid` component as a collection. The `Lineitem` collection variable is used in the right panel ticket's `dataTable`.

CSS and styling

The presentation of code can be a work of art, attracting the customer in many ways. Before you even buy a product, the first thing to consider is the appearance or the look and feel. CSS plays a vital role in how you feel as a customer when you come across a product in the web application industry. To overcome this situation, PrimeFaces has a readymade solution that contains many themes. Even though you have access to PrimeFaces' own themes, there may be some situations where the user might have some specific requirements regarding the appearance. If this is the case, you may need to override PrimeFaces' CSS to fulfill this requirement. The following CSS code snippet is applied for each panelGrid component created using PrimeFaces. (This is not relevant to the implementation). This code has to replaced with user specific CSS:

```css
.ui-panelgrid td {
  border-width: 1px;
  border-style: solid;
  border-color: inherit;
  padding: 4px 10px;
}
```

The preceding code can be overridden by using user-specific styles that are defined in the `styles.css` file:

```css
.aligns {
  margin: auto 0px;
  width: 100%;
  height: 100%;
  padding: 10px 10px !important;
}
```

In the preceding sample snippet, you are overriding the padding values, which is currently in the default PrimeFaces' theme. The `styles.css` file has class aligns. In this case, you are just using `!important`, which is the CSS property that needs to override the PrimeFaces theme. There are also many more ways to do this using CSS tricks.

There are many way to do this kind of fix, another one common practice is as follows:

- Find the default PrimeFaces theme CSS class name
- Write one user defined class name as a parent class
- Add the default class name as child and define new override CSS
- Use the user defined class for your component that you like to override

This following CSS snippet will override the default.

```
.user-define-grid .ui-panelgrid td {
    border: none;
    padding: 0;
}
```

In the preceding CSS snippet you have created `user-define-grid` as parent, and `ui-panelgrid` is defined as child. You just need to add a space between two class names, the second one will become child.

Working with sample code

If you wish to work on the sample code, all you need to do is just download it from the Git repository at `https://github.com/sudheerj/primefaces-blueprints` and use your preferred IDE. From there, you can start playing with the code. You can run the code using the `mvn jetty:run` command in the Maven console and then navigate to `http://localhost:8080/web`, using `admin/admin` as the credentials to log into the application.

Summary

This chapter showed you to how to develop your own restaurant business model application. Please note that in this chapter, the examples used were for demonstration purposes only, and the business may vary from restaurant to restaurant. The topics covered were the Facelet-templating features and the layout tag and its usage with the use of the default template file. You learned how to group elements in UI using the PrimeFaces' grouping components, which include accordion, `panelGrid`, `dataGrid`, `dataTable`, column, `columnGroup`, and row components.

The next chapter will provide you with a procedure to create another real-time business model called an employee registration application, which aims to explain the `Input` component of PrimeFaces.

4
Global Mutual Funds Tracking

This chapter teaches you how to create a simple online application to track mutual funds over a particular period. The PrimeFaces library provides you with the most-used data container components that have a very large and complex feature set, which you can use to hold big data sets. An important goal of this chapter is to also demonstrate the features of PrimeFaces' dataTable, dataList, and dataGrid components. To explain these components, you will be using the global mutual funds tracking application where either the service center user, dealer, advisor, or investor logs in to the application depending on their role to view specific related information. The topics that will be covered are as follows:

- A brief introduction to global mutual funds tracking application, including use cases and the architectural design
- Project creation and the implementation of the application screens using data container components
- Working with the global mutual funds tracking project code

An introduction to the global mutual funds tracking project

A mutual fund represents a professionally managed investment scheme that pools money from different investors to purchase various securities. Sometimes, we call them registered investment companies (or investment companies) that are controlled under securities and exchange commissions. These investment companies need to maintain a mutual funds application to display the various levels of user information and to perform their activities or operations. For example, the mutual fund organization will store the fund manager's information, service center, dealers, advisors, representatives, and their account values information, among other data, in a hierarchical order.

The global mutual funds tracking application

In this section, we will show you how to create an online global funds tracking application using the PrimeFaces library. The mutual funds tracking application is used to track the service center, dealer, advisor, as well as the representatives and their account details over the long run. Different levels of mutual fund users can log on to this application to view their data and perform their regular tasks.

Before you implement the various data container components using the PrimeFaces library, you should take a brief look at the project requirements and architectural designs explained in the following subsections.

Application use cases

The purpose of this application is to track global mutual funds information easily from the big data sets. At first, the mutual fund user needs to log in to the application in order to view the different landing pages based on the user roles, as follows:

- **Service center user**: This role can be used to view the service center information
- **Dealer user**: This role can be used to check the dealer information
- **Advisor user**: This role can be used to view the advisor information
- **Investor role**: This role can be used to access the accounts details for different types of accounts

The mutual funds information can also be viewed in a hierarchical manner from the top-to-bottom levels (service center to dealer, dealer to advisor, and advisor to accounts summary) of different user roles in the organization.

Sketching the UML use case diagram

The following use case diagram is used to represent the various functionalities that occur in the application with the help of **actors** and their roles. These functionalities, such as logging on to the application using service center, dealer, advisor, and investor roles; viewing the service center information using a multifeatured data table format; viewing the dealer's information using combined dataTable and dataList formats; viewing the advisor's information using the dataGrid format; and viewing the investors accounts information using the lazy data table are treated as individual use cases, which is exactly how they will be adopted in this application:

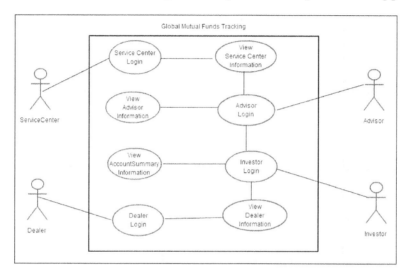

There are four actors who perform these functionalities in this application. They are the **ServiceCenter** user, **Dealer**, **Advisor**, and **Investor**.

The architectural design

The architecture of this application can be presented as follows:

- The presentation layer will be composed of standard JSF and PrimeFaces components
- **XHTML** or **Facelets** are used as the view technology in order to render the UI components
- You will use the PrimeFaces built-in **start** theme to skin or style the web pages

- The managed beans will be used to hold the session information and event handling as well as executing the business logic
- The data access layer is used to interact with the MySQL database using the JPA (specification) **hibernate** (**ORM Tool**) framework
- The Apache Maven build tool will be used to build the project and for dependency management

The following architecture diagram represents the three major layers of the web application and their interaction with the **MySQL** database. The flow from the presentation layer to the other layer components and database is represented by straight lines:

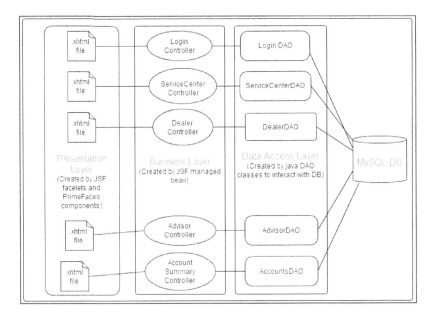

Here, hibernate is an ORM that implements the JPA standard used between the **DAO** layer and the MySQL database.

Creating a project and implementing the application screens

This section will show you how to implement the global mutual funds tracking application using the PrimeFaces data iteration components. The first step to is to start the project by creating the template structure using standard JSF Facelets. Then, you need to apply the multifeatured dataTable component for the creation of the service center information; enhanced dataTable filtering, which contains a dataList inside the expanded row, to represent additional dealer information; advisor information in a data grid format; and at the end, to apply RTL-supported lazy loading of the account summary information for a very large amount of data. We can also use the few supported components to complete the full-fledged reporting application.

Before the actual implementation, you should first create the project structure with the complete folder structure.

The project structure

The structure of the application should consider the MVC design pattern (which is used to separate the presentation, business, and data access layers) in order to make a proper web application. After you have properly implemented these sections, the Eclipse IDE project structure in the navigator view should look as shown in the following screenshot:

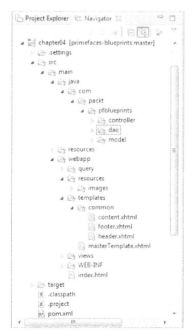

Next, you need to make sure that you have configured the entire web project using the step-by-step configurations detailed in *Chapter 1, Creating a "Hello World" Application*.

Understanding the application template design

You are going to use a single main template formed by the combination of three smaller template files. The `masterTemplate.xhtml` file uses Facelets' `ui:insert` and `ui:include` tags for the header, content, and footer sections, as shown in the following code snippet:

```
<div id="header">
    <ui:insert name="header">
    <ui:include src="/templates/common/header.xhtml" />
    </ui:insert>
</div>
<div id="content">
    <ui:insert name="content">
    <ui:include src="/templates/common/content.xhtml" />
    </ui:insert>
</div>
<div id="footer">
    <ui:insert name="footer">
    <ui:include src="/templates/common/footer.xhtml" />
    </ui:insert>
</div>
```

The `header` section deals with the website logo, advertisements, and logout functionalities. On the other hand, the `footer` section deals with the application information through the command links. Finally, the `content` section or template is just provided for default content.

Database configurations

The hibernate ORM is used to map between Java entities and RDBMS. The hibernate application can be created in two ways, as follows:

- XML configurations
- Annotations

We will use the XML configurations mechanism. In this approach, we have to configure the hibernate MySQL dialect and other configuration details in the hibernate configuration file, whereas the entity mapping information for each screen needs to be added to its respective hibernate mapping file. Please take a look at the hibernate configuration code in the blueprint's GitHub repository for reference.

> Remember to run all the SQL commands of `mysqlquery.txt` (which exist under query folder) before proceeding with the front end application design.

Implementing the application screens using data iteration components

Before we use the actual data iteration components, we will take a look at the login screen development.

Implementing the login screen

Here, you will be able to create a login screen where the mutual fund user can log on to the application. The mutual fund user needs to select the role first when logging in to the application. Before navigating to the other screens of this application, the login screen needs to validate whether the login user has been authenticated or not based on the role mentioned.

You can create the login form containing the user role, username, and password fields with the help of the PrimeFaces select, input, and keyboard components, as shown in the following code snippet:

```
<h:form id="loginform">
<p:panel style="width:30%;height:30%;margin-left:35%">
  <p:messages id="login"></p:messages>
  <h:panelGrid columns="3" cellpadding="5">
    <h:outputText value="LoginUser:"></h:outputText>
    <p:selectOneMenu value="#{loginController.userrole}"
    label="LoginUser:">
      <f:selectItem itemLabel="Service Center" itemValue="S" />
      <f:selectItem itemLabel="Dealer" itemValue="D" />
      <f:selectItem itemLabel="Advisor" itemValue="A" />
      <f:selectItem itemLabel="Investor" itemValue="I" />
    </p:selectOneMenu>
    <h:outputText/>

    <h:outputLabel for="username" value="Username:" />
```

```
<p:inputText value="#{loginController.username}" id="username"
  required="true" requiredMessage="Username cannot be empty"
  label="username">
</p:inputText>
<p:watermark for="username" value="Enter username" />

<h:outputLabel for="password" value="Password:" />
<p:keyboard value="#{loginController.password}" id="password"
  required="true" requiredMessage="Password cannot be empty"
  password="true" />
<p:watermark for="password" value="Enter password" />

<h:outputText></h:outputText>
<p:commandButton id="loginButton" value="Login" update="login"
  style="float:right"
  action="#{loginController.validateUser}" ajax="false" />
<h:outputText/>
    </h:panelGrid>
  </p:panel>
</h:form>
```

In the preceding code, after the user role, username, and password fields, you can see the login command button that is used to navigate mutual funds screens. The backing managed bean is defined with the user role, username, and passwords fields, along with the `validateUser()` method. This method validates the different types of user authentication by accessing the data access layer as follows:

```
public String validateUser() throws SQLException {
    FacesMessage msg = null;
    boolean isValidUser = false;
    LoginDAO dao = new LoginDAO();
    isValidUser = dao.validateUser(username, password,userrole);

    ExternalContext externalContext = FacesContext.
    getCurrentInstance().getExternalContext();
    Map<String, Object> sessionMap = externalContext.getSessionMap();

    if (isValidUser) {
    if(userrole.equalsIgnoreCase("S")){
    return "/views/servicecenterinfo?faces-redirect=true";
       }
    else if(userrole.equalsIgnoreCase("D")){
    sessionMap.put("dealertinnumber", username);
    return "/views/dealerinfo?faces-redirect=true";
    }
```

```
      else if(userrole.equalsIgnoreCase("A")){
        sessionMap.put("advisornumber", username);
        return "/views/advisorinfo?faces-redirect=true";
        }
      else {
        return "/views/accountsinfo?faces-redirect=true";
        }

        } else {
          msg = new FacesMessage(FacesMessage.SEVERITY_WARN,
          "Login Error","Invalid credentials");
          FacesContext.getCurrentInstance().addMessage(null, msg);
          return null;
     }
  }
```

In the data access layer (in this case, `loginDAO.java`), you need to create the hibernate session factory as shown in the following code snippet. It creates `SessionFactory` from the `hibernate.cfg.xml` file, which is located under the resources folder:

```
private   SessionFactory sessionFactory;
private   SessionFactory configureSessionFactory() throws
HibernateException {
    Configuration configuration = new Configuration();
    configuration.configure();
    StandardServiceRegistryBuilder
    builder = new StandardServiceRegistryBuilder()
        .applySettings(configuration.getProperties());
    SessionFactory sessionfactory = configuration.
    buildSessionFactory(builder.build());
    return sessionfactory;
}
```

To validate the user, you just need to make a MySQL-HQL query with the provided username and password details. Based on the role and login credentials, the service center and account summary screens will be authenticated by a true value being returned directly for a valid user role. For the other roles (the dealer and advisor roles), if the count variable is greater than one, then it represents that the logged in user is valid; it does this by returning a `true` Boolean value. Otherwise, the application can't be accessed as it returns a `false` Boolean value. The following code snippet validates the logged user in the data access layer as follows:

```
public boolean validateUser(String userid, String password, String
userrole) {
    try {
```

```
    sessionFactory = configureSessionFactory();
    Session session = sessionFactory.openSession();
    session.beginTransaction();
    String query = null;
    if (userrole.equalsIgnoreCase("S") &&
    userid.equalsIgnoreCase("servicecenter")
    &&password.equalsIgnoreCase("servicecenter")) {
       return true;
     }
    else if (userrole.equalsIgnoreCase("I") &&
    userid.equalsIgnoreCase("investor")
    &&password.equalsIgnoreCase("investor")) {
       return true;
    }
    else if (userrole.equalsIgnoreCase("D")) {
      query = "from Dealer where dealernumber='" + userid + "'
      and dealernumber='" + password + "' ";;
    }
    else if (userrole.equalsIgnoreCase("A")) {
      query = "from Advisor where advisornumber='" + userid + "'
      and advisornumber='" + password + "' ";;
    }
    else {
      return false;
     }
    Query queryObj = session.createQuery(query);
    List<Object> list = queryObj.list();
    int count = 0;
    if (list != null) {
    count = list.size();
    }
    session.getTransaction().commit();
    if (count > 0) {
    return true;
    } else {
    return false;
        }
      } catch (Exception e) {
    return false;         }
}
```

You should now find the login screen, with the preceding required functionalities, as shown in the following screenshot:

For the preceding login form, you will find that the non-empty and length validations have been applied.

Login credentials

The application has been provided with four different levels of login credentials based on user roles. They are as follows:

- **Service center and investor user roles**: The service center and investor users can log in with the `servicecenter/servicecenter` and `investor/investor` credentials, respectively.
- **Dealer user roles**: A particular dealer who is logging in to this application (using the dealer number as the username and password) will be authenticated from the list of dealers available in the dealer information. For example, if 111 is a dealer number, then the credentials to authenticate the dealer role are as follows:
    - **Username**: `111`
    - **Password**: `111`

- **Advisor user roles**: A particular advisor who is logging in to this application (using the advisor number as the username and password) will be authenticated from the list of advisors available in the advisor information. For example, if 1111 is a advisor number, then the credentials to authenticate the advisor role are as follows:
    - **Username**: 1111
    - **Password**: 1111

Exploring the mutual funds screens

The mutual funds screens contain a huge set of data in the form of data tables, data lists, and data grids with their useful features. The features available on these data containers display the information as per the user requirements. The mutual fund user can find the commonly used sorting, filtering, and pagination features in the data container components. Apart from these regular features, there will be component-specific features as well.

Implementing the service center information screen

The service center screen holds the list of dealers, along with the important required details of each dealer. You can find the list of dealers in a table format with the most-used sorting, filtering, and pagination features. The authenticated service center user can also select a particular dealer and navigate to view the dealer's information, view and edit the dealer's profile, and delete the dealer from the list of available dealers.

The service center table contains the dealer's TIN/CST number, dealer name, dealer branch name, date of registration, PAN number, status, number of advisors with the sorting, filtering, pagination, context menu, multisorting, draggable columns, and draggable rows features.

The draggable columns and draggable rows features are provided by setting the `draggableRows="true"` and `draggableColumns="true"` properties, respectively, as shown in the following code snippet:

```
<p:dataTable id="servicecenterinfo" widgetVar="$servicecenterinfo"
  var="dealer" value="#{serviceCenterController.servicecenterInfo}"
  paginator="true" rows="10"
  paginatorTemplate="{CurrentPageReport} {FirstPageLink}
  {PreviousPageLink} {PageLinks} {NextPageLink} {LastPageLink}
  {RowsPerPageDropdown}"
  rowsPerPageTemplate="5,10,15" draggableColumns="true"
  draggableRows="true" rowKey="#{dealer.dealertinnumber}"
```

```xml
paginatorPosition="bottom" sortMode="multiple"
selection="#{serviceCenterController.dealerobj}"
selectionMode="single">
  <f:facet name="header">
          Service Center Information-List of Dealers
      </f:facet>

  <p:ajax event="rowReorder"
  listener="#{serviceCenterController.onRowReorder}"
  update=":servicecenterform:messages" />

  <p:column sortBy="#{dealer.dealertinnumber}"
     filterBy="#{dealer.dealertinnumber}" id="dealertinnumber">
  <f:facet name="header">
    <h:outputText value="Dealer TIN/CST Number" />
  </f:facet>
  <h:outputText value="#{dealer.dealertinnumber}" />
  </p:column>

  <p:column sortBy="#{dealer.dealerfirstname}
    #{dealer.dealerlastname}"
    filterBy="#{dealer.dealerfirstname}
    #{dealer.dealerlastname}" id="dealername">
  <f:facet name="header">
    <h:outputText value="Dealer Name" />
  </f:facet>
  <h:outputText value="#{dealer.dealerfirstname}
  #{dealer.dealerlastname}" />
  </p:column>

  <p:column sortBy="#{dealer.branchname}"
  filterBy="#{dealer.branchname}" id="branchname">
  <f:facet name="header">
    <h:outputText value="Dealer Branch name" />
  </f:facet>
  <h:outputText value="#{dealer.branchname}" />
  </p:column>

  <p:column sortBy="#{dealer.dor}">
  <f:facet name="header">
    <h:outputText value="Date of registration" />
  </f:facet>
  <h:outputText value="#{dealer.dor}" />
  </p:column>
```

```
      <p:column sortBy="#{dealer.pan}">
      <f:facet name="header">
        <h:outputText value="PAN Number" />
      </f:facet>
        <h:outputText value="#{dealer.pan}" />
      </p:column>

      <p:column sortBy="#{dealer.status}">
      <f:facet name="header">
        <h:outputText value="Status" />
      </f:facet>
      <h:outputText value="#{dealer.status}" />
          <f:facet name="footer">
        <h:outputText value="Total Advisors:" />
          </f:facet>
      </p:column>

      <p:column sortBy="#{dealer.noofadvisors}">
      <f:facet name="header">
        <h:outputText value="Number of Advisors" />
      </f:facet>
      <h:outputText value="#{dealer.noofadvisors}" />
          <f:facet name="footer">
        <h:outputText
        value="#{serviceCenterController.advisorsCount}" />
          </f:facet>
      </p:column>

    </p:dataTable>
```

In the preceding code, the multisorting feature is enabled by setting the `sortMode` property as `multiple` (that is, `sortMode="multiple"`).

The `ServiceCenterController` managed bean holds the list as a backing bean by accessing `ServiceCenterDAO` and calculates the total advisor count under the service center.

Remember that from Java EE 7 (or JSF 2.2 release) onwards, managed beans have been deprecated and you need to use CDI instead. For example, the `@Named` annotation is recommended over the `@ManagedBean` annotation.

The following code snippet represents the backing bean for the service center screen as follows:

```
@ManagedBean
@ViewScoped
public class ServiceCenterController implements Serializable{

    private static final long serialVersionUID = 1L;
    private List<Dealer> servicecenterInfo=new ArrayList<Dealer>();
    private Dealer dealerobj=new Dealer();
    ServiceCenterDAO dao = new ServiceCenterDAO();
    private int advisorsCount=0;

    @PostConstruct
    public void init() {

        servicecenterInfo=dao.getAllDealers();
        advisorsCountCalc();
    }
    ......
}
```

`ServiceCenterDAO` retrieves all the dealers listed under the service center user as follows:

```
public List<Dealer> getAllDealers() {
    sessionFactory = configureSessionFactory();
    Session session = sessionFactory.openSession();
    session.beginTransaction();
    Query queryResult = session.createQuery("from Dealer");
    List<Dealer> allDealers = queryResult.list();
    session.getTransaction().commit();
    return allDealers;
}
```

The following screenshot shows how the service center screen will look with the list of dealers' information displayed:

Dealer TIN/CST Number	Dealer Name	Dealer Branch name	Date of registration	PAN Number	Status	Number of Advisors
111	Jonathan smith	california	02/02/2002	AFME009	ACTIVE	30
222	Manki John	Newyork	02/07/2007	AFGG023	ACTIVE	13
333	Jim Rock	Washington	02/12/2002	AFTT002	ACTIVE	32
444	Ricky Authorton	Newjersy	05/02/2005	AFME019	ACTIVE	10
555	Tom Terrin	viyanna	09/02/2006	FFME003	ACTIVE	40
666	Van Gosling	Chester	06/06/2002	HHME019	ACTIVE	70
777	Meta Sorug	Marion	08/08/2007	AFYY001	ACTIVE	20
888	Nicky Boyy	Salem	02/05/2009	AFME009	ACTIVE	70
999	Aldon Thomson	Alabama	10/02/2001	AFME109	ACTIVE	60
1001	Ricky Ponting	Washington	04/04/2010	AFFF019	ACTIVE	50
					Total Advisors:	395

The `contextMenu` component references the target data table using the `for` attribute, and a dialog will pop up once you right-click on a particular dealer. The `menuItems` child component of `contextMenu` is used to navigate the list of advisors page, view the dealer's profile, and delete a particular dealer, as follows:

```
<p:contextMenu for="servicecenterinfo">
  <p:menuitem value="View Advisors List"
    action="#{serviceCenterController.storeSelectedDealer}"
    ajax="false" icon="ui-icon-search" />
  <p:menuitem value="Dealer Profile" update=":dealerprofileform"
    oncomplete="PF('$dealerprofile').show()" icon="ui-icon-close" />
  <p:menuitem value="Delete Dealer"
    icon="ui-icon-close" update="servicecenterinfo"
    actionListener="#{serviceCenterController.deleteDealer}" />
</p:contextMenu>
```

The dealer's profile will be displayed in a pop-up dialog by just clicking on the **view dealer profile** link under `contextMenu`. The dealer's profile data can be edited and saved at any time by the service center user. The following code snippet represents dealer profile details in a dialog pop up as follows:

```
<p:dialog id="dealerprofile" header="Dealer Profile"
  widgetVar="$dealerprofile" modal="true" resizable="false">
  <h:form id="dealerprofileform">
```

```
<p:messages id="messages"></p:messages>
<h:panelGrid columns="3" cellpadding="5">
   <h:outputLabel for="firstname" value="Firstname:" />
   <p:inputText
   value="#{serviceCenterController.dealerobj.dealerfirstname}"
   id="firstname" required="true"
   requiredMessage="Firstname cannot be empty" label="username">
   </p:inputText>
   <p:watermark for="firstname" value="Enter firstname" />

   <h:outputLabel for="lastname" value="Lastname:" />
   <p:inputText
   value="#{serviceCenterController.dealerobj.dealerlastname}"
   id="lastname" required="true"
   requiredMessage="Firstname cannot be empty" label="username">
   </p:inputText>
   <p:watermark for="lastname" value="Enter lastname" />

   <h:outputLabel for="address1" value="Address1:" />
   <p:inputText
   value="#{serviceCenterController.dealerobj.address1}"
   id="address1" required="true"
   requiredMessage="Address cannot be empty" label="Address">
   </p:inputText>
   <p:watermark for="address1" value="Enter address" />

   <h:outputLabel for="address2" value="Address2:" />
   <p:inputText
   value="#{serviceCenterController.dealerobj.address2}"
   id="address2" label="Address"/>
   <p:watermark for="address2" value="Enter address" />

   <h:outputLabel for="country" value="Country:" />
   <p:inputText
   value="#{serviceCenterController.dealerobj.country}"
   id="country" label="country" />
   <p:watermark for="country" value="Enter Country" />

   <h:outputLabel for="city" value="City:" />
   <p:inputText
   value="#{serviceCenterController.dealerobj.city}"
   id="city" label="City" />
   <p:watermark for="city" value="Enter City" />
```

```
            <h:outputLabel for="contactnumber" value="Contact Number:" />
            <p:inputText
            value="#{serviceCenterController.dealerobj.contactnumber}"
            id="contactnumber" label="Contact Number" />
            <p:watermark for="contactnumber" value="Enter Contact number" />
            <h:outputLabel for="postalcode" value="Postal Code:" />
            <p:inputText
            value="#{serviceCenterController.dealerobj.postalcode}"
            id="postalcode" label="Postal Code" />
            <p:watermark for="postalcode" value="Enter Postal Code" />

            <f:facet name="footer">
            <p:commandButton id="update" value="Save"
            update=":servicecenterform"
            actionListener="#{serviceCenterController.updateDealerProfile}" />
            </f:facet>
        </h:panelGrid>
      </h:form>
</p:dialog>
```

`ServiceCenterDAO` updates the dealer's profile information as follows:

```
    public void updateDealerProfile(Dealer serviceCenterObj){
      sessionFactory = configureSessionFactory();
      Session session = sessionFactory.openSession();
      session.beginTransaction();
      session.update(serviceCenterObj);
      session.getTransaction().commit();
    }
```

When you click on any particular dealer, the dealer profile dialog with edit mode will pop up as follows:

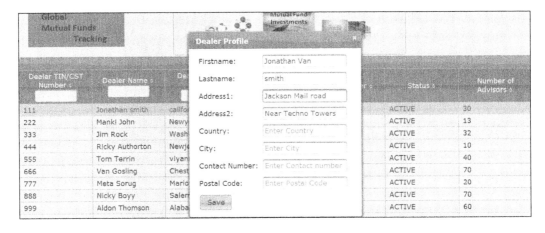

On the other hand, a particular dealer under the service center can be deleted by accessing the service center's data access layer, as shown in the following code snippet:

```
public List<Dealer> deleteDealer(Dealer object) {
   sessionFactory = configureSessionFactory();
   Session session = sessionFactory.openSession();
   session.beginTransaction();
   session.delete(object);
   Query queryResult = session.createQuery("from Dealer");
   List<Dealer> allDealers = queryResult.list();
   session.getTransaction().commit();
   return allDealers;
}
```

Apart from these specific features, you can also find the regular sorting, filtering, and pagination dataTable features.

Implementing the dealer information screen

The dealer screen holds the list of advisors with the basic information about the advisors displayed. You can find the list of advisors in a table format, with the additional information hidden by default. Clicking on the row toggler on the left-hand side displays the progress status details with the progress percentage for each year in a list format.

The dealers' information can be viewed either by navigating from the selected dealer in the service center screen or by directly logging in through the advisor role.

The advanced customized filtering features have recently been added in the PrimeFaces 5.0 release. The facet filter, new filter match modes, and custom filtering will be covered under this enhanced filtering.

The dealer table contains a dealer number, advisor name, advisor number, management company, branch, year of registration, status, and revenue using the row expansion feature, dataList component, and advanced customized filtering features.

The dealer information screen displays the list of advisors data using the dataTable expanded row and paginated dataList features. To enable the row expansion feature, the `rowToggler` component (`p:rowToggler`) should be placed under the column component. The `dataList` component under the `rowExpansion` component (`p:rowExpansion`) will be toggled (expanded/collapsed) based on the toggle icon action in each row.

The following code snippet represents the dealers' information screen with the list of advisors available:

```
<p:dataTable id="dealerinfo" widgetVar="$dealerinfo" var="advisor"
  value="#{dealerController.dealerInfo}" paginator="true" rows="10"
  paginatorTemplate="{CurrentPageReport} {FirstPageLink}
  {PreviousPageLink} {PageLinks} {NextPageLink} {LastPageLink}
  {RowsPerPageDropdown}"
  rowsPerPageTemplate="5,10,15" paginatorPosition="bottom"
  rowKey="#{advisor.advisornumber}"
  selection="#{dealerController.advisorobj}" selectionMode="single">

<f:facet name="header">
          Dealer Information-List of Advisors
     </f:facet>
<p:column style="width:2%">
  <p:rowToggler />
</p:column>
<p:column id="dealernumber" sortBy="#{advisor.dealernumber}"
  filterBy="#{advisor.dealernumber}" >
    <f:facet name="header">
   <h:outputText value="Dealer Number" />
     </f:facet>
   <h:outputText value="#{advisor.dealernumber}" />
</p:column>

<p:column id="advisorname" sortBy="#{advisor.advisorname}"
filterBy="#{advisor.advisorname}" >
     <f:facet name="header">
   <h:outputText value="Advisor Name" />
     </f:facet>
   <h:outputText value="#{advisor.advisorname}" />
</p:column>

<p:column id="advisornumber" sortBy="#{advisor.advisornumber}"
filterBy="#{advisor.advisornumber}" >
     <f:facet name="header">
   <h:outputText value="Advisor Number" />
     </f:facet>
   <h:outputText value="#{advisor.advisornumber}" />
</p:column>
<p:column id="managementcompany"
filterBy="#{advisor.managementcompany}" filterMatchMode="exact"
```

```
            headerText="Management Company" >
            <f:facet name="filter">
       <p:selectOneMenu onchange="PF('$dealerinfo').filter()">
        <f:selectItems value="#{dealerController.managementcompanies}" />
       </p:selectOneMenu>
            </f:facet>
       <h:outputText value="#{advisor.managementcompany}" />
</p:column>
<p:column id="branch"   filterBy="#{advisor.branch}"
headerText="Branch" filterMatchMode="in">
         <f:facet name="filter">
           <p:selectCheckboxMenu label="Branches"
           onchange="PF('$dealerinfo').filter()"
           panelStyle="width:150px" scrollHeight="150">
         <f:selectItems value="#{dealerController.branches}" />
           </p:selectCheckboxMenu>
         </f:facet>
       <h:outputText value="#{advisor.branch}" />
           </p:column>
<p:column id="year"   filterBy="#{advisor.year}"
filterMatchMode="lte" headerText="Year of registration">
        <f:facet name="filter">
         <p:spinner onchange="PF('$dealerinfo').filter()" min="2000"
         max="2010" size="5">
        <f:converter converterId="javax.faces.Integer" />
         </p:spinner>
        </f:facet>
      <h:outputText value="#{advisor.year}" />
</p:column>

<p:column  id="status" filterBy="#{advisor.status}"
headerText="Status" filterMatchMode="equals" width="290">
       <f:facet name="filter">
       <p:selectOneButton onchange="PF('$dealerinfo').filter()" >
       <f:converter converterId="javax.faces.Boolean" />
       <f:selectItem itemLabel="All" itemValue="" />
       <f:selectItem itemLabel="ACTIVE" itemValue="true" />
       <f:selectItem itemLabel="CLOSED" itemValue="false" />
       </p:selectOneButton>
       </f:facet>
    <h:outputText value="#{advisor.status? 'ACTIVE':'CLOSED'}" />
</p:column>
```

```xml
<p:column id="revenue" sortBy="#{advisor.revenue}"
filterBy="#{advisor.revenue}"
  filterFunction="#{dealerController.filterByRevenue}">
    <f:facet name="header">
  <h:outputText value="Revenue" />
    </f:facet>
  <h:outputText value="#{advisor.revenue}">
    <f:convertNumber currencySymbol="$" type="currency" />
  </h:outputText>
    </p:column>

<p:rowExpansion>
    <p:dataList value="#{advisor.progressStatus}" var="progress"
    paginator="true" rows="5"
  paginatorTemplate="{PreviousPageLink} {CurrentPageReport}
  {NextPageLink} {RowsPerPageDropdown}"
  rowsPerPageTemplate="5,10,15" type="none">
  <f:facet name="header">
   Progress Status
  </f:facet>
        Year:#{progress.year},Profit percentage:
        #{progress.percentage}%
    <br />
    </p:dataList>
    </p:rowExpansion>

</p:dataTable>
```

The `DealerController` managed bean holds the advisors list by retrieving the data from the dealer's data access layer as follows:

```java
@ManagedBean
@ViewScoped
public class DealerController implements Serializable{

  private static final long serialVersionUID = 1L;
  private List<Advisor> dealerInfo=new ArrayList<Advisor>();
  private SelectItem[] managementcompanies;
  private String[] branches;
  private Advisor advisorobj=new Advisor();
  DealerDAO dao = new DealerDAO();

  @PostConstruct
  public void init() {
    dealerInfo=dao.getAllAdvisors();
```

```
      createFilterCompanies();
      createFilterBranches();
  }
          .....
}
```

`DealerDAO` retrieves the list of details of the advisors either by logging in with a particular dealer or by selecting the dealer in the service center screen as follows:

```
public List<Advisor> getAllAdvisors() {
   sessionFactory = configureSessionFactory();
   Session session = sessionFactory.openSession();
   session.beginTransaction();
   Query queryResult=null;
   if(dealerNumber!=""){
      queryResult = session.createQuery("from Advisor where
      dealernumber = :dealerNum");
      queryResult.setParameter("dealerNum", dealerNumber);
   }else{
      queryResult = session.createQuery("from Advisor");
   }
   List<Advisor> allDealers = queryResult.list();
   for(Advisor dealerobj:allDealers){
      List<ProgressStatus> progressStatus=generateProgressStatus();
      dealerobj.setProgressStatus(progressStatus);
   }
   session.getTransaction().commit();
   return allDealers;
}
```

Now, the dealer's screen with the list of advisors will be displayed with additional progress status information, as follows:

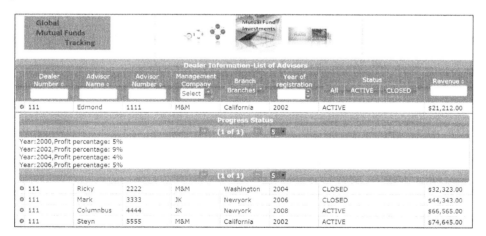

The enhanced dataTable filtering has been introduced with the filter facet, new filter match modes, and custom filtering as the major features. These features can be described as follows:

- The filter facet supports customized UI components, Ajax updates to filters, and objects instead of simple strings as filter values
- In addition to the existing options of the `filterMatchMode` attribute, new options/modes such as `lt, lte, gt, gte, equals,` and `in` are added
- Similar to the `sortFunction` property of the sorting implementation, the new `filterFunction` refers to a method that takes three parameters and the expected result is a Boolean that decides whether the value matches the filter

The dealers' information will be displayed after filtering with the various UI components as follows:

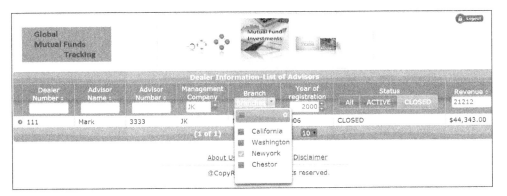

Implementing the advisor information screen

The advisor screen holds the list of representatives, with basic details on each representative. The list of representatives is represented in the form of grids/cells. Each cell contains representative details, additional details, and a way to navigate to the account information of a particular representative.

The advisor table contains the representative name, representative logo, advisor name, advisor number, and date of registration using the `dataGrid` component.

The `dataGrid` component holds the list of representatives in the grid format with the representative details. Clicking on the additional details pop up with representative information and on the account summary link navigates you to the account summary screen. The following code snippet represents advisor information with the list of available representatives in a table format:

```
<p:dataGrid id="advisorinfo" var="representative" columns="3"
  rows="9" value="#{advisorController.advisorInfo}" paginator="true"
  paginatorTemplate="{CurrentPageReport} {FirstPageLink}
  {PreviousPageLink} {PageLinks} {NextPageLink} {LastPageLink}
  {RowsPerPageDropdown}"
  rowsPerPageTemplate="4,6,9">
    <f:facet name="header">
          Advisor Information-List of Representatives
         </f:facet>

    <p:panel header="#{representative.repname}"
     style="text-align:center">
       <h:panelGrid columns="1" style="width:100%">
    <p:graphicImage
    value="/resources/images/reps/#{representative.repname}.png" />
      <h:outputText value="#{representative.repnumber}" />
      <h:outputText value="#{representative.advisornumber}" />
      <h:outputText value="#{representative.dor}" />

      <p:commandLink oncomplete="PF('$repInfo').show()"
      title="View Detail" update=":repDetails">
         <f:setPropertyActionListener
          target="#{advisorController.representativeobj}"
        value="#{representative}" />
           <h:outputText styleClass="ui-icon ui-icon-search"
           style="margin:0 auto;" />
      </p:commandLink>
      <p:commandLink value="View Account Summary"
          action="#{advisorController.navigateAccountSummary}"
          ajax="false"
          title="Navigate Account Summary page" />
       </h:panelGrid>
     </p:panel>
</p:dataGrid>
```

The `AdvisorController` managed bean holds the list of representatives as a backing bean, as follows:

```
@ManagedBean
@ViewScoped
public class AdvisorController implements Serializable{

  private static final long serialVersionUID = 1L;
  private List<Representative>
  advisorInfo=new ArrayList<Representative>();
  Representative repobj=new Representative();
  AdvisorDAO dao = new AdvisorDAO();

  @PostConstruct
  public void init() {

    advisorInfo=dao.getAllRepresentatives();
  }
  ......
}
```

`AdvisorDAO` is used to retrieve all the information from the list of representatives in the form of grids/cells as follows:

```
public List<Representative> getAllRepresentatives() {
  sessionFactory = configureSessionFactory();
  Session session = sessionFactory.openSession();
  session.beginTransaction();
  Query queryResult=null;
  if(advisorNumber!=""){
    queryResult = session.createQuery("from Representative where
    advisornumber = :advisorNum");
    queryResult.setParameter("advisorNum", advisorNumber);
  }else{
    queryResult = session.createQuery("from Representative");
  }
  List<Representative> allAdvisors = queryResult.list();
  session.getTransaction().commit();
        return allAdvisors;
}
```

Now, the advisor screen displays the list of representatives in the grid format and additional details in a pop up as follows:

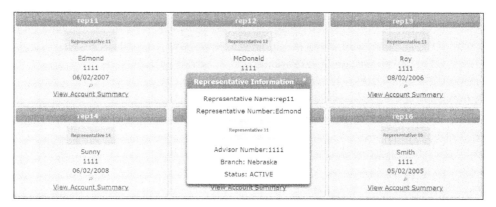

The number of rows in the `dataGrid` component are controlled/modified by using the `RowsPerPageDropdown` template.

Implementing the account summary information screen

The account summary screen holds the list of accounts with the mandatory details on each account. The list of accounts is retrieved from the database on demand lazily when there exist a large amount of data. Each basic operation such as sorting, filtering, and pagination makes the DB call to retrieve the requested data. The `table` header is grouped using the `columnGroup` and `row` components/tags, whereas the **RTL** support is provided with the help of the `selectBooleanButton` component/tag in the header.

The account summary table contains the investor name, account number, account holder name, UK balance, and US balances in a table format using the lazy-loading implementation.

The account summary table displays the list of account details referring the lazy data model named `lazyAccSummaryDataModel`, as follows:

```
<p:dataTable id="accountsummary" var="account"
  value="#{accountSummaryController.lazyAccSummaryDataModel}"
  paginator="true" rows="5" paginatorPosition="bottom" lazy="true"
  paginatorTemplate="{CurrentPageReport} {FirstPageLink}
  {PreviousPageLink} {PageLinks} {NextPageLink} {LastPageLink}
  {RowsPerPageDropdown}"
  rowsPerPageTemplate="5,10,15" rowKey="#{account.id}"
  filterEvent="enter"
```

```xml
         selection="#{accountSummaryController.accountobj}"
         selectionMode="single"
         dir="#{accountSummaryController.directionSupport}">
   <f:facet name="header">
         <p:outputLabel for="direction"
         value="Do you want RTL Support?"/>
         <p:selectBooleanButton  id="direction"
         value="#{accountSummaryController.direction}"
    onLabel="Yes" offLabel="No" onIcon="ui-icon-check"
    offIcon="ui-icon-close" >
      <p:ajax update="accountsummary"
      listener="#{accountSummaryController.addRTLsupport}" />
     </p:selectBooleanButton>
   </f:facet>
<p:columnGroup type="header">
   <p:row>
     <p:column colspan="6" headerText="Account Summary" />
   </p:row>
   <p:row>
     <p:column rowspan="2" headerText="InvestorName" />
     <p:column colspan="3" headerText="Account Details" />
     <p:column colspan="2" headerText="Market Value" />
   </p:row>
   <p:row>
     <p:column headerText="Account Number" />
     <p:column headerText="Account Type" />
     <p:column headerText="Accountholder Name" />
     <p:column headerText="Balance(US)" />
     <p:column headerText="Balance(UK)" />
   </p:row>
</p:columnGroup>
      <p:ajax event="rowSelect"
      oncomplete="PF('$accountdetails').show()"
      update=":accountdetails" />
     <p:column sortBy="investorName" filterBy="investorName"
     filterMatchMode="exact" id="investorName">
     <h:outputText value="#{account.investorName}" />
     </p:column>

     <p:column sortBy="accountNumber" filterBy="accountNumber"
     filterMatchMode="exact" id="accountNumber">
     <h:outputText value="#{account.accountNumber}" />
     </p:column>
```

```
            <p:column sortBy="accountType" id="accountType">
                <h:outputText value="#{account.accountType}" />
            </p:column>

            <p:column sortBy="registeredAccholderName"
            id="registeredAccholderName">
                <h:outputText value="#{account.registeredAccholderName}" />
            </p:column>

            <p:column sortBy="balanceUS" id="balanceUS">
                <h:outputText value="#{account.balanceUS}" />
            </p:column>

            <p:column sortBy="balanceUK" id="balanceUK">
                <h:outputText value="#{account.balanceUK}" />
            </p:column>
    </p:dataTable>
```

In the preceding code, you can find the rowSpan and colSpan properties applied to the column tags that are placed under the row tags. The list of row tags is grouped under the columngGroup component with the header type.

The accountSummary managed bean holds the lazy data model by overriding the load method of the lazyDataModel implementation. The basic dataTable operations such as sorting, filtering, and pagination result in a call to the load method. The following code snippet represents the account summary screen's backing bean with lazy loading implementation:

```
@ManagedBean
@ViewScoped
public class AccountSummaryController implements Serializable {

    private static final long serialVersionUID = 1L;
    private List<AccountSummary>
    accountsInfo = new ArrayList<AccountSummary>();
    private AccountSummary accountobj = new AccountSummary();
    AccountsDAO dao = new AccountsDAO();
    private LazyDataModel<AccountSummary> lazyAccSummaryDataModel;
    private Boolean direction = false;
    private String directionSupport = "ltr";

    @PostConstruct
    public void init() {
```

```java
      lazyAccSummaryDataModel = new LazyDataModel<AccountSummary>() {
      @Override
      public List<AccountSummary> load(int first, int pageSize,
        String sortField, SortOrder sortOrder,Map<String,
        Object> filters) {

        String sortOrderValue = null;
        if (sortField == null) {
          sortField = "investorName";
        }
        if (sortOrder.ASCENDING.equals("A")) {
          sortOrderValue = "ASC";
        } else if (sortOrder.DESCENDING.equals("D")) {
          sortOrderValue = "DSC";
        } else {
          sortOrderValue = "default";
        }

        accountsInfo = dao.getAllAccounts(first, pageSize,
        sortField,sortOrderValue, filters);
        this.setRowCount(20);
        return accountsInfo;
          }
        };
    }
    ....
    }
```

`AccountsDAO` filters the total accounts list by passing the sorting, filtering, and pagination fields in a query format, as follows:

```java
    public List<AccountSummary> getAllAccounts(int first,int
    pageSize,String sortField,String sortOrder,Map<String,Object> filters)
    {
      sessionFactory = configureSessionFactory();
      Session session = sessionFactory.openSession();
      session.beginTransaction();

      String investorname=null;
      String accountnumber=null;
      for(Iterator<String> it = filters.keySet().iterator();
      it.hasNext();) {
            String filterProperty = it.next();
```

```
            if(filterProperty.equalsIgnoreCase("investorName")){
                investorname = (String)filters.get(filterProperty);
            }
            if(filterProperty.equalsIgnoreCase("accountNumber")){
                accountnumber = (String)filters.get(filterProperty);
            }
        }
    String query=null;
    int end=0;
    if(sortOrder.equalsIgnoreCase("default")){
      end=20;
      sortOrder="ASC";
    }
    if(filters.isEmpty() ){
      end=first+pageSize;}
    else{
      end=20;
    }

    if(investorname!=null && accountnumber!=null){
      query="from AccountSummary WHERE (id BETWEEN "+(first+1)+"
      AND "+end+") AND ((investorName="+investorname+") AND
      (accountNumber="+accountnumber+")) ORDER BY
      "+sortField+" "+sortOrder;
    } else if(investorname!=null) {
      query="from AccountSummary WHERE (id BETWEEN "+(first+1)+" AND
      "+end+") AND (investorName="+investorname+") ORDER BY
      "+sortField+" "+sortOrder;
    } else if(accountnumber!=null) {
      query="from AccountSummary WHERE (id BETWEEN "+(first+1)+" AND
      "+end+") AND (accountNumber="+accountnumber+") ORDER BY
      "+sortField+" "+sortOrder;
    } else{
      query="from AccountSummary WHERE (id BETWEEN "+(first+1)+" AND
      "+end+") ORDER BY "+sortField+" "+sortOrder;
    }
    Query queryResult = session.createQuery(query);
    List<AccountSummary> allAccounts = queryResult.list();
    session.getTransaction().commit();
    return allAccounts;

}
```

Now the account summary screen displays all the accounts either by directly logging in the investor or navigating from the advisor information screen as follows:

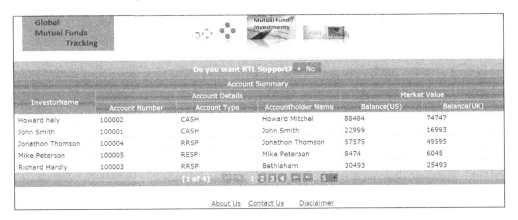

The RTL support in the **Account Summary** screen is enabled by turning the Boolean button from **No** to **Yes**. The RTL support is provided by setting the `dir` dataTable attribute to `rtl` (`dir="rtl"`). The supported values of the `dir` attribute are `rtl` and `ltr`. By default, its value is `ltr`.

The account summary screen with RTL support will be as follows:

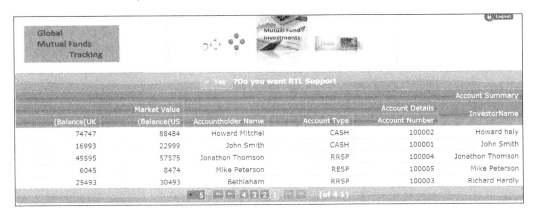

You can also configure RTL support at the application level using `contextParam` as follows:

```
<context-param>
    <param-name>primefaces.DIR</param-name>
    <param-value>RTL</param-value>
</context-param>
```

By default, the dataTable supports the `ltr` direction.

Working with the project code of the global mutual funds tracking application

If you wish to work on the sample code, all you need to do is download it from the Git repository at `https://github.com/sudheerj/primefaces-blueprints`, where you can use your preferred IDE. From there, you can start playing with the code. You can run it by using the `mvn jetty:run` command in the Maven console, and navigate your browser to `http://localhost:8080/web`, using either the service center, dealer, advisor, or investor credentials based on the user role type when logging in to the application.

Summary

In this chapter, you learned how to develop a global mutual funds tracking application. The topics covered in this chapter showed you how to create service center, dealer, advisor, and account summary screens with data iteration components such as dataTable, dataList, and dataGrid to hold the big data sets with all the available features in order to achieve the necessary functional requirements.

In the next chapter, you will learn to create an investor information analysis and reporting application, which will also show you how the export and chart export components of PrimeFaces work.

5
Investor Information Analysis and Reporting

This chapter teaches you how to create a simple investor information analysis and reporting application using PrimeFaces components. The PrimeFaces library provides a huge set of components to analyze and track big data sets for the reporting type of applications. It is difficult to analyze and track bulky information available in table format and when you are always required to log in to the application in order to check the information from time-to-time. Reporting components such as `dataExporter` are introduced to export the data in popular file formats and in various types of charts, displayed for analyzing big data. The client-side API is also available to download the same charts in image formats. Now the data can be stored, and we will be able to check the information in offline mode as well. The specific topics that will be covered are as follows:

- A brief introduction to the investor information analysis application, use cases, and architectural design
- The project creation and application screen implementation using export and chart components
- How to obtain the source code and work on the project

Understanding the investor information analysis and reporting project

The analysis and reporting applications are commonly used in the business and financial sectors to track large amounts of information quickly. The various types of charts such as pie charts, bar charts, line charts, and others can be used to compare and distinguish different categories of information. On the other hand, the `dataExporter` reporting component is used to export the bulky information to various popular file formats (PDF, Excel, XML, and CSV) in order to track and share the information in offline mode easily. Typical examples of analyzing and reporting applications include growth statistics and analysis of census information, employee performance tracking, business projects' gains and losses, share market analysis, investor information tracking, and many others.

About the application

In this section, you will see how to create an investor information analysis and reporting application using the PrimeFaces library. This application is used to analyze and track the following details over a particular period of time:

- Investor accounts
- Investments
- Transactions

Each investor can see their account's information just by logging in to the application. There will be multiple investments under each account, and there will be multiple transactions for each investment as well. The investment and transaction information will be available under the **Investment Summary** and **Transaction Summary** sections, respectively. As an investor, you can export the information in PDF, Excel, CSV, and XML formats. An investor can analyze the information with the help of charts and can download the charts when necessary.

You will make use of the export components to export the data in your favorite file formats and use the interactive chart components to give a fancy look and feel to your data. Based on the ease of use and functional requirements, you can select any of the export formats and chart components to apply them in this application.

Before you implement the various analysis and reporting components using the PrimeFaces library, you should take a brief look at the project requirements and architectural designs in the following sections.

Application use cases

The purpose of this application is to track and analyze investor information easily from big data sets. First, the investor needs to log in to the application to check their accounts' details for the different types of accounts. The investor is also allowed to view the optional accounts' information through the checkboxes menu. All the accounts' tabular data can be exported to PDF, Excel, CSV, or XML formats, with customizations such as adding a logo and disclaimer information. You can select pie charts or bar charts to analyze the market values for multiple account types.

After this, the investor can select any particular account to view all the investments under that account. The investments data can be exported by choosing the optional columns from the checkbox menu. Here, the fund investments and their market values are interpreted through a line chart, and this chart can be downloaded as an image as well.

Finally, the investor can also view all the transactions by selecting a particular fund investment in the investment summary. The investor has the option to export data from either a particular page or all the pages. All the transaction payment types and their net amounts are interpreted through a donut chart and it can be downloaded as an image.

The UML use case diagram

The following use case diagram is used to represent the various functionalities occurring in the entire application process. These functionalities, such as logging in to the application, viewing the investor's accounts information, exporting customized accounts data, analyzing the various account types and their balances using charts, viewing the account's investments information, exporting the investment data, the line chart interpretation on fund investments and market values, viewing the investments' transaction information, exporting the transactions data, and analyzing the various transaction payment types and their market values, are treated as individual use cases, which is exactly how they will be adopted in this application:

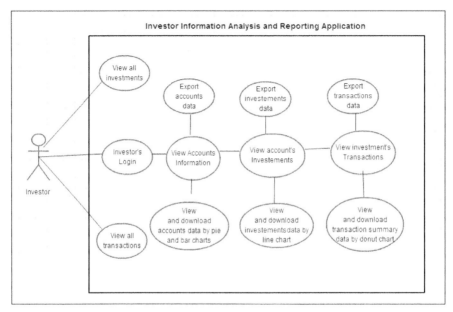

A diagram illustrating the responsibilities of the investor in the investor information analysis and reporting application

The only role that performs all these functionalities in this application is the **Investor**.

The architectural design

The architecture of this application can be presented as follows:

- The presentation layer will be composed of standard JSF and PrimeFaces components
- **XHTML** or **Facelets** are used as the view technology in order to render the UI components

- You will use PrimeFaces' built-in **ui-lightness** theme to skin or style the web pages
- The managed beans will be used to hold session information and event handling as well as to execute the business logic
- The data access layer is used to interact with the MySQL database using the **hibernate** framework
- The Apache Maven build tool will be used to build the project and for dependency management

The following architectural diagram represents the three major layers of the web application and their interaction with the **MySQL** database. The flow from the presentation layer to the other layer components and database is represented by straight lines.

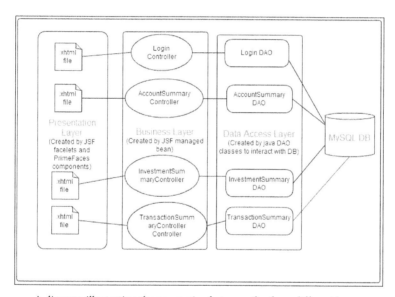

A diagram illustrating the connection between the three different layers

Here, hibernate is used as a JPA implementation to communicate between the DAO layer and the MySQL database.

Creating the project and implementing the application screens

This section will show you how to implement an investor information analysis and reporting application using PrimeFaces' export and chart components. The first step is to start the project by creating the template structure using standard JSF Facelets. Then, you need to apply dataTable components for the creation of the account summary, investment summary, and transaction summary screens. Later, you will find the functionalities such as export tables for all the three screens, apply different types of charts in all the screens, and export these charts as images. We can also use the few supported components to complete the full-fledged reporting application.

Before the actual implementation, prepare your project structure with a proper folder structure.

The project structure

For the structure of the application, you should consider presentation, business, and data access layers in order to make a proper web application. After you have properly implemented these sections, the project structure in the navigator view should look as shown in the following screenshot:

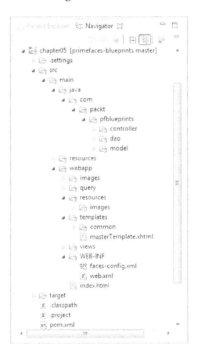

Next, you need to make sure that you have configured them all using the step-by-step configurations detailed in *Chapter 1, Creating a "Hello World" Application*.

The application template design

You are going to use a single main template formed by the combination of three smaller template files. The `masterTemplate.xhtml` file uses Facelets' `ui:insert` and `ui:include` tags for the header, content, and footer sections, as shown in the following code snippet:

```
<div id="header">
    <ui:insert name="header">
      <ui:include src="/templates/common/header.xhtml" />
    </ui:insert>
</div>
<div id="content">
    <ui:insert name="content">
      <ui:include src="/templates/common/content.xhtml" />
    </ui:insert>
</div>
<div id="footer">
    <ui:insert name="footer">
      <ui:include src="/templates/common/footer.xhtml" />
    </ui:insert>
</div>
```

The `header` section deals with the website logo, advertisements, and logout functionalities. On the other hand, the `footer` section deals with the application information through the command links. Finally, the `content` section or template is just provided for the default content.

Database configurations

The JPA provider or implementation called hibernate is used to map between Java entities and RDBMS. The hibernate application can be created in the following two ways:

- Using XML configurations
- Using annotations

We will use the XML configuration mechanism. In this approach, we have to configure the hibernate MySQL dialect details in the hibernate configuration file, whereas the entity mapping information by screen level. Please take a look at the hibernate configuration code in the blueprint's GitHub repository for reference.

> Remember to run all the SQL commands of mysqlquery.txt file (which exist under query folder of the project) before proceeding with the front end application design.

Implementing application screens using analysis and reporting components

Before we use the actual analysis and reporting components, we will take a look at the login screen development and the dataTables implementation for the summary screens.

Implementing the login screen

Here, we will create a login screen where the investor can log in to the application. Before navigating to the other screens of this application, you will have to validate whether the login user has been authenticated or not. Step-by-step instructions to create the login screen are provided as follows:

1. You can create the login form containing the username and password fields with the help of the PrimeFaces input and password components, as shown in the following code:

```
<h:form id="loginform">
   <p:panel style="width:30%;height:30%;margin-left:35%">
  <p:messages id="login"></p:messages>
    <h:panelGrid columns="3" cellpadding="5">
      <h:outputLabel for="username" value="Username:" />
      <p:inputText value="#{loginController.username}"
      id="username"
         required="true" requiredMessage="Username cannot be empty"
         validatorMessage="The length of the username
         should not be less than 4  chapters"
         label="username">
     <f:validateLength minimum="4"/>
        </p:inputText>
        <p:watermark for="username" value="Enter username" />
        <h:outputLabel for="password" value="Password:" />
```

```
            <p:password value="#{loginController.password}"
            id="password"
            required="true" requiredMessage="Password cannot be empty"/>
            <p:watermark for="password" value="Enter password" />
            <h:outputText/>
            <p:commandButton id="loginButton" value="Login"
            update="login" style="float:right"
            action="{loginController.validateUser}"
                        ajax="false" />
    </h:panelGrid>
  </p:panel>
</h:form>
```

In the preceding code, after the username and password fields, you can see the login command button that is used to navigate the account summary page.

2. The backing managed bean is defined with the username and password fields, along with the `validateUser()` method. This method validates the investor authentication by accessing the data access layer, as follows:

```
public String validateUser() throws SQLException {
   FacesMessage msg = null;
   boolean isValidUser = false;
   LoginDAO dao = new LoginDAO();
   isValidUser = dao.validateUser(username, password);
   if (isValidUser) {
     return "/views/accountsummary?faces-redirect=true";
   } else {
     msg = new FacesMessage(FacesMessage.SEVERITY_WARN,
     "Login Error",
          "Invalid credentials");
   FacesContext.getCurrentInstance().addMessage(null, msg);
   return null;
   }
}
```

3. In the data access layer (in this case, `loginDAO.java`), you need to create the hibernate session factory as follows:

```
private  SessionFactory sessionFactory;
private  SessionFactory configureSessionFactory()
      throws HibernateException {
   Configuration configuration = new Configuration();
   configuration.configure();
```

```
            StandardServiceRegistryBuilder builder =
            new StandardServiceRegistryBuilder().applySettings
           (configuration.getProperties());
            SessionFactory sessionfactory =
            configuration.buildSessionFactory(builder.build());
            return sessionfactory;
}
```

4. To validate the user, you just need to make a MySQL-HQL query with the provided username and password details. If the `count` variable is greater than one, then it represents that the logged in user is valid; it does this by returning a true Boolean value. Otherwise, the application can't be accessed as it returns a false Boolean value. The following code snippet is used to validate the logged user in the data access layer:

```
public boolean validateUser(String userid, String password) {
   try {
   sessionFactory = configureSessionFactory();
   Session session = sessionFactory.openSession();
   session.beginTransaction();
   String query = "from InvestorsList  where username='"
   + userid + "' and   password='" + password + "'";
         Query queryobj = session.createQuery(query);
         List<InvestorsList> list=queryobj.list();
         int count=0;
         if(list!=null){
     count= list.size();
}
         session.getTransaction().commit();
   if (count > 0) {
      return true;
   } else {
      return false;
   }
      } catch (Exception e) {
            e.printStackTrace();
      }
      return false;
}
```

5. You should now find the login screen, with the preceding required functionalities, as shown in the following screenshot:

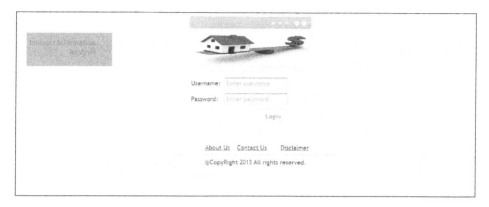

For the preceding login form, you will find that the nonempty and length validations have been applied.

The login credentials

The application has been provided with 10 login credentials, starting from *investor01* to *investor10* with the same username and password values. So, the credentials should be any one of these 10 values; otherwise, the application will display an invalid validation message.

For example, the first investor needs to login as `investor01/investor01`.

Exploring the summary tables

Before you use the export and chart components, you can find the account summary, investment summary, and transaction summary tables to hold the bulky data sets. The same data of the summary tables can be used to report and analyze the data in a simpler way.

Implementing the account summary table

The account summary table contains the investor name, account holder name, account number, account type, status, registration date, open date, end date, joint account, US balance, and UK balance amount fields. The table also has the optional fields such as registration date, open date, and end date using the column toggle feature. The step-by-step procedure to implement the account summary table is as follows:

1. The account summary table is defined with all the required fields using the column toggle feature as follows:

```
<p:dataTable id="accountsummary" var="account" value="#{accountSum
maryController.accountsInfo}"
   paginator="true" rows="5" paginatorPosition="bottom"
   paginatorTemplate="{CurrentPageReport} {FirstPageLink}
   {PreviousPageLink} {PageLinks} {NextPageLink} {LastPageLink}
   {RowsPerPageDropdown}"
   rowsPerPageTemplate="5,10,15" rowKey="#{account.id}"
   selection="#{accountSummaryController.accountobj}"
   selectionMode="single">
    <f:facet name="header">
        Account Summary
        <p:commandButton id="toggler" type="button"
      value="Columns" style="float:right"
      icon="ui-icon-calculator" />
 <p:columnToggler datasource="accountsummary"
 trigger="toggler" />
 <div style="clear: both" />
   </f:facet>
 <p:column sortBy="investorName" filterBy="investorName"
     toggleable="false" id="investorName">
     <f:facet name="header">
        <h:outputText value="Investor Name" />
     </f:facet>
     <h:outputText value="#{account.investorName}" />
</p:column>
<p:column sortBy="registeredAccholderName"
    filterBy="registeredAccholderName" toggleable="false"
    id="registeredAccholderName">
    <f:facet name="header">
        <h:outputText value="Accountholder Name" />
    </f:facet>
        <h:outputText
        value="#{account.registeredAccholderName}" />
```

```
                </p:column>
                <p:column sortBy="accountNumber" filterBy="accountNumber"
                    toggleable="false" id="accountNumber">
                  <f:facet name="header">
                      <h:outputText value="Account Number" />
                  </f:facet>
                      <h:outputText value="#{account.accountNumber}" />
                </p:column>
                <p:column sortBy="accountType" filterBy="accountType"
                    toggleable="false" id="accountType">
                  <f:facet name="header">
                      <h:outputText value="Account Type" />
                  </f:facet>
                      <h:outputText value="#{account.accountType}" />
                </p:column>
                <p:column sortBy="status" filterBy="status" id="status"
                     toggleable="false">
                   <f:facet name="header">
                      <h:outputText value="Status" />
                   </f:facet>
                      <h:outputText value="#{account.status}" />
                </p:column>
                <p:column sortBy="registrationDate" id="registrationDate">
                    <f:facet name="header">
                       <h:outputText value="Registration Date" />
                    </f:facet>
                       <h:outputText value="#{account.registrationDate}" />
                </p:column>
                <p:column sortBy="openDate" id="openDate">
                    <f:facet name="header">
                       <h:outputText value="Open Date" />
                    </f:facet>
                       <h:outputText value="#{account.openDate}" />
                </p:column>
                <p:column sortBy="closeDate" id="closeDate">
                    <f:facet name="header">
                       <h:outputText value="Close Date" />
                    </f:facet>
                       <h:outputText value="#{account.closeDate}" />
                </p:column>
                <p:column sortBy="jointAccount" id="jointAccount">
                    <f:facet name="header">
```

Investor Information Analysis and Reporting

```
                <h:outputText value="Joint Account" />
            </f:facet>
                <h:outputText value="#{account.jointAccount}" />
        </p:column>
        <p:column sortBy="balanceUS" id="balanceUS" toggleable="false">
            <f:facet name="header">
                <h:outputText value="Balance US" />
            </f:facet>
                <h:outputText value="#{account.balanceUS}" />
        </p:column>
             <p:column sortBy="Balance UK" id="balanceUK"
             toggleable="false">
            <f:facet name="header">
                <h:outputText value="balanceUK" />
            </f:facet>
                <h:outputText value="#{account.balanceUK}" />
        </p:column>
</p:dataTable>
```

2. The backing bean is defined with the account summary fields, getters, setters, accounts list, and the `PostConstruct` call to retrieve the account summary information from the data access layer. The investor can also navigate to the investment summary by selecting a particular account and storing the account in the session to retrieve the data. Based on the stored account number, the investments will be retrieved from the database as follows:

```
@ManagedBean
@ViewScoped
public class AccountSummaryController implements Serializable{
    // Account summary fields
    // Getters and setters
private List<AccountSummary>
accountsInfo=new ArrayList<AccountSummary>();
AccountSummaryDAO dao = new AccountSummaryDAO();
private AccountSummary accountObj=new AccountSummary();
    @PostConstruct
    public void init() {
    accountsInfo=dao.getAllAccounts();
    createPieModel();
    createCategoryModel();
    }
public String storeSelectedAccount(){
  ExternalContext externalContext =
  FacesContext.getCurrentInstance().getExternalContext();
```

Chapter 5

```
    Map<String, Object> sessionMap =
    externalContext.getSessionMap();
    sessionMap.put("accountNumber", accountObj.getAccountNumber());
    return "investmentsummary.xhtml?faces-redirect=true";
     }
    ....
}
```

3. The `getAllAccounts()` method of `AccountSummaryDAO` is used to retrieve all the accounts under a particular investor as follows:

```
public List<AccountSummary> getAllAccounts() {
  sessionFactory = configureSessionFactory();
  Session session = sessionFactory.openSession();
  session.beginTransaction();
  Query queryResult = session.createQuery("from AccountSummary");
  List<AccountSummary> allAccounts = queryResult.list();
  session.getTransaction().commit();
  return allAccounts;
}
```

4. Now, the account summary information is displayed in the table format after the investor logs in, as follows:

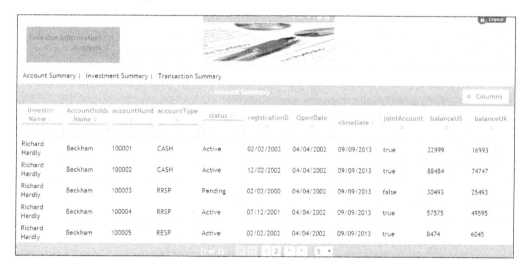

5. Right-click on each record popup with the investment summary navigation link to display the investments under that account.

The investment summary table implementation

The investment summary table contains the fund name, investment number, investment manager, marketing company, average unit price, market value1, market value2, market value3, market value4, and market value5 fields. The step-by-step procedure to create the investment summary table is as follows:

1. The investment summary table is defined with all the required fields as follows:

```
<p:dataTable id="investmentsummary" var="investment"
  value="#{investmentSummaryController.investmentsInfo}"
  paginator="true" rows="5"
  paginatorTemplate="{CurrentPageReport} {FirstPageLink}
  {PreviousPageLink} {PageLinks} {NextPageLink}
  {LastPageLink} {RowsPerPageDropdown}"
  rowsPerPageTemplate="5,10,15" rowKey="#{investment.id}"
  selection="#{investmentSummaryController.investmentobj}"
  selectionMode="single">
<f:facet name="header">
            Investment Summary
     </f:facet>
<p:column sortBy="fundname" filterBy="fundname" id="fundname">
   <f:facet name="header">
        <h:outputText value="Fund Name" />
   </f:facet>
        <h:outputText value="#{investment.fundname}" />
</p:column>
<p:column sortBy="investmentNumber" filterBy="investmentNumber"
   id="investmentNumber">
   <f:facet name="header">
        <h:outputText value="Investment Number" />
   </f:facet>
        <h:outputText value="#{investment.investmentNumber}" />
</p:column>
<p:column sortBy="investmentManager"
filterBy="investmentManager"
    id="investmentManager"
    exportable="#{investmentSummaryController.
    exportInvestmentManager}">
    <f:facet name="header">
        <h:outputText value="Investment Manager" />
    </f:facet>
        <h:outputText value="#{investment.investmentManager}"
/>
```

```xml
</p:column>
<p:column sortBy="marketingCompany" filterBy="marketingCompany"
   id="marketingCompany"
   exportable="#{investmentSummaryController.
   exportMarketingCompany}">
    <f:facet name="header">
        <h:outputText value="Marketing Company" />
    </f:facet>
        <h:outputText value="#{investment.marketingCompany}" />
</p:column>
<p:column sortBy="avgUnitPrice" filterBy="avgUnitPrice"
   id="avgUnitPrice"
   exportable="#{investmentSummaryController.
   exportAvgUnitPrice}">
  <f:facet name="header">
        <h:outputText value="Average UnitPrice" />
  </f:facet>
        <h:outputText value="#{investment.avgUnitPrice}" />
</p:column>
<p:column sortBy="marketValue1" id="marketValue1">
    <f:facet name="header">
        <h:outputText value="Market Value(1st Time Period)" />
    </f:facet>
        <h:outputText value="#{investment.marketValue1}" />
</p:column>
<p:column sortBy="marketValue2" id="marketValue2">
    <f:facet name="header">
        <h:outputText value="Market Value(2nd Time Period)" />
    </f:facet>
        <h:outputText value="#{investment.marketValue2}" />
</p:column>
<p:column sortBy="marketValue3" id="marketValue3">
    <f:facet name="header">
        <h:outputText value="Market Value(3rd Time Period)" />
    </f:facet>
        <h:outputText value="#{investment.marketValue3}" />
</p:column>
<p:column sortBy="marketValue4" id="marketValue4">
    <f:facet name="header">
        <h:outputText value="Market Value(4th Time Period)" />
    </f:facet>
```

```
            <h:outputText value="#{investment.marketValue4}" />
    </p:column>
    <p:column sortBy="marketValue5" id="marketValue5">
        <f:facet name="header">
            <h:outputText value="Market Value(5th Time Period)" />
        </f:facet>
            <h:outputText value="#{investment.marketValue5}" />
    </p:column>
</p:dataTable>
```

2. The backing bean is defined with the investment summary fields, getters, setters, investment list, and the `PostConstruct` call to retrieve the investment summary information from the data access layer. The investor can also navigate to the transaction summary by selecting a particular investor and storing the investment number in the session to retrieve the data. The following code snippet represents the investment summary screen's backing bean:

```
@ManagedBean
@ViewScoped
public class InvestmentSummaryController implements Serializable{
    //Investment summary fields
    //Getters and Setters
    private List<InvestmentSummary>
    investmentsInfo=new   ArrayList<InvestmentSummary>();
    private InvestmentSummary
    investmentobj=new InvestmentSummary();
    InvestmentSummaryDAO dao = new InvestmentSummaryDAO();

    @PostConstruct
    public void init() {
    investmentsInfo=dao.getAllInvestments();
    createLinearModel();
    exportColumns();
    }
    public String storeSelectedInvestornum(){
    ExternalContext externalContext =
    FacesContext.getCurrentInstance().getExternalContext();
    Map<String, Object> sessionMap =
    externalContext.getSessionMap();
    sessionMap.put("investmentNumber",
    investmentobj.getInvestmentNumber());
    return "transactionsummary.xhtml?faces-redirect=true";
    }
    .....
}
```

3. The `getAllInvestments()` method of `InvestmentSummaryDAO` is used to retrieve all the investments under a particular investor. If the investor selects any particular account, then the investments under that account get displayed; if the investor selects the **Investment Summary** link in the menu bar, then all the investments get displayed. The following code snippet is used to retrieve all the investments in the data access layer:

```
public List<InvestmentSummary> getAllInvestments() {
      sessionFactory = configureSessionFactory();
      Session session = sessionFactory.openSession();
      session.beginTransaction();
      Query queryResult=null;
      if(accountNumber!=""){
         queryResult = session.createQuery("from InvestmentSummary
         where accountNumber = :accNum");
         queryResult.setParameter("accNum", accountNumber);
      }else{
         queryResult = session.createQuery
         ("from InvestmentSummary");
      }
      List<InvestmentSummary> allInvestments = queryResult.list();
      session.getTransaction().commit();
      return allInvestments;
}
```

4. Now the investment summary information is displayed in the table format when the investor navigates from the account summary, as follows:

Fund Name	Investment Number	Investment Manager	Marketing Company	Average UnitPrice	Market Value(1st Time Period)	Market Value(2nd Time Period)	Market Value(3rd Time Period)	Market Value(4th Time Period)	Market Value(5th Time Period)
Moderate Balanced Fund	111	BlackRock	US savings and retirements	10	2000.0	1000.0	1200.0	2200.0	2500.0
Capital Research management LLC	112	Quantitative management associates	UK Fidelity markets	7	1000.0	1100.0	1200.0	1200.0	1500.0
Money market Fund	113	AIS capital management	German Prudentials	5	500.0	800.0	400.0	1100.0	1500.0
Aggressive balanced fund	114	Active passive funds	NationWide	8	1300.0	1000.0	1200.0	2200.0	1500.0
conservative Balanced Fund	115	BlackRock	LIC retirements	13	200.0	1000.0	1200.0	2200.0	2700.0

5. Right-click on each record pop up with the transaction summary navigation link to display the transactions under that investment.

The transaction summary table implementation

The transaction summary table contains the transaction ID, transaction type, transaction date, payment type, status, unit price of a transaction, transaction units, gross amount, deductions, and net amount fields.

The step-by-step procedure to implement the transaction summary table is as follows:

1. The transaction summary table can be created with all the required fields as follows:

```
<p:dataTable id="transactionsummary" var="transaction"
   value="#{transactionSummaryController.transactionsInfo}"
   paginator="true" rows="5"
   paginatorTemplate="{CurrentPageReport} {FirstPageLink}
   {PreviousPageLink} {PageLinks} {NextPageLink} {LastPageLink}
   {RowsPerPageDropdown}"
   rowsPerPageTemplate="5,10,15">
   <f:facet name="header">
                Transaction Summary
   </f:facet>
   <p:column sortBy="transactionid" filterBy="transactionid"
       id="transactionid">
       <f:facet name="header">
           <h:outputText value="TransactionID" />
       </f:facet>
           <h:outputText value="#{transaction.transactionid}" />
   </p:column>
   <p:column sortBy="transactiontype" filterBy="transactiontype"
       id="transactiontype">
       <f:facet name="header">
           <h:outputText value="Transaction Type" />
       </f:facet>
           <h:outputText value="#{transaction.transactiontype}" />
   </p:column>
   <p:column sortBy="transactiondate" filterBy="transactiondate"
       id="transactiondate">
       <f:facet name="header">
           <h:outputText value="Transaction Date" />
       </f:facet>
           <h:outputText value="#{transaction.transactiondate}" />
   </p:column>
   <p:column sortBy="paymenttype" filterBy="paymenttype"
       id="paymenttype">
```

```xml
        <f:facet name="header">
            <h:outputText value="Payment Type" />
        </f:facet>
            <h:outputText value="#{transaction.paymenttype}" />
</p:column>
<p:column sortBy="status" filterBy="status" id="status">
    <f:facet name="header">
        <h:outputText value="Status" />
    </f:facet>
        <h:outputText value="#{transaction.status}" />
</p:column>
<p:column sortBy="transactionunitprice"
  id="transactionunitprice">
    <f:facet name="header">
        <h:outputText value="Transaction Unitprice" />
    </f:facet>
        <h:outputText
        value="#{transaction.transactionunitprice}" />
</p:column>
<p:column sortBy="transactionunits" id="transactionunits">
    <f:facet name="header">
        <h:outputText value="Transaction Units" />
    </f:facet>
        <h:outputText value="#{transaction.transactionunits}" />
</p:column>
<p:column sortBy="grossamount" id="grossamount">
    <f:facet name="header">
        <h:outputText value="Grossamount" />
    </f:facet>
        <h:outputText value="#{transaction.grossamount}" />
</p:column>
<p:column sortBy="deductions" id="deductions">
    <f:facet name="header">
        <h:outputText value="Deductions" />
    </f:facet>
        <h:outputText value="#{transaction.deductions}" />
</p:column>
<p:column sortBy="netamount" id="netamount">
    <f:facet name="header">
        <h:outputText value="Net Amount" />
    </f:facet>
```

```
            <h:outputText value="#{transaction.netamount}" />
        </p:column>
    </p:dataTable>
```

2. The backing bean is defined with the transaction summary fields, getters, setters, transactions list, and the `PostConstruct` call to retrieve the transaction summary information from the data access layer. The following code snippet represents the transaction summary screen's backing bean:

```
@ManagedBean
@ViewScoped
public class TransactionSummaryController implements Serializable
{
    // Transaction Summary fields
    // Getters and Setters
  private List<TransactionSummary>
  transactionsInfo = new ArrayList<TransactionSummary>();
    TransactionSummaryDAO dao = new TransactionSummaryDAO();
    @PostConstruct
  public void init() {
     transactionsInfo = dao.getAllTransactions();
     createDonutModel();
  }
     ...
  }
```

3. The `getAllTransactions()` method of `TransactionSummaryDAO` is used to retrieve all the transactions under a particular investor. If the investor selects any particular investment, then the transactions under that investment get displayed; if the investor selects the **Transaction Summary** link in the menu bar at the top, then all the transactions get displayed. The following code snippet is used to retrieve all the transactions in the data access layer:

```
public List<TransactionSummary> getAllTransactions() {
        sessionFactory = configureSessionFactory();
        Session session = sessionFactory.openSession();
        session.beginTransaction();
        Query queryResult=null;
        if(investmentNumber!=""){
          queryResult = session.createQuery("from TransactionSummary
          where investmentNumber = :invNum");
          queryResult.setParameter("invNum", investmentNumber);
        }else{
          queryResult = session.createQuery
          ("from TransactionSummary");
        }
```

```
        List<TransactionSummary> allTransactions = queryResult.list();
        session.getTransaction().commit();
        return allTransactions;
    }
```

4. Now the transaction summary information is displayed in the table format when the investor navigates from the investment summary, as follows:

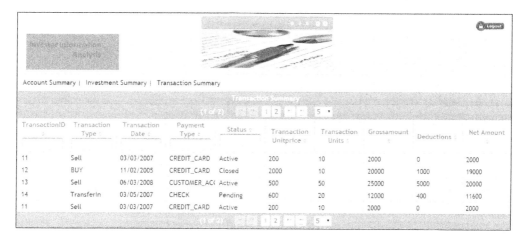

Along with the filtering and sorting options, you can find the pagination on both the top and bottom sections of the summary screen.

Implementing the export functionality in summary screens

The export functionality is used to export the bulky data sets to the summary screens. The `dataExporter` component from PrimeFaces is used to export the `dataTable` information. The data can be exported to any one of the popular formats (PDF, Excel, CSV, and XML) based on the investor's selection.

The PDF export requires `iText-2.1.7.jar`, whereas the Excel export requires `poi-3.7.jar` as the mandatory libraries. Please refer to the first chapter optional dependencies section for more details.

Exporting the account summary data

The account summary information is exported to multiple file formats (PDF, Excel, CSV, and XML) using the `p:dataExporter` component, targeting the account summary component ID. The PDF and Excel formats support customizations through the `preProcessor` and `postProcessor` method expressions. The application logo and screen titles are exported in the header section using `preProcessor`, whereas the application disclaimer is exported in the footer section with the help of `postProcessor`. The following code represents the export section of account summary screen:

```
<p:panel header="Export Accounts Data">
    <h:commandLink>
  <p:graphicImage value="/images/excel.png" />
  <p:dataExporter type="xls" target="accountsummary"
     postProcessor="#{accountSummaryController.postProcessXLS}"
     fileName="AccountSummary" />
    </h:commandLink>
    <h:commandLink>
  <p:graphicImage value="/images/pdf.png" />
  <p:dataExporter type="pdf" target="accountsummary"
     preProcessor="#{accountSummaryController.preProcessPDF}"
     postProcessor="#{accountSummaryController.postProcessPDF}"
     fileName="AccountSummary" />
    </h:commandLink>
    <h:commandLink>
  <p:graphicImage value="/images/csv.png" />
  <p:dataExporter type="csv" target="accountsummary"
  fileName="AccountSummary" />
    </h:commandLink>
    <h:commandLink>
  <p:graphicImage value="/images/xml.png" />
  <p:dataExporter type="xml" target="accountsummary"
     fileName="AccountSummary" />
    </h:commandLink>
</p:panel>
```

The managed bean is defined with the `preProcessor` and `postProcessor` methods to customize the PDF document with the logo and disclaimer sections, whereas the Excel document is customized with the disclaimer section using the `postProcessor` attribute. The following code represents the export PDF's `preProcessor` section:

```
public void preProcessPDF(Object document) throws IOException,
   BadElementException, DocumentException {
    Document pdf = (Document) document;
```

```
        pdf.setPageSize(PageSize.A3);
        pdf.open();
        ServletContext servletContext = (ServletContext)
        FacesContext.getCurrentInstance().getExternalContext().
        getContext();
        String logo = servletContext.getRealPath("") + File.separator
        +"resources" + File.separator + "images" + File.separator +"logo"
        + File.separator + "logo.png";
        Image image=Image.getInstance(logo);
        image.scaleAbsolute(100f, 50f);
        pdf.add(image);
        // add a couple of blank lines
        pdf.add( Chunk.NEWLINE );
        pdf.add( Chunk.NEWLINE );
        Font fontbold = FontFactory.getFont("Times-Roman", 16, Font.BOLD);
        fontbold.setColor(55, 55, 55);;
        pdf.add(new Paragraph("Account Summary",fontbold));
        // add a couple of blank lines
        pdf.add( Chunk.NEWLINE );
        pdf.add( Chunk.NEWLINE );
    }
    public void postProcessPDF(Object document) throws IOException,
BadElementException, DocumentException {
        Document pdf = (Document) document;
        pdf.add( Chunk.NEWLINE );
        Font fontbold = FontFactory.getFont("Times-Roman", 14, Font.BOLD);
        pdf.add(new Paragraph("Disclaimer",fontbold));
        pdf.add( Chunk.NEWLINE );
        pdf.add(new Paragraph("The information contained in this website
        is for information purposes only, and does not constitute, nor
        is it intended to constitute, the     provision of financial
        product advice."));
        pdf.add(new Paragraph("This website is intended to track the
        investor account summary information,investments and transaction
        in a particular period of time. "));
    }
    public void postProcessXLS(Object document) {
        HSSFWorkbook wb = (HSSFWorkbook) document;
        HSSFSheet sheet = wb.getSheetAt(0);
        HSSFRow header = sheet.getRow(0);
        HSSFCellStyle cellStyle = wb.createCellStyle();
        cellStyle.setFillForegroundColor(HSSFColor.GREEN.index);
        cellStyle.setFillPattern(HSSFCellStyle.SOLID_FOREGROUND);
```

Investor Information Analysis and Reporting

```
            for(int i=0; i < header.getPhysicalNumberOfCells();i++) {
            HSSFCell cell = header.getCell(i);
            cell.setCellStyle(cellStyle);
             }
            Row row=sheet.createRow((short)sheet.getLastRowNum()+3);
            Cell cellDisclaimer = row.createCell(0);
            HSSFFont customFont= wb.createFont();
            customFont.setFontHeightInPoints((short)10);
            customFont.setFontName("Arial");
            customFont.setColor(IndexedColors.BLACK.getIndex());
            customFont.setBoldweight(HSSFFont.BOLDWEIGHT_BOLD);
            customFont.setItalic(true);

            cellDisclaimer.setCellValue("Disclaimer");
            HSSFCellStyle cellStyleDisclaimer = wb.createCellStyle();
            cellStyleDisclaimer.setFont(customFont);
            cellDisclaimer.setCellStyle(cellStyleDisclaimer);

            Row row1=sheet.createRow(sheet.getLastRowNum()+2);
            Cell cellDisclaimerContent1 = row1.createCell(0);
            cellDisclaimerContent1.setCellValue("The information contained
            in this website is for information purposes only, and does not
            constitute, nor is it intended to constitute, the provision of
            financial product advice.");
            Row row2=sheet.createRow(sheet.getLastRowNum()+1);
            Cell cellDisclaimerContent2 = row2.createCell(0);
            cellDisclaimerContent2.setCellValue("This website is intended
            to track the investor account summary information,investments and
            transaction in a partcular period of time. ");
    }
```

Now the generated customized output is represented in the form of Excel and PDF formats in a step-by-step manner as follows:

1. The exported Excel document with a customized disclaimer using `postProcessor` is shown in the following screenshot:

Chapter 5

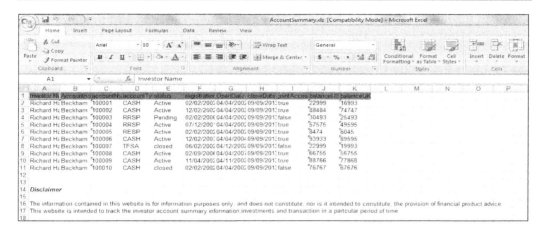

2. The exported PDF document with the customized logo and disclaimer using `preProcessor` and `postProcessor` is shown as follows:

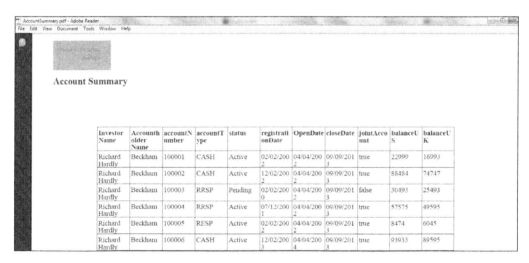

[147]

Investor Information Analysis and Reporting

3. In the following screenshot, we applied `postProcessor` to add the disclaimer just after the account summary dataTable:

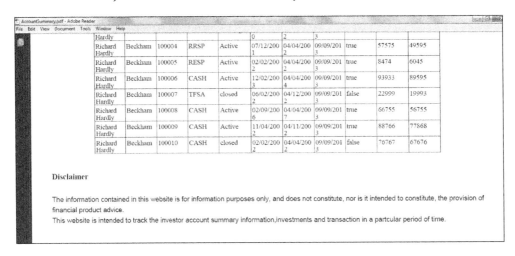

 Remember, both CSV and XML documents don't support the `preProcessor` and `postProcessor` expressions.

4. The exported CSV document with the account summary information is shown in the following screenshot:

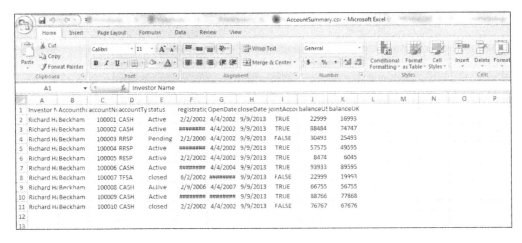

[148]

5. The exported XML document with the account summary information will look as shown in the following screenshot:

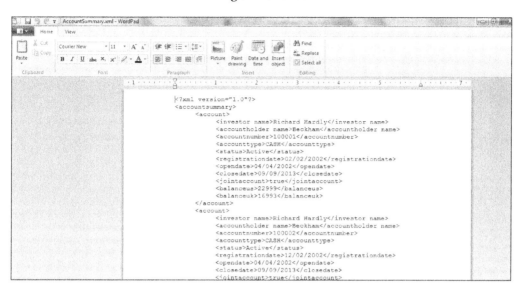

In the preceding XML format, each record is displayed as one node in the document. The record's information will be displayed in the tree nodes format.

Exporting the investment summary data

The investment summary information is exported to multiple file formats (PDF, Excel, CSV, and XML) where some optional columns are omitted by setting `exportable="false"` on `p:column`. Here, the `p:dataExporter` component targets the investment summary component ID. The following code represents the export section of the investment summary screen:

```
<p:panel header="Export Investment Summary">
    <p:selectCheckboxMenu
    value="#{investmentSummaryController.selectedColumns}"
    label="Export columns"  panelStyle="width:220px">
    <f:selectItems value="#{investmentSummaryController.allcolumns}" />
    <p:ajax event="change"
    listener="#{investmentSummaryController.changeOptions}"
    update="investmentsummary"/>
    </p:selectCheckboxMenu>

    <p:separator style="margin-bottom:10px" />
    <h:commandLink
```

```
            <p:graphicImage value="/images/excel.png" />
            <p:dataExporter type="xls" target="investmentsummary"
                postProcessor="#{investmentSummaryController.postProcessXLS}"
                fileName="InvestmentSummary" />
          </h:commandLink>
          <h:commandLink>
            <p:graphicImage value="/images/pdf.png" />
            <p:dataExporter type="pdf" target="investmentsummary"
                preProcessor="#{investmentSummaryController.preProcessPDF}"
                postProcessor="#{investmentSummaryController.postProcessPDF}"
                fileName="InvestmentSummary" />
          </h:commandLink>
          <h:commandLink>
            <p:graphicImage value="/images/csv.png" />
            <p:dataExporter type="csv" target="investmentsummary"
                fileName="InvestmentSummary" />
          </h:commandLink>
          <h:commandLink>
            <p:graphicImage value="/images/xml.png" />
            <p:dataExporter type="xml" target="investmentsummary"
                fileName="InvestmentSummary" />
          </h:commandLink>
        </p:panel>
```

The export column's selection in the investment summary page is shown in the following screenshot:

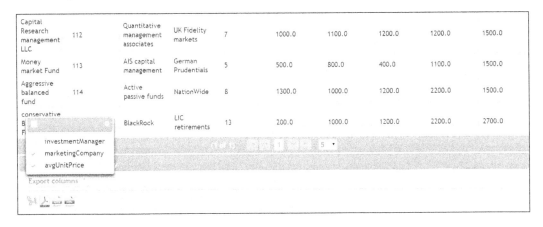

In the preceding investment summary screen, we need to select/unselect whether the optional columns are to be exported or not.

Exporting the transaction summary data

The transaction summary information is exported to multiple file formats (PDF, Excel, CSV, and XML) where the investor can select either the current page or all the pages' data to be exported. The `pageOnly="true"` setting on `p:dataExporter` enables the current page export. Here, the `p:dataExporter` component targets the transaction summary component ID. The following code represents the export section of the transaction summary screen:

```
<p:panel header="Export Transactions Information">
    <h:panelGrid columns="2" style="margin-bottom:10px"
    cellpadding="5">
 <h:outputLabel value="Export Options: " for="options" />
 <p:selectOneRadio id="options"
 value="#{transactionSummaryController.optionValue}"
         label="Export Options:">
   <f:selectItem itemLabel="Export All" itemValue="1" />
   <f:selectItem itemLabel="Export PageOnly" itemValue="2" />
   <p:ajax event="change" update="exportOptions"
   listener="#{transactionSummaryController.changeExportOption}" />
 </p:selectOneRadio>
   </h:panelGrid>
   <p:separator></p:separator>
   <p:outputPanel id="exportOptions">
   <h:commandLink>
 <p:graphicImage value="/images/excel.png" />
 <p:dataExporter type="xls" target="transactionsummary"
     postProcessor="#{transactionSummaryController.postProcessXLS}"
     fileName="TransactionSummary"
     pageOnly="#{transactionSummaryController.pageOnly}" />
   </h:commandLink>
   <h:commandLink>
 <p:graphicImage value="/images/pdf.png" />
 <p:dataExporter type="pdf" target="transactionsummary"
     preProcessor="#{transactionSummaryController.preProcessPDF}"
     postProcessor="#{transactionSummaryController.postProcessPDF}"
     pageOnly="#{transactionSummaryController.pageOnly}"
     fileName="TransactionSummary" />
   </h:commandLink>
   <h:commandLink>
 <p:graphicImage value="/images/csv.png" />
 <p:dataExporter type="csv" target="transactionsummary"
```

Investor Information Analysis and Reporting

```
      fileName="TransactionSummary"
      pageOnly="#{transactionSummaryController.pageOnly}" />
  </h:commandLink>
  <h:commandLink>
<p:graphicImage value="/images/xml.png" />
<p:dataExporter type="xml" target="transactionsummary"
      fileName="TransactionSummary"
      pageOnly="#{transactionSummaryController.pageOnly}" />
  </h:commandLink>
  </p:outputPanel>
</p:panel>
```

The investor can select either the current page or all the pages in the transaction summary, as shown in the following screenshot:

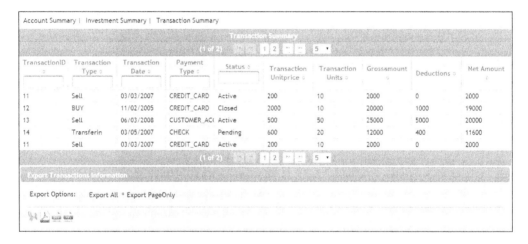

In the preceding transaction summary screen, the investor needs to select either the **Export All** or **Export PageOnly** option using radio buttons. Apart from the **PageOnly** options, `dataExporter` can also export the selected records using the `selectionOnly="true"` setting.

Export tips and tricks

We provided a few export recommendations or the tips and tricks section to optimize the behavior of the export functionality as follows:

- Always use JSF's `h:outputText` component to hold and export the data because inline expressions cannot be exported
- Use header and footer facets to export because `headerText` and `footerText` won't be supported yet

- Components other than `h:outputText` and `graphicImage` inside the `dataTable` component will be ignored during the export
- All the `dataTable` features are not yet supported by the `dataExporter` component

Implementing the charts functionality in summary screens

Charts are very useful components for analyzing and tracking different types of information. Comparing the different categories of data is not easy with huge data represented in a tabular form. The PrimeFaces library created various types of charts based on the `jqPlot` JavaScript library. The summary screen's data can be tracked using various types of available charts. The investor also has the option to download the charts as images.

From the PrimeFaces 5.0 release onwards, the charts API is enhanced with a model-driven API that has additional features such as multi axis, date axis, and custom axis support.

The account summary data analysis using pie and bar charts

The market value of the amounts in different currencies under each account type can be tracked by either using pie charts or bar charts based on the selection type. The first pie chart is used to track the US market values, whereas the second pie chart is used to track the UK market values. A single bar chart will be used to analyze both the market values.

The `p:chart` component is used for all the types of charts, and the type attribute is used to identify the chart type.

The account summary contains the pie and bar charts (based on user selection) based on the account type and balances as shown in the following code snippet. Here, the possible values of the type attribute are `pie` and `bar`:

```
<h:panelGrid columns="3">
    <h:panelGrid columns="2" style="margin-left:150px"
    rendered="#{accountSummaryController.pieChartFlag}">
    <p:chart type="pie" id="pieUS" widgetVar="$pieUS"
model="#{accountSummaryController.pieModelUS}" style="width:400px;
height:300px" />
    <p:chart type="pie" id="pieUK" widgetVar="$pieUK"
model="#{accountSummaryController.pieModelUK}" style="width:400px;
height:300px" />
```

Investor Information Analysis and Reporting

```
        </h:panelGrid>
        <h:panelGrid columns="2" style="margin-left:150px"
    rendered="#{!accountSummaryController.pieChartFlag}">
        <p:chart type="bar" id="barChart" widgetVar="$barChart"
      model="#{accountSummaryController.categoryModel}"
      style="width:400px;height:300px" />
        <p:spacer width="400" height="300"></p:spacer>
        </h:panelGrid>
        <p:spacer width="50"></p:spacer>
        <p:outputPanel style="margin-top: -100px">
   <h:outputText value="Select chart type " />
   <p:selectOneMenu value="#{accountSummaryController.type}">
        <p:ajax event="change"
        listener="#{accountSummaryController.changeOption}"
            update="accsummarycharts"></p:ajax>
       <f:selectItem itemLabel="Pie Chart" itemValue="1" />
       <f:selectItem itemLabel="Bar Chart" itemValue="2" />
   </p:selectOneMenu>
        </p:outputPanel>
</h:panelGrid>
```

The managed bean needs to be defined with the pie chart and bar chart models. The model API allows the chart options such as title, legend position, `showDataLabels`, fill, and `sliceMargin` in these models, instead of using tag attributes. The following code snippet is used to create the pie and bar chart models:

```
private PieChartModel pieModelUS;
private PieChartModel pieModelUK;
private BarChartModel categoryModel;

private void createPieModel() {
      pieModelUS = new PieChartModel();
  pieModelUK = new PieChartModel();

        for(AccountSummary obj:accountsInfo){
            pieModelUS.set(obj.getAccountType(),
            new Double(obj.getBalanceUS()));
            pieModelUK.set(obj.getAccountType(),
            new Double(obj.getBalanceUK()));
        }

        pieModelUS.setTitle("USD Marketvalue");
        pieModelUS.setLegendPosition("w");
        pieModelUS.setShowDataLabels(true);
```

Chapter 5

```
            pieModelUK.setTitle("UK Marketvalue");
            pieModelUK.setLegendPosition("e");
            pieModelUK.setFill(false);
            pieModelUK.setShowDataLabels(true);
            pieModelUK.setSliceMargin(5);
    }

    private void createCategoryModel() {
            categoryModel = new BarChartModel();
            ChartSeries balanceUS = new ChartSeries();
            ChartSeries balanceUK = new ChartSeries();

            for(AccountSummary obj:accountsInfo){
               balanceUS.set(obj.getAccountType(),
               new Double(obj.getBalanceUS()));
               balanceUK.set(obj.getAccountType(),
               new Double(obj.getBalanceUK()));
            }
            balanceUS.setLabel("US_Balance");
            balanceUK.setLabel("UK_Balance");
            categoryModel.addSeries(balanceUS);
            categoryModel.addSeries(balanceUK);
            categoryModel.setTitle("Marketvalue");
            categoryModel.setLegendPosition("w");
            categoryModel.setShowPointLabels(true);
    }
```

Now the pie charts of the account summary screen are rendered as follows:

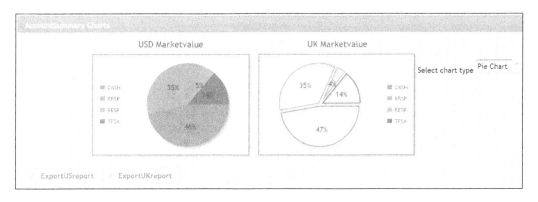

After selecting the bar chart option from the drop-down menu on the right-hand side, we get a bar chart as shown in the following screenshot:

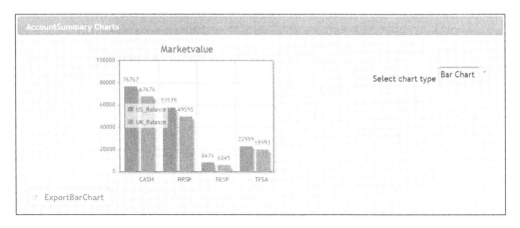

All the charts are provided with an additional option named the **extender client-side** function to export the chart with low-level **jQplot** options. The following line chart example uses the extender option to increase the shadow depth:

```
<p:chart type="line" model="#{bean.model}" extender="ext" />
```

```
function ext() {
//this refers to chart widget instance
//this.cfg refers to chart options
this.cfg.seriesDefaults = {
shadowDepth: 5
};
}
```

Please take a look at the following link to get all the jQplot options: http://www.jqplot.com/docs/files/jqPlotOptions-txt.html.

The investor can also export the canvas-based charts in the image format using the client-side API. The exportAsImage() function is used on a chart widget, which will return a base64 png encoded string. The encoded string is converted to a decoded string using the Apache commons codec library. Finally, the decoded byte stream is created as a PNG file.

The fileDownload component of PrimeFaces is used to download the PNG images created in the application context.

The account summary view should be defined with three command buttons (corresponding to each chart) to invoke the client-side script using their on-click client-side JS callbacks. The `fileDownload` components are defined as the children of the three command buttons to download the chart images. Remember that we also need to define the hidden input fields to store the encoded Base64 codes derived from the client-side script. The following code represents the various charts export section:

```
<p:outputPanel rendered="#{accountSummaryController.pieChartFlag}">
    <p:commandButton value="ExportUSreport " icon="ui-icon-extlink"
   ajax="false" onclick="exportPieChart()"
    actionListener="#{accountSummaryController.piechartUSBase64Str}">
        <p:fileDownload value="#{accountSummaryController.file1}" />
    </p:commandButton>
    <p:commandButton value="ExportUKreport " icon="ui-icon-extlink"
   ajax="false" onclick="exportPieChart()"
    actionListener="#{accountSummaryController.piechartUKBase64Str}">
        <p:fileDownload value="#{accountSummaryController.file2}" />
    </p:commandButton>
</p:outputPanel>
<p:outputPanel rendered="#{!accountSummaryController.pieChartFlag}">
    <p:commandButton value="ExportBarChart" icon="ui-icon-extlink"
   ajax="false" onclick="exportBarChart()"
    actionListener="#{accountSummaryController.barchartBase64Str}">
        <p:fileDownload value="#{accountSummaryController.file3}" />
    </p:commandButton>
</p:outputPanel>
// InputHidden fields to store the Base64 encoded strings
<h:inputHidden id="pie1" value="#{accountSummaryController.base64Str1}" />
<h:inputHidden id="pie2" value="#{accountSummaryController.base64Str2}" />
<h:inputHidden id="bar" value="#{accountSummaryController.base64Str3}" />
```

The client-side script returns the Base64 encoded strings and stores them in the hidden input fields to create images as follows:

```
<script>
  function exportPieChart() {
  // exportAsImage() will return a base64 png encoded string
  var img1 = PF('$pieUS').exportAsImage();
  var img2 = PF('$pieUK').exportAsImage();
  document.getElementById('accountform:pie1').value = img1.src;
  document.getElementById('accountform:pie2').value = img2.src;
  }
```

```
    function exportBarChart() {
    // exportAsImage() will return a base64 png encoded string
    var img1 = PF('$barChart').exportAsImage();
    document.getElementById('accountform:bar').value = img1.src;
    }
</script>
```

In the `actionListener` methods of the managed bean, we will define `inputStreams`, referring to the empty image files that are located in the project filesystem. After this, the encoded strings from the client-side are converted to decoded byte strings. Finally, the decoded byte strings are rendered as PNG files in the managed bean, as follows:

```
public void piechartUSBase64Str(){
    InputStream stream1 = servletContext.getResourceAsStream
    ("/images/pie1.png");
    file1 = new DefaultStreamedContent(stream1, "image/png",
    "US_Piechart.png");
    if(base64Str1.split(",").length > 1){
    String encoded = base64Str1.split(",")[1];
    byte[] decoded = Base64.decodeBase64(encoded);
    // Write to a .png file
    try {
        RenderedImage renderedImage =
        ImageIO.read(new ByteArrayInputStream(decoded));
        ImageIO.write(renderedImage, "png",
        new File(servletContext.getRealPath("images/pie1.png")));
      } catch (IOException e) {
        e.printStackTrace();
      }
     }
}
public void piechartUKBase64Str(){
    InputStream stream2 = servletContext.getResourceAsStream
    ("/images/pie2.png");
    file2 = new DefaultStreamedContent(stream2, "image/png",
    "Uk_Piechart.png");
    if(base64Str2.split(",").length > 1){
    String encoded = base64Str2.split(",")[1];
    byte[] decoded = Base64.decodeBase64(encoded);
    // Write to a .png file
    try {
        RenderedImage renderedImage =
        ImageIO.read(new ByteArrayInputStream(decoded));
        ImageIO.write(renderedImage, "png",
        new File(servletContext.getRealPath("images/pie2.png")));
      } catch (IOException e) {
```

```
                e.printStackTrace();
            }
        }
    }
    public void barchartBase64Str(){
        InputStream stream2 =
        servletContext.getResourceAsStream("/images/bar.png");
        file3 = new DefaultStreamedContent(stream2,
        "image/png", "BarChart.png");
        if(base64Str3.split(",").length > 1){
        String encoded = base64Str3.split(",")[1];
        byte[] decoded = Base64.decodeBase64(encoded);
        // Write to a .png file
        try {
            RenderedImage renderedImage =
            ImageIO.read(new ByteArrayInputStream(decoded));
            ImageIO.write(renderedImage, "png",
            new File(servletContext.getRealPath("images/bar.png")));
        } catch (IOException e) {
          e.printStackTrace();
        }
      }
    }
}
```

In total, we have created three `actionListener` methods in the managed bean that correspond to each chart in the frontend side.

Now when you click on the export charts button, the images will be downloaded as follows:

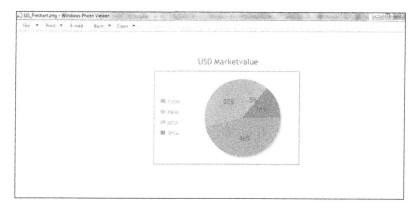

The chart images can be exported to different file formats based on necessity.

The investment summary data analysis using line charts

Each investment fund name with market values at different periods of time can be interpreted as a line chart in the investment summary screen. The `p:chart` component with `type="line"` can be used to create a line chart, and each line in the chart is treated as a separate line chart series. The line chart can be created and can be made interactive with the animation and zoom facilities.

The investment summary contains the line chart based on the fund name and different market values as follows:

```
<p:chart type="line" id="linechart" widgetVar="$linechart"
    model="#{investmentSummaryController.lineModel}"
style="height:300px" />
```

The managed bean holds `lineModel` with custom options such as animation, zooming, legend position, title, and showing point labels. Here, the market values of the same fund are summed up as a single fund to compare it with other funds values as follows:

```
private CartesianChartModel lineModel;
private void createLinearModel() {
    lineModel = new CategoryChartModel();

    for(InvestmentSummary obj:investmentsInfo){
      if((chartMap.keySet()).contains(obj.getFundname())){
         chartMap.get(obj.getFundname()).setMarketValue1
         (chartMap.get(obj.getFundname()).getMarketValue1()
         +obj.getMarketValue1()); ;
         chartMap.get(obj.getFundname()).setMarketValue2
         (chartMap.get(obj.getFundname()).getMarketValue2()
         +obj.getMarketValue2()); ;
         chartMap.get(obj.getFundname()).setMarketValue3
         (chartMap.get(obj.getFundname()).getMarketValue3()
         +obj.getMarketValue3()); ;
         chartMap.get(obj.getFundname()).setMarketValue4
         (chartMap.get(obj.getFundname()).getMarketValue4()
         +obj.getMarketValue4()); ;
         chartMap.get(obj.getFundname()).setMarketValue5
         (chartMap.get(obj.getFundname()).getMarketValue5()
         +obj.getMarketValue5()); ;
          } else {
            chartMap.put(obj.getFundname(), obj);
          }
    }
    for (String key : chartMap.keySet()) {
       InvestmentSummary obj = chartMap.get(key);
       LineChartSeries series = new LineChartSeries();
```

```
            series.setLabel(obj.getFundname());
            series.set("MarketValue1", obj.getMarketValue1());
            series.set("MarketValue2", obj.getMarketValue2());
            series.set("MarketValue3", obj.getMarketValue3());
            series.set("MarketValue4", obj.getMarketValue4());
            series.set("MarketValue5", obj.getMarketValue5());
        lineModel.addSeries(series);
    }
            lineModel.setAnimate(true);
            lineModel.setZoom(true);
            lineModel.setLegendPosition("e");
            lineModel.setTitle("Linear Chart");
            lineModel.setShowPointLabels(true);
}
```

The line chart will be displayed under the investment summary screen as follows:

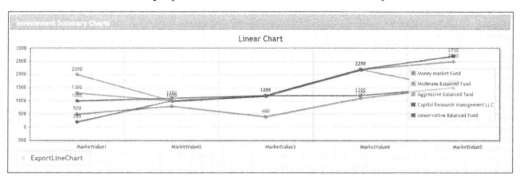

The export chart feature is also available in this investment summary, similar to the account summary screen.

The transaction summary data analysis using donut charts

Each transaction's payment type and its total net amount can be interpreted with the donut chart in the transaction summary screen. The `p:chart` component with `type="donut"` can be used to create a donut chart, and the data is represented in the form of multiple rings.

The transaction summary screen's donut chart is created based on the payment types and their net amount values as follows:

```
<p:outputPanel style="margin-left:30%">
   <p:chart type="donut" id="chart"
   model="#{transactionSummaryController.donutModel}"
   style="width:400px;height:300px" widgetVar="$chart" />
</p:outputPanel>
```

The managed bean holds `donutModel` with custom options such as title, legend position, slice margin, show data labels, data format, and shadow, as follows:

```java
private DonutChartModel donutModel;
private void createDonutModel() {
    donutModel = new DonutChartModel();
    Map<String, Number> circle1 = new LinkedHashMap<String, Number>();
    Map<String, Number> circle2 = new LinkedHashMap<String, Number>();
    Map<String, Number> circle3 = new LinkedHashMap<String, Number>();
    Map<String, Number> circle4 = new LinkedHashMap<String, Number>();
   for (TransactionSummary obj : transactionsInfo) {
  if (obj.getTransactiontype().equalsIgnoreCase("Sell")) {
       circle1.put(obj.getPaymenttype(),
       new Integer(obj.getNetamount()));
     }
   if (obj.getTransactiontype().equalsIgnoreCase("BUY")) {
       circle2.put(obj.getPaymenttype(),
       new Integer(obj.getNetamount()));
   }
       if (obj.getTransactiontype().equalsIgnoreCase("TransferIn")) {
       circle3.put(obj.getPaymenttype(),
       new Integer(obj.getNetamount()));
     }
   if (obj.getTransactiontype().equalsIgnoreCase("TransferOut")) {
       circle4.put(obj.getPaymenttype(),
       new Integer(obj.getNetamount()));
     }

   }
   donutModel.addCircle(circle1);
   donutModel.addCircle(circle2);
   donutModel.addCircle(circle3);
   donutModel.addCircle(circle4);

   donutModel.setTitle("Transaction Summary");
   donutModel.setLegendPosition("e");
   donutModel.setSliceMargin(5);
   donutModel.setShowDataLabels(true);
   donutModel.setDataFormat("percent");
   donutModel.setShadow(false);
}
```

Now the donut chart of the transaction summary will be rendered as follows:

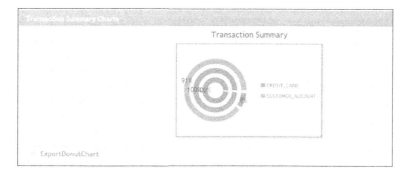

The export chart feature is also available in this transaction summary, similar to the account summary screen.

Working with investor information analysis and reporting the application project code

If you wish to work on the sample code, all you need to do is download it from the Git repository at https://github.com/sudheerj/primefaces-blueprints where you can use your preferred IDE. From there, you can start playing with the code. You can run it by using the mvn jetty:run command in the Maven console and then navigate your browser to http://localhost:8080/web, using the investor credentials to log in to the application.

Summary

In this chapter, you learned how to develop an investor information analysis and reporting application. The topics covered in this chapter are how to create summary screens, how to export big data sets with possible features, how to interpret and analyze the summary data using charts, and how to export the charts as image files.

In the next chapter, you will learn the procedure to create an online shopping cart application, which will also show you how the major menu variations and the drag-and-drop components of PrimeFaces work.

6
Creating a Simple Online Shopping Cart Application

This chapter explains the step-by-step procedure to design and develop an online shopping cart application. The highlight of this chapter is dealing with the **menu** component and the **drag-and-drop** component from PrimeFaces. During the development, you will learn how to use the menu and drag-and-drop components and their variations.

Understanding the application

Online shopping applications changed the way that it was before in shopping trends. Online shopping or e-shopping is a form of electronic commerce that allows consumers to directly buy goods or services from a seller's shop over the Internet using a web browser. Today's digital era makes this process very simple, such that most of the retail companies have their own online shopping systems to increase their sales; for example, `amazon.com`, `buy.com`, and `ebay.com` are some of the giants in market sales. You only need to look at Amazon, eBay, and buy to see how successful online shopping can be.

Let's see how you can design and develop your own online shopping application. Imagine that your client, a retail company, has provided you with the requirements in order to build their online shopping application.

The application use case

Our client is an electronic products retail company that serves throughout North Texas, aiming to establish their business online using a product showcase website in order to increase their business nationwide. They are in need of a website to list their products and services, which will eventually sell their products, while monitoring their financial status through a single system called **Next Generation Ordering System** (**NGOS**). This system has two different parts: the storefront and the administration:

- **Storefront**: This is the area of the web store that is accessed publicly, or in other words, it is a digital shop or an e-store. Based on the information saved in the store's database, the e-store will dynamically populate the product catalogs and categories in the appropriate pages. The store owners are responsible for changing the store-wide products and categories via the store's administration.

- **Administration**: This is the area of the web store that is accessed by the merchant in order to manage the online shop. The number of store management features depend on the sophistication of the shopping cart software, but in general, a store manager is able to add and edit products as well as control the settings for categories, discounts, shipping, and payments. It is also possible to control the order management features. The administration area can be of either of the following types:

    ○ Web-based, such that it is accessed through a web browser
    ○ Desktop-based, such that a desktop application runs on the user's computer and then transfers changes to the storefront component

Functional requirements

The shopping cart application needs to fulfill the following criteria:

- NGOS is designed to be used by two different types of users. The first type is an internal user who will perform the order processing as well as add and update their products. The other type is the customer who intends to buy or browse products online through the shopping cart system using their credit card or any other available source for payment.

- It needs to display all the products grouped by category.

- It needs a product showcase that will be present to show the products and their related description.

- It needs an integrated shopping cart that will allow the purchase of the product through the system using a payment gateway.

- It needs to have a dashboard to show all the activities of the online shop.
- Finally, it needs to have a platform to add, update, and delete products and categories with restricted user access.

The architecture

You will be using the same architecture as discussed in the previous chapters. For the sake of continuity, the architecture of this project should be as follows:

- The JSF web application
- PrimeFaces as the view component (XHTML)
- A managed bean as the controller
- Hibernate as the persistence layer
- MySQL as the database

The following diagram shows you the entire application's workflow:

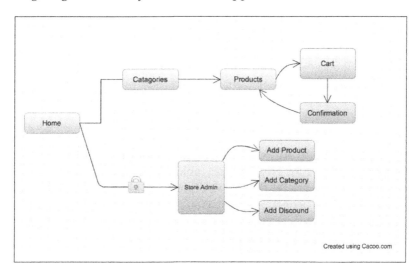

The preceding flow diagram shows you how a user can purchase their desired product online through the website. First, the user needs to select their favorite browser, navigate to the NGOS web application, and select the category from the available category list. Then, they need to select the desired product from the product catalog page and click on the **add to cart** button (alternatively, they can also drag-and-drop the product to the cart). Once the shopping is completed, the user can check out by selecting a **checkout** option on the cart page. They would select an available and convenient payment option before paying the correct amount. This would conclude with a confirmation page saying that the payment was successful.

The ER diagram

The following ER diagram shows the entities required in this project, such that products can be stored and information can be organized for processing:

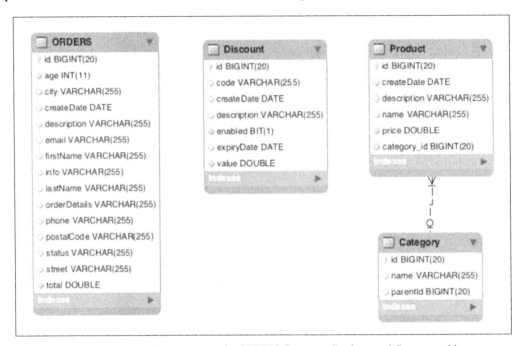

The entity diagram that represents the ORDERS, Discount, Product, and Category tables

The **Category** table is used to add various categories to categorize the available products in a grouped fashion. The **Product** table holds all the information related to the product. Finally, the **ORDERS** table will hold all the information related to an order. In particular, the **orderDetails** field in the **ORDERS** table is used to store all the information related to a particular order, such as the selected products and payment details. The shipping address and related information are stored in the **ORDERS** table itself.

The implementation

In this section, you will learn how to implement the preceding requirements in the JSF 2 web application project using PrimeFaces.

Every shopping cart application consists of the storefront and the administration (also known as the back office). These two areas are intended to perform certain operations in a store in order to sell products. To summarize this, a visitor can browse through the available products, which are added through the back office. Only an internal store user or store admin can access the back office.

The persistence layer

You will be using hibernate as the persistent layer. Here, you will see how the persistent layer is configured and coded in this shopping cart application. The following is the code snippet to configure hibernate:

```
<hibernate-configuration>
 <session-factory>
    <property name="hibernate.bytecode.use_reflection_optimizer">
false
    </property>
    <property name="hibernate.connection.driver_class">
com.mysql.jdbc.Driver
    </property>
    <property name="hibernate.connection.url">
jdbc:mysql://localhost:3306/pocketdb?createDatabaseIfNotExist=true
    </property>
    <property name="hibernate.connection.username">root</property>
    <property name="hibernate.connection.password">root</property>
    <property name="hibernate.dialect">
org.hibernate.dialect.MySQLDialect
    </property>
  <property name="hibernate.connection.autocommit">true</property>
    <property name="hibernate.show_sql">true</property>
    <property name="hibernate.format_sql">true</property>
    <property name="hibernate.hbm2ddl.auto">create-drop</property>
    <property name="hibernate.hbm2ddl.import_files">
classpath:import.sql
    </property>
    <property name="hibernate.current_session_context_class">
org.hibernate.context.internal.ThreadLocalSessionContext
</property>
    <mapping class="com.packtpub.pf.blueprint.persistence.entity.
Category"/>
<mapping class="com.packtpub.pf.blueprint.persistence.entity.
Discount"/>
    <mapping class="com.packtpub.pf.blueprint.persistence.entity.
Product"/>
    <mapping class="com.packtpub.pf.blueprint.persistence.entity.
Order"/>
```

```
    </session-factory>
</hibernate-configuration>
```

You can also find the same code in the `hibernate.cfg.xml` file under the `Project_home/src/main/resources/hibernate.cfg.xml` resource directory.

The `HibernateUtil.java` file is used to hold the connection factory that enables on-demand connections to the specified database. This utility reads the configuration from the `hibernate.cfg.xml` file and opens the hibernate session factory. The advantage of hibernate is that it is a container that handles connection pools, transactions, security, and so on. Hibernate also has a lot of other advantages over ordinary JDBC, such as writing complicated SQL queries, handling transactions, and many more. In this chapter, you will be using annotation-driven hibernate entity mapping.

```java
public class HibernateUtil {
   private static final SessionFactory sessionFactory
         = buildSessionFactory();
   private static SessionFactory buildSessionFactory()
             throws  HibernateException {
     Configuration configuration = new Configuration()
             .configure();
     // configures settings from hibernate.cfg.xml
     StandardServiceRegistryBuilder serviceRegistryBuilder
           = new StandardServiceRegistryBuilder();
     // If you miss the below line then it will
     //complain about a missing dialect setting
     serviceRegistryBuilder.applySettings(
             configuration.getProperties());
     ServiceRegistry serviceRegistry = serviceRegistryBuilder.
             build();
        return configuration.buildSessionFactory(serviceRegistry);
   }

   public static SessionFactory getSessionFactory() {
          return sessionFactory;
   }

   public static void shutdown() {
        // Close caches and connection pools
        getSessionFactory().close();
   }
}
```

The administration / back office module

Let's see how you can design and develop the back office module, where we will focus on its functionalities first so that you can understand the process easily.

The presentation layer

You have two different template files: one for the storefront and the other for the back office. The admin template is designed to support the required layout for the back office. The back office should have a common navigation menu for all the different pages. The body content is defined in each of the pages of the administrator module. You will be using the `layout` and `layoutunit` components to implement the layout design requirement. The following code snippet is used in the application in order to design the layout:

```
<p:layout>
    <p:layoutUnit position="center">
        <div id="menubar">
            <ui:insert name="menubars">
                <h:form>
                    <p:menubar>
                        <p:menuitem value="Dashboard"
                        url="/pages/storeadmin.jsf" icon="ui-icon-home"/>
                            <p:submenu label="Store Management">
                                <p:menuitem value="Products"
                                url="/pages/products.jsf"/>
                                <p:menuitem value="Category"
                                url="/pages/categories.jsf"/>
                                <p:menuitem value="Discount"
                                url="/pages/discounts.jsf"/>
                            </p:submenu>
                            <p:submenu label="Order Management">
                                <p:menuitem value="Process Order"/>
                            </p:submenu>
                        <p:menuitem value="Logout"/>
                    </p:menubar>
                </h:form>
            </ui:insert>
        </div>
        <p:panel style="min-height: 200px;">
            <ui:insert name="bodyContent"/>
        </p:panel>
    </p:layoutUnit>
</p:layout>
```

Creating a Simple Online Shopping Cart Application

The objective of the back office module is to manipulate the products' catalog and make it available for public viewing the back office. The application will land on a dashboard page that shows all the recent orders and their status. The administrator can process the order by changing the appropriate order status directly in the table view. You will be using PrimeFaces's inline edit functionality of the dataTable component. This is where the user clicks on the appropriate order status, and the list will be populated as a drop-down menu. In the drop-down menu, the user can select from the available status types. The following screenshot shows you how it is designed:

When the user clicks on the order status in the data table, the field is made editable. The following screenshot shows that the field is actually editable. You can clearly see the drop-down menu in **Order Status**, so you can select an available status type. Similarly, more information is available by clicking on the down arrow near the **Order Id** field. In order to achieve this functional requirement, you will be using the dataTable component of PrimeFaces.

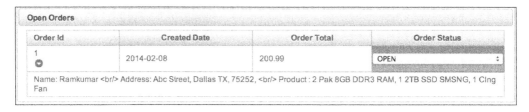

The menubar component

PrimeFaces provides a good feature called **menubar**. This component is used to render the menu in a horizontal style navigation for your application. This shopping cart application will contain a list of menu navigations, as depicted in the following screenshot:

You can clearly see the administrator module with the **Store Management** and **Order Management** options. Under **Store Management**, we have three different options: **Products**, **Categories**, and **Discounts**. These serve as page navigators in this application. We will make use of this menu navigation to perform tasks such as **Product Management**, **Category Management**, and **Discounts Management**, where each page will perform the CRUD operations for the appropriate selected menu option.

Store management

Let's see how the product management page looks, and how it is implemented using PrimeFaces's rich set of components. The following screenshot shows you the product management page:

Adding new products

Users can perform three operations here: add, edit, and delete. All of these are available on one single screen. When you click on the **Add New Product** button on the top-left hand side, a pop-up dialog appears, as seen in the following screenshot. You will be using PrimeFaces's `dialog` component. In this screen, the user will have to fill in all the necessary information for the product:

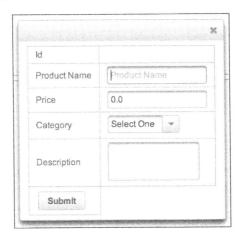

Once the user clicks on the **Submit** button, the information is saved in the database which is then populated dynamically in the storefront, as shown in the following screenshot. Similarly, the user can edit or delete the product using the appropriate button.

Similarly, when the user clicks on the edit icon, a menu pops up to show the product information to be edited. After the user clicks on the **Submit** button, this information will be updated in the database. You can delete the product by clicking on the minus button for the product.

The category page

Similar to the product manipulation page, you have the category page, which allows the user to perform the CRUD operations on the category table. The following screenshot shows how the category page looks as a shopping cart application:

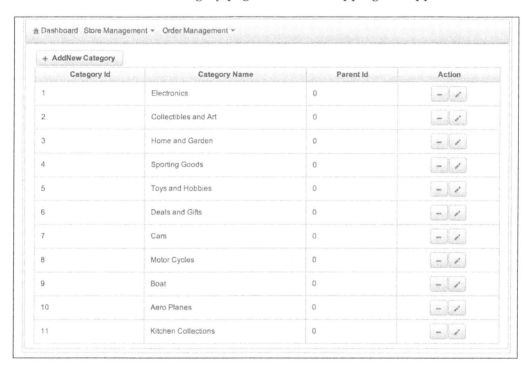

Similarly, you will find that the discount management page uses the same design pattern. Discounts are added; so, during the checkout, the code is validated against the database value and gives the user an appropriate discount value. The following screenshot shows the discount page in the edit mode:

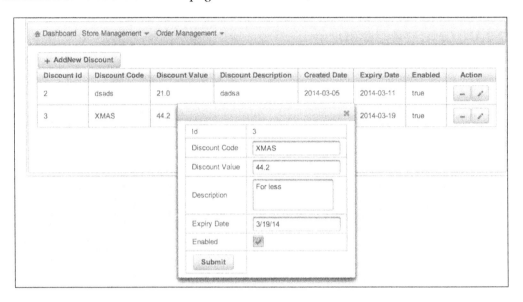

The flow diagram

The flow diagram summarizes the interactions between the presentation layer, the managed bean, the service layer, and the database; all of these use the hibernate persistence mechanism.

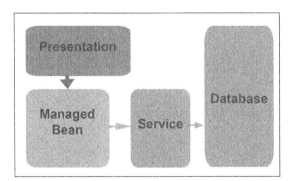

Let's see how the presentation layer interacts with the controller and the service layers:

```
<p:dataTable value="#{productController.categories}" var="cat"
id="cateTable">
        <p:column headerText="Category Id">
```

The preceding code snippet can be found in the `pages/categories.xhtml` file. The `productController.categories` method in `ProductController.java` is executed each time this page loads. There is another method called `populateCategory` that creates sample categories and products in a database and populates them as an application startup. Since this class is defined as a session scope, this category information will always reside in the memory until the application is destroyed or stopped.

The storefront

The storefront is responsible for showcasing all the products with help of the template. Customers visit the site, navigate to their favorite category, and add the product to the shopping cart. They can even drag the product and drop it in the shopping cart.

A representation of the storefront is shown in the following screenshot:

As you can see from the preceding screenshot, the left panel shows the categories, the right panel shows the products, and the shopping cart is at the bottom. The `leftPan` component is used to render all the categories, such that when a user clicks on a category, the center part of the screen is populated with the available products of the appropriate category. They can then select a product and drag-and-drop it in the cart.

Implementing the cart mechanism

You will see an explanation for each and every component of our shopping cart application in the following sections.

The drag-and-drop component

In this application, you will learn how to make a component draggable and learn some basic features of the `draggable` component. The following code snippet can be found in the `welcome.jsf` file, which uses the `draggable` tag inside the `column` tag. This means that each `column` tag inside the `dataGrid` component will behave as a draggable component, making the products draggable.

In order to implement the drag-and-drop functionality, you need to understand the following two draggable concepts:

- Draggable components can be created. In order to do this, you will need to specify which container is going to act as a draggable container. Any component can be enhanced with a draggable behavior. To enable the draggable behavior on any PrimeFaces component, you will need a component called `draggable`. The following code snippet shows the way to enable draggable behavior to a particular component. In this code, the draggable behavior is enabled for the panel component with the `pnl` ID:

```
<p:dataGrid id="availableProducts" var="item"
    value="#{storeController.products}" columns="3">
  <p:column>
    <p:panel id="pnl" header="#{item.name}"
       style="text-align:center">
    <h:panelGrid columns="1" style="width:100%">
      #{item.price}
    </h:panelGrid>
    <p:commandButton value="Add to Cart"
       update=":centerForm:dropArea"
       action="#{storeController.addToCart(item)}"/>
  </p:panel>
  <p:draggable for="pnl" revert="true"
      handle=".ui-panel-titlebar" stack=".ui-panel"/>
  </p:column>
</p:dataGrid>
```

- A component can be made draggable by using `p:draggable`. The component ID must match the `for` attribute of the `p:draggable` component. If the `for` attribute is omitted, the parent component will be selected as a draggable target. You can see that the `draggable` tag is inside the column tag in this application.

Droppable components have a special integration with the data iteration components; such PrimeFaces components are `dataTable`, `dataGrid`, `dataList`, `Carousel`, `Galleria`, `Ring`, and `Sheet`. Any component can be enhanced with a droppable behavior. Droppable components are the targets for the draggable panel, as we defined earlier. To enable the droppable functionality on any PrimeFaces component, we always need a component called droppable. The component tag, `p:droppable`, defines a data source option as an ID of the data iteration component that needs to be connected to droppable. The following code shows how it is used in this application:

```
<p:fieldset id="selectedProducts" style="margin-top:20px">
    <p:outputPanel id="dropArea">
......
    </p:outputPanel>
</p:fieldset>
<p:droppable for="selectedProducts" tolerance="touch"
        activeStyleClass="ui-state-highlight"
        datasource="availableProducts" onDrop="handleDrop"
        <p:ajax listener="#{storeController.onProdDrop}"
           update="dropArea :centerForm:availableProducts"/>
</p:droppable>
```

In the preceding code snippet, we introduced a `dataGrid` component containing all our listed products, using the `Grouping` component as `availableProducts`. These `availableProducts` components were then made draggable in order to drop them onto `selectedProducts`. The `dataGrid` component will act as a data source for the droppable `selectedProducts` component. Inside the `draggable` tag, there is a `p:ajax` tag that handles the target operation to be performed when the item is dropped in the target container. In the following screenshot, you can see the first item SmSng-Kybd is in drag state:

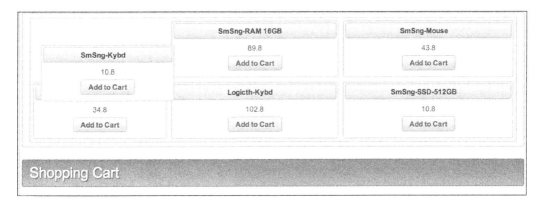

In the preceding screenshot, note that when you drag an item, the shopping cart will be highlighted and directs the user to drop the item inside this component. Once you drop the product, an Ajax call is fired to update the `target` component as well as add the particular item to another array called the selected array. Similarly, you can use the **Add to Cart** button for the same purpose. It automatically calls the method and updates the selected product list as well as updates the total number of products based on the selection.

Here, you can see how the code interacts while dropping the product in the cart:

```
public void onProdDrop(DragDropEvent ddEvent) {
    Product p = ((Product) ddEvent.getData());
    addItemNow(p);
}
private void addItemNow(Product p){
    cartProducts.add(p);
    productTotal += p.getPrice();
    _log.info("Product Name: "+p.getName() +" is added Successfully, Total is: "+ productTotal);
}
```

The checkout cart

Once the customer has selected products, the next step is to allow them to purchase these from the cart. The following screenshot shows the appearance of the checkout functionality using the PrimeFaces wizard component:

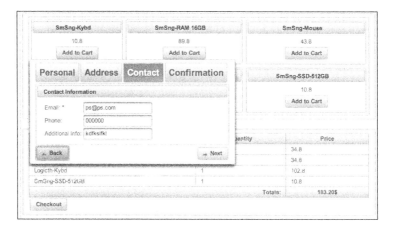

The **Checkout** button is enabled when the products are added to the cart. The customer can then click on the **Checkout** button and enter their information in the wizard format; finally, they will land on the confirmation screen and can submit their order. The order details will be added to the database, and the administrator can then process the order from the opened order list. The following code is used to implement the `wizard` component, which is used to collect information from the user in a sequential format:

```
<h:form>
<p:wizard>
  <p:tab id="personal" title="Personal">
    // .... Personal information
  </p:tab>
  <p:tab id="address" title="Address">
// .... Address information
  </p:tab>
  <p:tab id="contact" title="Contact">
    // .... Contact information
  </p:tab>
  <p:tab id="confirm" title="Confirmation">
    // .... Confirmation Screen
  </p:tab>
</p:wizard>
</h:form>
```

The `wizard` component makes a workflow by creating multiple steps out of a single page form. The process in the checkout page is implemented in four steps using the `wizard` component, namely the user information, address information, contact information, and finally, a summary page with a submit button. In the case of a validation error, the current step is processed partially and the user is prompted to correct the errors. The next step is displayed only when the current step passes validations. The wizard flow is sequential by default, and this can be managed by using the optional Ajax flow listeners, the outcome of which will be displayed in the next step.

When the user clicks on the **Submit** button, the `Checkout` method is executed in the managed bean. Then, the collected information will be added in the `order` table to the database.

Code walk-through

The following screenshot shows a list of the files that are used in the NGOS application, followed by a detailed explanation:

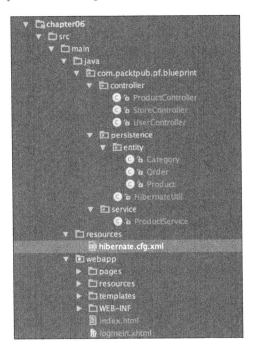

From the file structure, you will notice that there are three controllers. Each controller is working for a separate purpose:

- `ProductController.java` is used to perform operations related to the back office process
- `StoreController.java` is used to handle operations related to the storefront
- `UserController.java` serves as a user management process, which holds the session information of the user-related process

The preceding three controllers are session scopes.

Now, the next major part is the entity. You have three different tables, where each table is associated and mapped to one entity. You can see that it is fully coded using the hibernate3 annotation. The advantage is that it is easy to control, and it automatically creates the **Data Definition Language** (**DDL**) on demand in the database.

The `ProductService.java` class is the middle business layer, enabling the bridge between the persistent layer and the presentation layer.

The `HibernateUtil.java` class is used to perform all sorts of hibernate operations and also holds the hibernate session factory.

Working with the sample code

If you wish to work on the sample code, all you need to do is just clone it from the Git repository at `https://github.com/sudheerj/primefaces-blueprints` where you can use your preferred IDE. Please refer to *Chapter 1, Creating a "Hello World" Application*, for prerequisites to run the application. Change the MySQL user ID and password and then you can start playing with the code. You can run the code for this chapter by using the `mvn jetty:run` command under the `chapter06` folder in the Maven console and then navigate to `http://localhost:8080/web`. You should use `admin/admin` as the user credentials. You can use the following URL to work on the back office process as well as on all kinds of administrator processes, such as adding products, editing categories, and much more: `http://localhost:8080/web/pages/storeadmin.jsf`.

Summary

In this chapter, you have learned how to develop your own shopping cart application and the major functionality of a retail business. You also learned the usage of the `menu` component, the drag-and-drop component, the `dataTable` inline edit, and the `wizard` component provided by the PrimeFaces library.

In the next chapter, you will learn how to create your own online video portal application used by a dance company for their customers to share their videos. From this application, you will learn how to leverage the use of the media components from PrimeFaces.

7
Creating an Online Video Portal Application

In the previous chapter, you learned about an online shopping cart application, where you learned major menu variations and the drag-and-drop components of PrimeFaces. This chapter will walk you through the design and development process of an online video portal application. It will also explain some of the advanced PrimeFaces components that are used to handle media files. With this chapter, you will get a good grip on the components of PrimeFaces, such as multimedia, maps, and schedule components. This chapter guides you through the process of creating an online video portal application. This application can be used in the entertainment world, such as nightlife, special events, and dance concerts; and to book events that occur seasonally, such as special events in the summer or winter. Customers can pick the event that interests them and book it accordingly.

A quick overview

In this chapter, you will design and develop an application for a dance studio that is spread across the country in different locations. This application aims to share the users' thoughts, videos, and events globally. The customers from various locations are virtually connected with the help of this portal. The main intention of building this app is to market their business throughout the world in order to attract more viewers and eventually increase their customers by establishing new locations.

Portal users will be able to share their videos and comment on other videos. The videos will be tagged with keywords such that the users will later be able to search throughout the database. This portal includes two sections: one section is for the content editors, and the other is for the content viewers. The content editors are responsible for the approval process. Any authenticated user can post their videos and make them public; they can also edit their videos temporarily.

Understanding our requirements

The dance studio company provided the following requirements, which lists their need to develop a website and make their business available worldwide. This chapter follows the international corporate standard in order to help the reader understand the requirement structure and its standards. The resolution field in the following table will be filled on the go:

Functional requirement ID	Description	Resolution	Status: Accept/ Denied
FRQ-1	Design and develop a video portal for the dance studio		Accept
FRQ-1.1	Video blogging and forum		Accept
FRQ-1.1.1	Anyone can submit their videos, subject to approval		Accept
FRQ-1.1.2	The logged-in user can comment their suggestions		Accept
FRQ-1.1.3	Public can view all the comments		Accept
FRQ-1.1.4	If a user is not logged in, the system needs to prompt them to log in before posting the videos		Accept
FRQ-1.1.5	The comments section should have the name, date, and time fields along with the comments		Accept
FRQ-1.1.6	A video can be deleted and edited by the owner		Accept
FRQ-1.1.7	A logged-in user will have a dashboard link, which populates all the information related to the current user, and the user can perform all the operations		Accept
FRQ-1.2	User profile management		Accept
FRQ-1.2.1	Need the user profile registration page, which needs to have an option to capture the picture of the user		Accept
FRQ-1.2.2	Need to have a **captcha** in order to avoid nonhuman operations		Accept
FRQ-1.3	A video scheduler or an event scheduler		Accept

Functional requirement ID	Description	Resolution	Status: Accept/ Denied
FRQ-1.3.1	Users can schedule their own events in the site to be displayed publically		Accept
FRQ-1.3.2	Any user can view the events; this scheduler should can just be viewed		Accept
FRQ-1.4	The location map		Accept
FRQ-1.4.1	The location map allows the company to show all their locations on Google Map		Accept
FRQ-1.4.2	Shows the head office's location as the center when the user navigates to the location page		
FRQ-1.5	The video gallery		Accept
FRQ-1.5.1	The video gallery to display all the available videos for various sources, such as YouTube, mp4 files, and wma files		Accept

The system architecture

You will be using the **MySQL** database server as your backend for this application. This project is built on the JSF 2 web application. In this chapter, you will be learning a new framework called **Project Lombok**, which helps you to reduce boilerplate coding. You can get more information at www.projectlombok.org. **Project Lombok** will automatically create all the getter and setter methods for you when you follow the instructions; all you need to do is just define the *@Data annotation* for your **Plain Old Java Object** (**POJO**) class. In order to make this framework work, you will have to install the Project Lombok plugin; it supports both **Eclipse** and **Intellij**. Follow the instructions provided at the **Project Lombok** website.

Implementations

Now, you will learn how to implement the given requirements using the PrimeFaces framework. In this section, you will learn more about the design implementation. Based on the requirements, you will have to design and develop the blocks one by one; this will cover the complete life cycle of the design and implementation phase.

The ER diagram

In this section, you will learn how to design the required database tables and their relationships. In order to design the ER diagram, you can use **MySQL Workbench**; you will have the option to perform forward engineering and reverse engineering. You can get more information on **MySQL Workbench** at `http://www.mysql.com/products/workbench/`. The following diagram shows the design diagram of the database tables and their relationships:

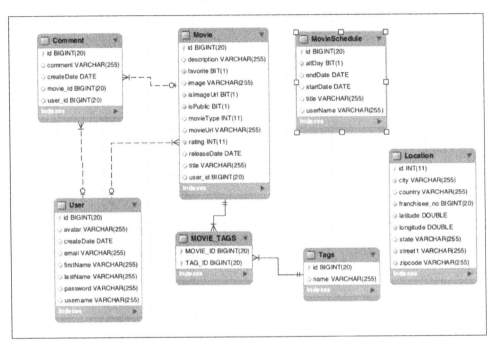

The preceding diagram depicts the database design, which describes the relational schema between all the tables associated with this application. You can see that the **Movie** table holds all the information related to the movie, the **Comment** table holds all the comments that the users commented on the movies, and the **Tags** table holds all the tags that are associated with the movie. These tags are provided when the user adds a movie; this tag has a many-to-many relationship and that is the reason of the **MOVIE_TAGS** table's existence. As you know, the **User** table will hold the user profiles with the login credentials. Both the **Location** table and the **MovieSchedule** table are used to store the location information and event information, respectively. In the following sections, you will learn more about the usage of these tables.

Working on the application persistence layer

Like previous chapters, you will be using hibernate as the persistence layer. In this application, you will be using only one service class as a **Data Access Object** (**DAO**), which will define all the required methods to pull and push data from and to the database.

The following code snippet is used to pull the list of available locations from the database. Each of the methods in this class will be encapsulated with a hibernate transaction in order to avoid data losses:

```
public List<Location> getAllLocations(){
    org.hibernate.Transaction tx = getSession().beginTransaction();
    List list = getSession().createCriteria(Location.class).list();
    tx.commit();
    getSession().close();
    _log.info("Listed Successfully....");
    return list;
}
```

The first line of this method starts the transaction-aware hibernate session. The hibernate `util` class holds the current session by using the connection parameters provided in the hibernate configuration file. Once the transaction is enabled, you can perform all the DB operations. Hibernate provides a lot of ready-made utilities that help you to perform the **Data Manipulation Language** (DML) operations in an efficient way. Once the DML operations are done, it is better to close the connection and the session in order to release the allocated resources.

Possible errors in hibernate DML

When you perform the DML operations, you sometimes see an error that is related to the hibernate session. One of the reasons for this error is because the hibernate session is always closed after the execution of each DML, and when you perform the lazy fetch, the operation will fail as the current session is already closed. To overcome this situation, you should always query the lazy load separately with a new transaction. That is, you can query the relational associates separately when you require it.

Working on the presentation layer

Now it is time to explain the UI functionality of the dance company's web application. As mentioned previously, this application is intended to demonstrate some of the advanced components of PrimeFaces, such as the media, schedule, and map, and also covers some additional supporting components.

The home page

On the home page, you will see all the videos in the order of their published dates. When the user selects any one of the videos, it will take him or her to the showroom where it uses the appropriate video player and will give them the option to play the video. The following screenshot shows the home page of this application:

The following screenshot shows you the showroom page with a video playing option. This screen will have a back button that will allow you to choose another video. And, if the user is logged in, then the commenting option is enabled; otherwise, the commenting option will be disabled. The comment section will list all the comments associated with that particular video.

Chapter 7

You will use the PrimeFaces **toolbar** component for the menu navigation. The buttons present in this toolbar appear conditionally. That is, since the public user does not have the permission to perform certain operations, those are enabled only when the user is logged in.

The home page also has a good feature called ring. This PrimeFaces `ring` component will display the movie titles and their images in a ring fashion, and the user can click and enjoy the animation. The following screenshot shows the `ring` component at the bottom of the page:

When the user selects any of the images in the ring, the image will slide to the center of the ring and get highlighted. This feature is there to impart a rich UI experience.

Code walk-through – the home page

In the following code snippet, you can see how to get the list of movies and render them with the help of CSS in the presentation layer. You will be iterating the list using the `ui:repeat` tab from Facelets, as follows:

```
<h:form id="centerForm">
<p:panelGrid columns="1" style="width: 100%;">
<p:panel style="text-align: center; border: none;">
<ui:repeat value="#{movieController.movies}" var="movs">
<p:commandLink style="a:link { text-decoration:none; }"
                              actionListener="#{movieControll
er.setSelectedMovie(movs)}"
                              action="showcase.jsf?faces-
redirect=true">

<div id="col1" class="twoCols">
<h2>#{movs.title}</h2>
<hr/>
<h2>Alphabetic List</h2>

<p style="text-align: center;">
<p:graphicImage library="images" name="#{movs.image}"
 style="width: 90%;"/>
<strong>Euler angels</strong>
</p>
<hr/>
<h2>Description</h2>

<div id="tip">
<p>#{movs.description}</p>
</div>
</div>
</p:commandLink>
</ui:repeat>
</p:panel>
<p:panel style=" text-align: center; border: none;">
<p:ring id="custom" value="#{movieController.movies}"
                      var="favs" styleClass="li
{height:200px;}">
<p:graphicImage library="images" name="#{favs.image}"
                              width="130px"/>
</p:ring>
</p:panel>
</p:panelGrid>
</h:form>
```

The preceding code snippet is used in the `welcome.xhtml` file. The main aim of this is to render all the available videos in the order in which they were created. You can also see that the `ring` component will show only the videos that are marked as favorites. Here, you have the `panelGrid` component that holds two panel components. One panel has the `repeat` tag that iterates the video list generated from the DB and renders them as boxes. These boxes are aligned, and CSS is added to improve the look and feel. The other panel holds the `ring` component.

Enabling registration and login

Every portal usually requires user registration; similarly, this application has a user registration page. When the user clicks on the **Login** button at the top-right corner of the toolbar, a new screen appears where the user can provide their credentials and log in to the system. New users can click on the **Register** button and register for a new user profile.

Users are requested to perform the desired operation by selecting the appropriate button. The following screenshot shows the available **Login** option:

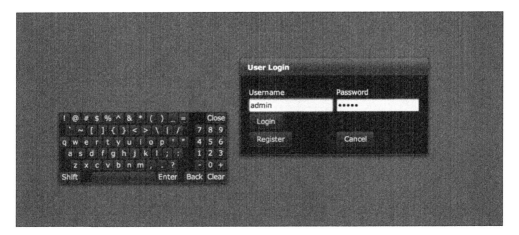

Creating an Online Video Portal Application

The user can enter their credentials using the keyboard, or they also have the option to use the onscreen keyboard that is provided by PrimeFaces. The **Register** button takes the user to the user registration page, where the user needs to provide all the information as expected. The user can also capture their photos using the online photo capture option, as shown in the following screenshot:

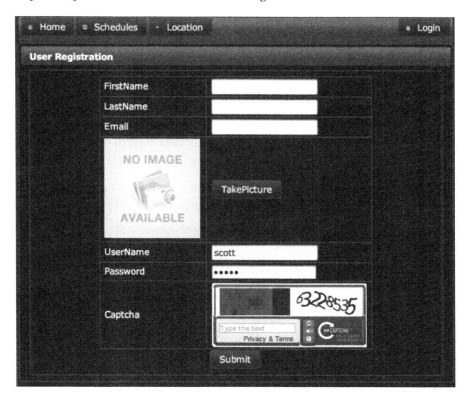

The **User Registration** page contains basic information. The user needs to provide full information, and using the `photoCam` component, the user can take a picture directly using their web camera. Also, note that the captcha component is used in this registration. Captcha is used in many public websites in order to avoid nonhuman entries.

> Each and every day, automated machines crawl through websites in order to make search engines work better. These crawlers often visit public webpages and read each and every possibility, and if applicable, they also submit pages. Google, Yahoo, and many other search engines perform these kind of tasks every now and then. If we don't use the captcha mechanism, our database will be full of junk information.

Code walk-through – the user registration page

On the user registration page, the `photoCam` component and the captcha component can be highlighted as follows:

```
<p:dialog id="picFrame" header="Take Picture" widgetVar="picFrame"
closeOnEscape="true" appendTo="@(body)" draggable="false"
position="center" resizable="false">
<p:photoCam widgetVar="pc" listener="#{userController.oncapture}"
update="ppict"/>
<p:commandButton type="button" value="Capture" onclick="PF('pc').
capture()" oncomplete="PF('pc').capture()" onsuccess="PF('picFrame').
close();"/>
</p:dialog>
```

The preceding code snippet is used to show or hide the `photoCam` component. Note that the `photoCam` component is added inside the `dialog` component; when the user clicks on the **TakePicture** button, the dialog will be displayed and the `photoCam` component will be enabled. The `photoCam` component will always prompt the user to allow or deny access to the camera. Due to security and privacy reasons, HTML5 added this functionality such that the user can either allow or deny access. The following screenshot shows how the privacy prompt looks:

The following code has the logic to store the captured image in the filesystem:

```java
public void oncapture(CaptureEvent captureEvent) {
        String photo = getRandomImageName();
        this.user.setAvatar(photo);
        byte[] data = captureEvent.getData();
        ServletContext servletContext = (ServletContext) FacesContext.getCurrentInstance().getExternalContext().getContext();
        String newFileName = servletContext.getRealPath("") + File.separator + "photocam" + File.separator + photo + ".png";
        FileImageOutputStream imageOutput;
        try {
            imageOutput = new FileImageOutputStream(new File(newFileName));
            imageOutput.write(data, 0, data.length);
            imageOutput.close();
        } catch (Exception e) {
            throw new FacesException("Error in writing captured image.");
        }
    }
```

You will be setting the filepath in the user object, and the update attribute will update the graphic image component and display the captured image. The following screenshot shows you how the screen will look after an image is captured:

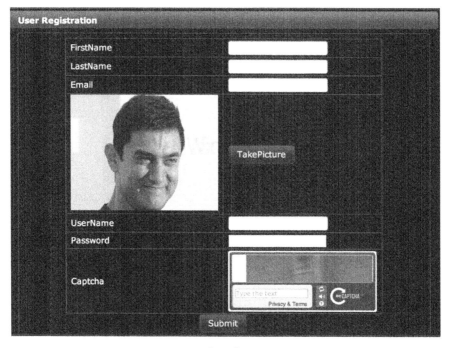

The photoCam component requires the Flash player.

Once the user registers with the website, he or she can use the same credentials to log in to the system and perform the operations allowed to the logged-in users.

The user dashboard page

The user dashboard is the place where the user will land when they log in to the system. Here, the user can add, edit, or delete videos. All the available videos are displayed in the user dashboard using PrimeFaces' dataTable component. This media component can have file formats such as YouTube URL, wma files, mp4 files, and many more. In the following example, you will get information on how to use the YouTube URL:

Creating an Online Video Portal Application

The preceding screenshot shows the user dashboard view. Here, we have listed all the available videos in a data table. The user can click on the **Add New** button at the top and at the bottom to add new videos. There is also an edit icon and a delete icon to perform the respective operations. When the user clicks on the edit icon, the `dialog` component immediately pops up, which is populated with all the information related to the appropriate video. The user can edit the information and click on the **Submit** button, as shown in the following screenshot:

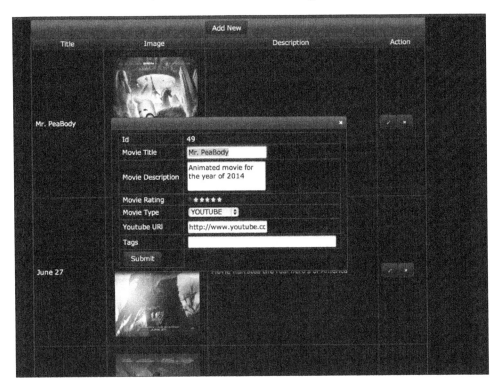

The preceding screenshot shows you the edit video option. PrimeFaces has provided two interesting components in this edit screen. One of these is the rating component; that is, the user can input their rating by selecting the exact number of stars from the display, which is automatically converted to the appropriate integer value that can be stored in the database. The second is the drop-down component; the highlight of this component is that you can directly use the `enum` data type in the drop-down list without converting the Java `enum` object to a list of strings. The following snippet shows the usage of both the components:

```
<p:rating value="#{movieController.movie.rating}"/>
<h:selectOneMenu value="#{movieController.movie.movieType}" >
<f:selectItems value="#{movieController.getMovieTypes()}" />
</h:selectOneMenu>
```

The preceding snippet has both the `rating` component and the drop-down component. The `rating` component is directly bound to an integer Java data type, and the `selectItems` tag is directly bound to the movie type enum object.

Scheduling the application components

In this section, you will learn how to use the PrimeFaces scheduler component. In the dance company's video portal application, the business requirement says that each registered user can share their events and schedules with all the other virtual users; the schedule component is one of the useful components provided by PrimeFaces. The schedule component provides an Outlook Calendar, iCal, like the JSF component to manage events. The following screenshot shows you how to use the schedule component in this application:

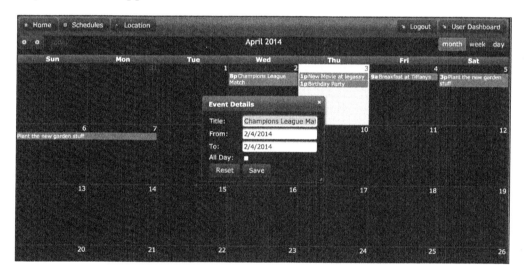

Logged-in users are allowed to edit any events from the display by double-clicking on the event directly, or they can add new events by double-clicking on the desired date as well. When the user double-clicks on the desired date, a pop up appears, and the user is requested to enter the event information. The pop-up panel will have the following information: title, start date, and end date. If the event is an all-day event, the user can also select the **All Day** option.

Code walk-through – the schedule page

The scheduler component in this application is implemented using the following code snippet:

```
<p:schedule id="schedule" value="#{scheduleController.eventModel}"
                  widgetVar="myschedule"
                  rendered="#{userController.loggedIn}">

<p:ajax event="dateSelect" listener="#{scheduleController.
onDateSelect}" update="eventDetails"
                  oncomplete="PF('eventDialog').show()"/>
<p:ajax event="eventSelect" listener="#{scheduleController.
onEventSelect}" update="eventDetails"
                  oncomplete="PF('eventDialog').show()"/>
<p:ajax event="eventMove" listener="#{scheduleController.onEventMove}"
update="messages"/>
<p:ajax event="eventResize" listener="#{scheduleController.
onEventResize}" update="messages"/>
</p:schedule>
<p:schedule id="readSchedule" value="#{scheduleController.
eventModel}"rendered="#{ not userController.loggedIn}"/>
```

In the preceding code snippet, two different scheduler components were used to display the calendar. Based on the user permissions, one of them is displayed and is for authenticated users who can add or edit events, and the other one is for public users with only the view option.

The scheduler component supports the following events: `dateSelect`, `eventSelect`, `eventMove`, `viewChange`, and `eventResize`. As the names state, these events are triggered when the user performs such operations on the component. These events are bound to the `controller` method to process the specific tasks. The following code snippet will show you how the Ajax events are bound with the component to listen:

```
<p:ajax event="dateSelect" listener="#{scheduleController.
onDateSelect}" update="eventDetails"
                  oncomplete="PF('eventDialog').show()"/>
        <p:ajax event="eventSelect"
listener="#{scheduleController.onEventSelect}" update="eventDetails"
                  oncomplete="PF('eventDialog').show()"/>
        <p:ajax event="eventMove"
listener="#{scheduleController.onEventMove}" update="messages"/>
        <p:ajax event="eventResize"
listener="#{scheduleController.onEventResize}" update="messages"/>
```

The scheduler component needs to be backed by an `org.PrimeFaces.model.ScheduleModel` instance; a schedule model consists of the `org.PrimeFaces.model.ScheduleEvent` instance. PrimeFaces provided `DefaultScheduleEvent`, which is the default implementation of the `ScheduleEvent` interface. The properties required to create a new event are the title, start date, and end date. Other properties are optional, such as `allDay` and the default values. The following code snippet will show you how to use `defaultScheduleEvent`:

```java
public void createSamples() {
        eventModel = new DefaultScheduleModel();
        MovieSchedule ms = new MovieSchedule("New Movie at legassy",
today1Pm(), today6Pm(), false, user.getUsername());
        ds.addOrUpdateEntity(ms);
        ms = new MovieSchedule("Champions League Match",
previousDay8Pm(), previousDay11Pm(), false, user.getUsername());
        ds.addOrUpdateEntity(ms);
        ms = new MovieSchedule("Birthday Party", today1Pm(),
today6Pm(), false, user.getUsername());
        ds.addOrUpdateEntity(ms);
        ms = new MovieSchedule("Breakfast at Tiffanys", nextDay9Am(),
nextDay11Am(), false, user.getUsername());
        ds.addOrUpdateEntity(ms);
        ms = new MovieSchedule("Plant the new garden stuff",
theDayAfter3Pm(), fourDaysLater3pm(), false, user.getUsername());
        ds.addOrUpdateEntity(ms);
        List<MovieSchedule> msL = ds.getAllEvents();
        for(MovieSchedule e : msL){
            eventModel.addEvent(e.toScheduleEvent());
        }
    }
```

Take a look at the preceding code; you will be creating a `MovieSchedule` entity object and adding it to the database. At the end of the method, you will populate the list from the database and update `eventModel`; thus, you can utilize the API from PrimeFaces to populate the scheduler components.

Implementing the location page

As mentioned at the beginning of this chapter, the client is a dance studio company that is spread across the country in various locations. In this application, the location page will show the users how to easily explore the company's various locations by picking the Google map view. The user can also calculate the nearest location from the map. PrimeFaces provides a gmap component that helps to achieve this requirement. The gmap component is a map component integrated with the Google Maps API v3. The following screenshot shows the location page in which all the company locations are plotted in Google Maps:

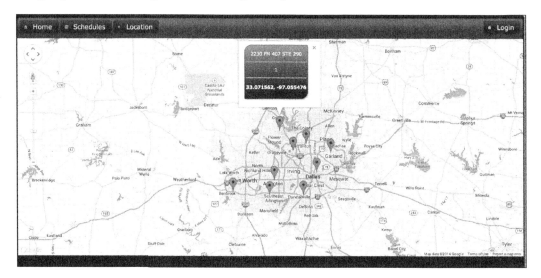

When the user clicks on the location marker, the pop up shows the information related to that location.

Integration

For integration, the first thing to do is to place the required JavaScript from the Google Maps API that the gmap component belongs to, usually v1.3. The ideal location to include the JavaScript API is at the head section of your page. This is a third-party JavaScript library provided by Google Inc.

The following snippet will do the rest of the job for your application in order to implement the `gmap` component:

```
<script src="http://maps.google.com/maps/api/js?sensor=true|false"
        type="text/javascript"></script>
```

As the Google Maps API states, the mandatory `sensor` parameter is used to specify whether your application requires a sensor such as a GPS locator. Based on this parameter, your application uses the current location and enables or disables the GPS. If the GPS is *on*, the user will be asked whether they want to allow this application to use Geo Location or not. Four options are required to place a `gmap` component on a page; these are center, zoom, type, and style:

- **Center**: The center of the map is represented in the latitude and longitude format
- **Zoom**: This represents the zoom level of the map
- **Type**: This shows the type of the map—valid values are hybrid, satellite, roadmap, and terrain
- **Style**: This represents the dimensions of the map

In order to make the `gmap` marker center to the current location, add the following snippet at the head of the page and also make sure to specify `sensor = true` in the JavaScript API parameter:

```
<script type="text/javascript">
$(function () {
navigator.geolocation.getCurrentPosition(
function (position) {
var map = PF('gmap').getMap(),
latlng = new google.maps.LatLng(
position.coords.latitude,
position.coords.longitude);
map.setCenter(latlng);
var marker = new google.maps.Marker({
position: latlng});
marker.setMap(map);
},
function (error) {alert(error.message); });
);
});
</script>
```

When you specify `sensor = true`, the application enables the GPS and the API will provide the current location coordinates. The preceding method is executed when the page is loaded and then sets the current location coordinates to the `gmap` component. Thus, the `gmap` component will be at the center of the current location. You can also manually specify the current coordinates to set them to a specific location. If the preceding method already exists, it will overwrite the current position to the current Geo Location at runtime.

The `MapModel` class and the `Marker` class are very important classes in `gmap` in order to set the proper value to the `gmap` component.

MapModel

The `gmap` component is backed by an `org.PrimeFaces.model.map.MapModel` instance. PrimeFaces provides `org.PrimeFaces.model.map.DefaultMapModel` as the default implementation. The API documents of all `gmap` related model classes are available at the end of the `gmap` section and also in Javadocs of PrimeFaces. This `MapModel` object will hold all the location coordinates. Here, you can see that the `LocationMap` property is an instance of `ModelMap`, and we will set all the available location information that we get from the database:

```
    private void populateLocationCoordinates(){
        List<Location> locations = ds.getAllLocations();
        if(locations == null) {
            return;
        }
        centerMap = "";
        locationMap = new DefaultMapModel();
        location = null;

        log.info("Too Many Map Locations: "+locations.size());

        for(Location loc: locations){
            LatLng ll = new LatLng( loc.getLatitude(), loc.
getLongitude());
            locationMap.addOverlay(new Marker(ll, loc.getStreet1(),
loc.getFranchiseeNo()));
        }
    }
```

Take a look at the preceding snippet; this method is responsible for populating all the location information and setting it to the `locationMap` property. We get all the location information from the DB using the `ds.getAllLocations()` method, iterate it, and populate the `ModelMap` object, which is referenced in the `gmap` component of the XHTML page.

Markers

A marker is represented by `org.PrimeFaces.model.map.Marker`. This marker will hold the location coordinates and the extra information, such as the address. The `Marker` class has a data property, which is of the `Java.lang.Object` type. You can carry any information with this data property; for example, you can hold an image URL, a full HTML snippet, and so on.

LatLng

You will be using the `LatLng` object from the PrimeFaces API to hold the latitude and longitude, and this object is set in the `Marker` object. You can refer to the same information from the GUI using the following code snippet:

```
<h:form styleClass="form-inline" prependId="false">
<p:gmap center="32.658669, -97.134435" zoom="13" type="ROADMAP" id="gmap"
                    mapTypeControl="false" navigationControl="false"
                    widgetVar="gmap" model="#{locationController.locationMap}"
                    style="width:100%; height:600px;"
streetView="true">
<p:ajax event="overlaySelect" listener="#{locationController.onMarkerSelect}"/>

<p:gmapInfoWindow>
<p:outputPanel id="col1" class="twoCols" style="text-align:center;display:block;margin:auto:">
<p>#{locationController.marker.title}</p>
<hr/>
<p>#{locationController.marker.data.toString()}</p>
<hr/>
<h4>#{locationController.marker.latlng.lat}, #{locationController.marker.latlng.lng}</h4>
</p:outputPanel>
</p:gmapInfoWindow>
</p:gmap>
</h:form>
```

Take a look at the code implementation in the GUI; you will have to provide all four parameters to initialize the `gmap` component. The marker has a `title` field that holds the title information for the given location.

In the following screenshot, you can see the table that is used to store the location's information:

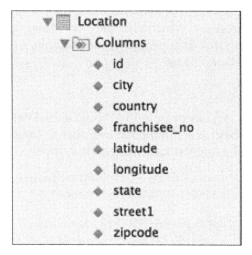

Working with the sample code

If you wish to work on the sample code, all you need to do is just clone it from the GitHub repository at https://github.com/sudheerj/PrimeFaces-blueprints, where you can use your preferred IDE. From there, change the MySQL user ID and password, and then you can start playing with the code. You can run the Chapter07 code by using the mvn jetty:run command under the chapter07 folder in the Maven console and then navigate to http://localhost:8080/web. You can use admin/admin as the user credentials, or you can create your own profile and use the user ID and password as credentials. For your convenience, here you can see some sample videos that will be created each time you run the application.

Summary

In this chapter, you learned how to develop an online video portal application. This application can be used by many different small-scale businesses, such as a dance studio, music company, and many more. As intended, you learned the advanced PrimeFaces components such as the media component, the gmap component, the scheduler component, the ring component, and some of the supporting components.

In the next chapter, you will learn another real-time business application that is used for an online printing station. It enables you to have a high-quality printer, which you can use from anywhere in the world at an affordable price, without owning the costly printer hardware.

8
Creating an Online Printing Station Application

In the previous chapter, you learned about the video portal application. You are now familiar with media tags and you also know how to handle media files. It is wonderful how PrimeFaces includes these tags to support the media files.

In this chapter, you will learn how to develop a real-time business application called an online printing station application. The highlight of this chapter is that you will be learning how easy it is to upload and download a file using PrimeFaces's variety components. You will also learn some of the new tags that have just been launched in PrimeFaces v5.0.

Understanding the need of this application

Everyone knows how today's world has changed with regards to technology. Leveraging the advanced use of modern technology is a good thing. Assume that you will be needing a printer at your place for all your printing needs, but for more advanced quality and features, you may end up paying more to buy a printer for your advanced printing usage. This usage might be for a day or for a week; just for a day or a week of usage, you will buy a costly printer, print as per your needs, and then keep it idle for years. Thus, you will be loosing your hard-earned money.

This client printing company is planning to launch a printing station in each town. The main aim of this printing station is to establish a chain of stores that maintain a wide variety of printers. These printers can be used for the public on demand, as a paid service for their printing needs. You will design and develop an application, which provides a platform to request and track the user printing needs. The printing company will use your application to connect, track, and schedule users' printing jobs. This application also enables you to share a single printer with other users on demand.

This application will allow its users to select a desired location and then help them to fine-tune the printing options before the actual printing is done. The print order will then be processed immediately and the user can collect the printed copies at the selected drive-through counter. Using this application, one can also send prints remotely to any person any where, and the person from another location can collect them when they're ready at the drive-through counter.

Requirement analysis

The printing company requires an online web application that can manage the entire process of tracking, ordering, and processing the user print jobs in a secure and faster way. This application will be capable of handling users' files without giving permissions to read or write the file to some anonymous users. The following specification requirements help you to understand the overall business process of the online printing station.

In this phase, many scheduled meetings will be held in order to draft the requirements. The meeting participants are the people involved in the business, such as team members including the business analyst, system designer, and team lead.

Functional requirements

The following are the functional requirements of this application:

- You need an online system to track and process the overall activity of the printing station.
- You need to have a platform where the user can see all the available services and their benefits.
- You need a fully-integrated system to handle more than 1,000 print jobs per minute from various locations.

- You need an option for the user to select their own location for their convenience to collect the finished jobs. You also need the administrator rights to add a new location.

- You need one user to act as an administrator who needs the permission to add the location and to display all the open jobs and their progress.

The architecture

In this chapter, you will be working on the same architecture that you've seen in the previous chapters. On top of that, you will also be using many advanced PrimeFaces components. Again, here you will be using MySQL as the database. As mentioned earlier, you will be using Project Lombok to reduce the effort to create boilerplate codes.

Fulfilling our application requirements using PrimeFaces

Now, let's see how to implement the requirements using the PrimeFaces components. In this section, you will learn everything about how to use the PrimeFaces components for the specified requirements. You will also learn about each component and its implementation one by one with a detailed description.

The ER diagram

First, you will have to understand the database design. Every project will start with the DB design. In order to design the DB, there are plenty of tools available. Designing a DB is not an easy task, since it involves all the business requirements and RDBMS concepts. The major parts in designing a DB are normalization, de-normalization, identity key, surrogate key, and so on. For more information, you can search on Google for RDBMS concepts.

The following diagram depicts the database design that is used in this project:

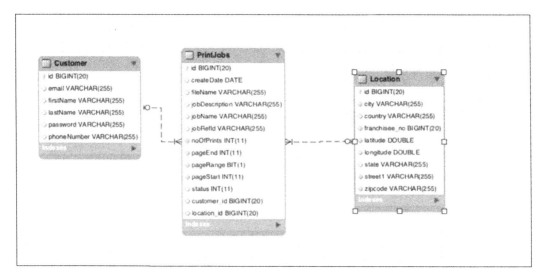

The preceding diagram depicts the database design. You will be using three main tables as described here. The **Customer** table holds all the customer details and their login credentials. In the **Location** table, you will see all the available locations; information about these locations will be displayed in the location map for easy navigation. The next table is the **PrintJobs** table; this is the real transaction table that holds the order details of the print jobs. Here is the use case of the entire project: customers register their basic information, chose the desired location, and then they place the print job order; while ordering, they upload the files to be printed and specify their comments.

Implementing our landing page

The landing page of this printing press application has company advertisements. When you run the sample application and navigate to the application root, you will land on the index.xhtml page, which showcases the company's products and attractive ads. The user can navigate to various options related to print jobs.

The following screenshot shows the landing page of this application:

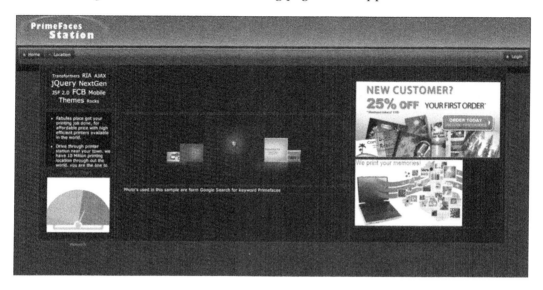

In this page, you will use the `chart` component, the content flow component, and the scroll panel component. This page is designed to attract the end user to buy their (the company's) products, listed service, and also educate the user on the different available services.

The TagCloud component

A tag cloud (word cloud or weighted list in visual design) is a visual representation of text data, typically used to depict keyword metadata (tags) on websites, or to visualize free form text. Tags are usually single words, and the importance of each tag is shown with font size or color. This format is useful to quickly perceive the most prominent terms and locate a term alphabetically to determine its relative prominence. When used as website navigation aids, the terms are hyperlinked to items associated with the tag. In those days, generating a tag cloud was a big headache for developers. The tag cloud component in PrimeFaces is used to show text visualization in different sizes to attract users. This will showcase the different tag text related to the content of the website.

In order to display `TagCloud` in the GUI page, you need to collect all the tags in the `TagCloudModel` object. The `TagCloudModel` object has a method to add tags. You will have to add each tag using the `addTag` method. PrimeFaces provides a `DefaultTagCloudItem` object implementation, which accepts three parameters: text, URL, and the strength. The text field is the display text that is used to render. The URL parameter enables the text as a hyperlink, and the strength parameter is an integer that defines the size of the keyword. You can specify any number, and based on the specified number, it will assign the font size.

Code walk-through

The following snippet can be found in the `GenericController`. This snippet is responsible for populating all the tag clouds:

```
Private TagCloudModel model = new DefaultTagCloudModel();
model.addTag(new DefaultTagCloudItem("Book Printing", 1));
      model.addTag(new DefaultTagCloudItem("Print Now",
      "location.jsf?faces-redirect=true", 3));
      model.addTag(new DefaultTagCloudItem("Ink Jet ", 2));
      model.addTag(new DefaultTagCloudItem("Dot Matrix",
      "location.jsf?faces-redirect=true", 5));
      model.addTag(new DefaultTagCloudItem("NextGen Printing",
      4));
      model.addTag(new DefaultTagCloudItem("Printing Orders",
      "location.jsf?faces-redirect=true", 2));
      model.addTag(new DefaultTagCloudItem("Laser Print", 5));
      model.addTag(new DefaultTagCloudItem("Flex Printing",
      3));
      model.addTag(new DefaultTagCloudItem("Vinyl Printing",
      "location.jsf?faces-redirect=true", 4));
      model.addTag(new DefaultTagCloudItem("Request Print",
      "location.jsf?faces-redirect=true", 1));
```

In the preceding snippet, the `TagCloudModel` object is initialized with `DefaultTagCloudModel`, and in the consecutive lines, you will be adding the `DefaultTagCloudItme` object to the model object. Finally, you will just bind the model object to the tag cloud component in the GUI page, as seen in the following code snippet:

```
<p:tagCloud model="#{genericController.model}">
<p:ajax event="select" update="msg" listener="#{genericController.
onSelect}"/>
</p:tagCloud>
```

You can find the preceding GUI code snippet in the `index.xhtml` file. You are using PrimeFaces's `tagCloud` component, and the `model` attribute is bound to the generic controller model object. You also have an interaction option, such as when and what the user performs on the `tagCloud` component. For example, if the user clicks on any of the `tagCloud` text, the `listener` method is immediately triggered, which performs the specified operation. This might be useful when you want to track the user operations.

The scrollPanel component

PrimeFaces provides more interesting components; one of the components that you will use in this project is the `scrollPanel` component. This component is used to limit the usage of the available page space. The `scrollPanel` component is used to display the overflowed content with theme-aware scroll bars instead of the native browsers scroll bars.

The `scrollPanel` component is used as a container component. That is, you can use the `scrollPanel` component to hold other components. This acts as a panel component in which you need to set the width and height. By default, `scrollPanel` displays theme-aware scrollbars, and setting the mode option to the native browser displays scroll bars. This setting allows the `scrollPanel` component to display the scroll bar the same as the browser window. In this project, the user had a requirement that there had to be one landing page that should not have any window scroll, and simultaneously, the terms and conditions had to be displayed to be scrolled separately inside the same page.

More usage for this component can found at http://www.primefaces.org/showcase/ui/panel/scrollPanel.xhtml.

Code walk-through

The section overviews how to implement the `scrollPanel` component, and you will also get an idea on how PrimeFaces supports the designing of a web page in a tight space crunch:

```
<p:scrollPanel mode="native" style="width:250px;height:200px">
. . . .
</p:scrollPanel>
```

The preceding snippet can be found in the `index.xhtml` file as mentioned above. The content inside these tags, which is beyond the size of the component, is viewable only on user scroll. This aims to utilize limited space to show more content.

The chart component

PrimeFaces provides the `chart` component that helps you to render the numeric value in a graphical representation. In this sample project, our user's requirement is to display how many users are visiting the site as a meter gauge, which allows the visitors to understand how many visitors are visiting the page every day. In order to achieve this, you will be using the `chart` component from PrimeFaces. The `chart` component allows you to render different types of charts such as the bar chart, the line chart, and so on. Similarly, the meter gauge chart component can be used to display the data in a meter gauge format. The following URL has more use cases for this component: http://www.primefaces.org/showcase/ui/chart/metergauge.xhtml. The following screenshot shows how the visitor gauge is displayed on the page:

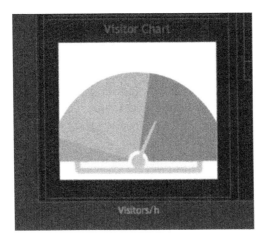

Let's see how to implement this in our page.

Code walk-through

In this section, you will get an idea about how the meter gauge chart is coded in our application. You can find the following code snippet in `index.xhtml`:

```
<p:chart type="metergauge"
model="#{genericController.meterGaugeModel}"style="width:250;height:2
50px"/>
```

In the `chart` component, you will specify the `type` attribute as `metergauge`, which enables the chart to be displayed as a meter gauge. The model attribute is bound to a meter gauge model from `genericController`.

The following code snippet is used to populate the `metergauge` chart from the backing bean:

```
Private MeterGaugeChartModel initMeterGaugeModel() {
        List<Number> intervals = new ArrayList<Number>(){{
add(20);
add(50);
add(120);
add(220);
        }};

return new MeterGaugeChartModel(140, intervals);
    }

private void createMeterGaugeModels() {
meterGaugeModel = initMeterGaugeModel();
meterGaugeModel.setTitle("Visitor Chart");
meterGaugeModel.setGaugeLabel("Visitors/h");
meterGaugeModel.setGaugeLabelPosition("bottom");
meterGaugeModel.setShowTickLabels(false);
meterGaugeModel.setLabelHeightAdjust(110);
meterGaugeModel.setIntervalOuterRadius(130);
    }
```

`MeterGaugeChart` can be customized using various options. You can specify your set of colors, enable and disable legends, and so on. If you would like to set your own colors, you can change the `seriesColors` attribute with a list of comma-separated color strings such as `seriesColors="66cc66, 93b75f, E7E658, cc6666"`.

The contentFlow component

The `contentFlow` component allows the user to display the contents with good animations. PrimeFaces has many components that allow the user to build a good animation in a matter of minutes, leveraging the use of the cross-browser support. This `contentFlow` component was introduced in PrimeFaces 5.0.

The `contentFlow` component requires content as children that can either be defined dynamically using iteration or one by one. Each item must have the `contentStyle` class applied as well. This component is used to create a gallery with sliding animations. In dynamic content, the picture URL is populated as a `collection` object, bound to its value attribute, and iterated as children.

Code walk-through

In this section, you will learn how to code the `contentFlow` component to render the sliding animated gallery:

```
<p:contentFlow value="#{genericController.images}" var="image"
style="width: 815px;">
<p:graphicImage library="images" name="#{image}"
styleClass="content"/>
</p:contentFlow>
```

The preceding code is used to render the `contentFlow` component, and the `value` attribute is bound to a list of image array. This will display the animated gallery as shown in the following screenshot:

The preceding screenshot shows what the content flow looks like and how the images are displayed with sliding animation.

Supporting components

In this chapter's example, you will use more common additional components such as the `panelGrid` and `growl` components.

The `growl` component is used in the same way as the message component. This component provides an overlay instead of showing the message inline. You can see an example at the following URL: http://www.primefaces.org/showcase/ui/message/growl.xhtml.

The login page

The login page provides a platform to authenticate the user, or the user can create a new user profile in the application. Based on the privilege granted, the user is able to perform the operation. An administrator and a customer are the two different categories. In this application, use `admin@admin.com`/`admin` to get the administrator privilege.

Administrators can perform the following operations:

- Edit and add content to the website
- Add a new location in the location page
- View the print order in the admin dashboard

If you use the normal customer/user credentials, you will have the permission to add print orders. The dashboard page is used to see all their order history and related information. The following screenshot shows the login page for this application:

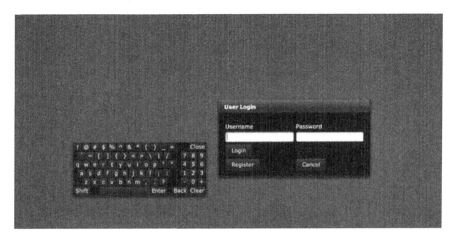

The user can also register their basic information by clicking on the **Register** button. The next section shows you how to design the registration page in order to get the basic information from the customer:

```
<div id="content" title="User Login">
<h:form id="login" prependId="false">
<p:dialog header="User Login"
id="dialog"
modal="true"
closable="false"
position="center"
widgetVar="modalLogin"
showEffect="slide"
draggable="false"
resizable="false"
visible="true">
<h:panelGrid id="loginBox" columns="2" cellpadding="3"
style="margin: 0 auto; border: 0px; padding-top: 20px;">
<h:outputLabel for="j_username" value="Username "/>
<h:outputLabel for="j_password" value="Password "/>
```

```
<p:keyboard id="j_username" required="true"
widgetVar="usernameKeyBoard"
value="#{customerController.useremail}"
onfocus="$('#keypad-div').css( 'z-index', 9999 );"/>
<p:keyboard id="j_password" required="true" password="true"
value="#{customerController.password}"
onblur="$('#keypad-div').css( 'z-index', 9999 );"/>
<p:commandButton id="loginBtn" value="Login" ajax="false"
action="#{customerController.loginMeIn()}"/>
<p:message for="loginBtn"/>

<p:commandButton value="Register" action="/userRegistration.jsf?faces-
redirect=true"
actionListener="#{customerController.prepareAddNewUser}"/>
<p:commandButton value="Cancel" action="/welcome.jsf?faces-
redirect=true"/>
<p:defaultCommand target="loginBtn"/>
</h:panelGrid>
</p:dialog>
</h:form>
</div>
```

The registration page

Customer registration is a common page that you can see in every web application. Some corporations use other sources to collect information such as SSO, account management, CRM portal, and so on. The following screenshot shows how this application designed the customer registration page:

Chapter 8

The preceding screenshot shows the customer registration page for the application. The first name, last name, and e-mail address fields use the common PrimeFaces input text field. The password field uses PrimeFaces's `inputSecret` component. This hides the characters from the users. The phone field uses PrimeFaces's `inputMask` component. This component has a special usage when you need to get information from the user, that is, you can specify the format in which you want the information from the user. In this registration page, the phone number is formatted as (000) 123-1234. PrimeFaces supports more different formatting options for the input components, namely the SSN number, product code, zip code, and also the ability to specify user-defined format using `regex`. You can see more patterns at http://www.primefaces.org/showcase/ui/input/inputMask.xhtml.

Code walk-through

In this section, you will learn how to code the user registration page:

```
<h:form styleClass="form-inline" prependId="false" id="thisform">
<p:fieldset rendered="#{not customerController.loggedIn}"
style="margin: 0 auto; text-align: center;
text-align: -webkit-center;">
<p:panelGrid columns="2">
<p:outputLabel for="txtFname" value="FirstName"/>
<p:inputText id="txtFname"
value="#{customerController.newCustomer.firstName}"/>

<p:outputLabel for="txtLname" value="LastName"/>
<p:inputText id="txtLname"
value="#{customerController.newCustomer.lastName}"/>

<p:outputLabel for="txtemail" value="Email"/>
<p:inputText id="txtemail"
value="#{customerController.newCustomer.email}"/>

<p:outputLabel for="txtpasswd" value="Password"/>
<h:inputSecret id="txtpasswd"
value="#{customerController.newCustomer.password}"/>

<p:outputLabel for="txtPhoneNumber" value="Phone Number"/>
<p:inputMask id="txtPhoneNumber"
value="#{customerController.newCustomer.phoneNumber}"
mask="(999) 999-9999"/>

</p:panelGrid>
<p:commandButton value="Submit" ajax="false" update="thisform"
action="#{customerController.saveCustomerInfo}"/>
</p:fieldset>
</h:form>
```

The user dashboard page

Dashboards often provide at-a-glance views of the **key performance indicators** (**KPIs**) relevant to a particular objective or a business process. As mentioned, this page serves as the main page for user activities in this application. The two different types of users, admin and customer, can perform different operations that they are allowed by the system. You will be using PrimeFaces's dashboard component, which helps you to show the print jobs in the widget windows. It is a single dashboard that will have all their active jobs as **dashlets**, and the users can perform their desired tasks.

The dashboard component and its implementation

The dashboard component in PrimeFaces provides a portal kind of layout with drag-and-drop based reorder capabilities. These kinds of applications are called dashboard applications. Normally, the dashboard will have more than one dashlet. In this application, each print job will be displayed as a dashlet.

The dashboard component will always bind to a backing bean by a dashboard model, which is provided by the PrimeFaces API. The DashboardModel class has a mandatory field called the widget ID; this is set and assigned to the panel component's ID. The same widget ID is assigned to the panel component, and the panels will displayed as dashlets.

Code walk-through

In this section, you will learn the implementation of the dashboard component, and get a detailed explanation of how to create the dashlet model in the backing bean as well as how to code it in the GUI. You will also get a tip on generating the dashboard widget dynamically:

```
public void populatePrintJobList(){
System.out.println("Populating List ");
if(customer.getEmail().equals("admin@admin.com")){
jobList = ds.getJobsBySubmittedStatus();
}else{
jobList = ds.getJobsByCustomerId(customer);
      }
model = new DefaultDashboardModel();

if(jobList != null && !jobList.isEmpty()){

for(inti=0;i<jobList.size();i++) {
DashboardColumn column = new DefaultDashboardColumn();
for(int j=0;j<4;j++) {
if(i<jobList.size()) {
```

```
                column.addWidget(jobList.get(i).getJobRefId());
                i++;
                            }
                        }
        model.addColumn(column);
                }
            }

        }
```

The dashboard model is used to define the number of columns and to populate the widgets to be placed in each column using the `addWidget` method. You can get the preceding code from the `DashboardController.java` file. This code snippet is responsible for populating all the available print jobs as dashlets. Here, the first thing you need to do is to specify the number of columns and then add an equal number of dashlets to each column.

The first iteration is to just loop through all the available print jobs, and the second iteration is to iterate the total number of columns. In each iteration, you will have to add the job as a widget to the column. Finally, the column is then added to the dashboard model.

Another thing that you can note in the preceding code is how we populate the print jobs based on the user type. If the current user is an administrator, then it will populate all the available jobs in the descending order of dates, and if the current user is a customer, then it will populate only the jobs for the current user.

The following code is used in the GUI to render the dashboard dynamically:

```
<p:dashboard id="board" model="#{dashboardController.model}" >
<p:ajax event="reorder" listener="#{dashboardController.
handleReorder}"/>

<c:forEach items="#{dashboardController.jobList}" var="job">
<p:panel id="#{job.jobRefId}" header="#{job.jobName}" style="width:
250px; height: 150px;">
<h:outputText value="#{job.createDate}" />
</p:panel>
</c:forEach>
</p:dashboard>
```

You can see the preceding code snippet in the `dashboard.xhtml` file. The `dashboard` tag will have the model attribute, which is bound to the backing bean's `dashboardModel` attribute. The model can be generated using the preceding backing bean snippet.

Creating an Online Printing Station Application

In this sample, you will be using the `forEach` tag instead of the `repeat` tag because the `panel` component is not allowed inside the `repeat` tag. When you attempt to use the `panel` component inside the `repeat` tag, you will get the following error screen. The reason for error is not relevant to what is shown in the error message:

```
An Error Occurred:

Empty id attribute is not allowed

- Stack Trace

java.lang.IllegalArgumentException: Empty id attribute is not allowed
    at javax.faces.component.UIComponentBase.validateId(UIComponentBase.java:580)
    at javax.faces.component.UIComponentBase.setId(UIComponentBase.java:412)
    at com.sun.faces.facelets.tag.jsf.ComponentTagHandlerDelegateImpl.assignUniqueId(ComponentTagHandlerDelegateImpl.java:434)
    at com.sun.faces.facelets.tag.jsf.ComponentTagHandlerDelegateImpl.apply(ComponentTagHandlerDelegateImpl.java:180)
    at javax.faces.view.facelets.DelegatingMetaTagHandler.apply(DelegatingMetaTagHandler.java:120)
    at javax.faces.view.facelets.DelegatingMetaTagHandler.applyNextHandler(DelegatingMetaTagHandler.java:137)
    at com.sun.faces.facelets.tag.jsf.ComponentTagHandlerDelegateImpl.apply(ComponentTagHandlerDelegateImpl.java:203)
    at javax.faces.view.facelets.DelegatingMetaTagHandler.apply(DelegatingMetaTagHandler.java:120)
    at javax.faces.view.facelets.CompositeFaceletHandler.apply(CompositeFaceletHandler.java:95)
```

The state of the dashboard is always stateful. Whenever a widget is reordered, the dashboard model will be updated automatically by capturing the current position and persisting the user changes, so, you can easily create a stateful dashboard with the use of this `dashboard` component. *reorder* is the one and only Ajax behavior that is supported by the `dashboard` component. This event is fired when the dashboard panels are reordered. The listener method will be invoked when the user rearranges the dashlet. This method will have the `org.primefaces.event` parameter. `DashboardReorderEvent` holds information about the model that is rearranged.

If a widget is reordered in the same column, `senderColumnIndex` will be always null. This field is populated only when a widget is transferred from one column to another. Also, when the listener is invoked, the dashboard model will automatically update the position of the column.

Chapter 8

In general, the dashlets presented in the dashboard can be closable, togglable, and can have an options menu as well. The dashboard doesn't implement these by itself, as these features are already provided by the `panel` component. By enabling the togglable and closable properties, we can use this option. Ultimately, the dashlets get toggled inside the dashboard. If you'd like to disable the reordering feature, you can set the disabled option to true.

Placing the print job order

The main purpose of this application is to provide a platform to upload the user files and to order prints at the chosen location. The logged-in customers will choose the nearest location from the location map, enter the information, and submit the order. Finally, they can upload their files and submit them for printing. Once the printing is done, the customer can drive to the location and collect the prints.

The following screenshot shows you how the order is implemented, with the file upload page:

An authenticated customer can select the desired location by clicking on the marker from the location map and can place their order by clicking on the **Order Now** button that appears in the pop-up box.

When the customer clicks on the **Order Now** button, the order page prompts for the print order details (which has many options to identify the print order), special instructions if any, number of prints, page range, and so on. The following screenshot is used to collect information about the customer's print details:

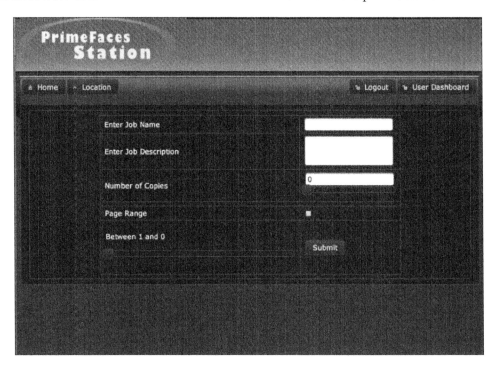

The **Enter Job Name** field is used for customer identification. The customer can easily remember the name that they have provided. The description can be anything that may be an instruction. In the **Number of Copies** field, you will be using the number slider. You can either enter the number, or you can slide the slider and increase the value. The slider can be used in different ways.

The slider component

The slider component is used in many ways. You can get more information on slider components at http://www.primefaces.org/showcase-labs/ui/slider.jsf. In the preceding screenshot, the slider component has been used in two different places.

Code walk-through

You can get the following code from the `joborder.xhtml` file:

```
<p:panel id="jobPanel">
<p:fieldset style="margin: 0 auto; text-align: center;
text-align: -webkit-center;">
<p:panelGrid columns="2">
<p:outputLabel value="Enter Job Name"/>
<p:inputTextvalue="#{fileUploadController.jobs.jobName}"/>
<p:outputLabel value="Enter Job Description"/>
<p:inputTextarea
value="#{fileUploadController.jobs.jobDescription}"/>
<p:outputLabel value="Number of Copies"/>
<h:panelGrid columns="1" style="margin-bottom:10px">
<p:inputText id="txt1" value="#{fileUploadController.jobs.
noOfPrints}"/>
<p:slider for="txt1"/>
</h:panelGrid>
<h:inputHidden id="txtstart" value="#{fileUploadController.jobs.
pageStart}"/>
<h:inputHidden id="txtend" value="#{fileUploadController.jobs.
pageEnd}"/>
<p:outputLabel value="Page Range"/>
<h:selectBooleanCheckbox
value="#{fileUploadController.jobs.pageRange}"/>
<h:panelGrid columns="1" style="margin-bottom:10px">
<h:outputText id="displayRange"value="Between #{fileUploadController.
jobs.pageStart} and #{fileUploadController.jobs.pageEnd}"/>
<p:slider for="txtstart,txtend" display="displayRange"
style="width:400px" range="true"
displayTemplate="Between {min} and {max}"/>
</h:panelGrid>
<p:commandButton action="#{fileUploadController.savePrintJobs}"
update="jobPanel" value="Submit"/>
</p:panelGrid>
</p:fieldset>
</p:panel>
```

The preceding code snippet is used to render various input components. The `slider` component is one of the advanced components used in this page, which provides a slider that is used to get input from the user without using the keyboard as the ultimate aim of PrimeFaces is to reduce the use of the keyboard. After filling the appropriate information, click on the **Submit** button, which saves the information to the database and proceeds to the `fileUpload` component page.

The fileUpload component

PrimeFaces provides the best file upload component in the web industry. Personally, I've never seen such a component elsewhere. The fileUpload component goes beyond the browser input type="file" functionality and features an HTML5-powered rich solution with graceful degradation for legacy browsers. This has a lot of advantages; usability is the main advantage. You can use the same component for many functionalities as follows:

- Basic usage by uploading one file at a time
- Can be enabled to upload more than one file from the user
- Can also enable the drag-and-drop support
- Can limit the user to the total upload size
- Can restrict the user to upload specific file formats

The following screenshot is used to get the files from the user using PrimeFaces's fileUpload component. The main advantage of this component is that the user can upload more than one file at the time.

Implementation

The fileUpload component needs some special attention with regards to the configuration since the upload component needs some third-party API such as the Apache common file upload utility and its associated settings.

The file upload engine on the server side can either be servlet 3.0 or a common file upload. PrimeFaces selects the most appropriate uploader engine by detection, and it is possible to force one or the other using an optional configuration context parameter in the web.xml file as follows:

```
<context-param>
<param-name>primefaces.UPLOADER</param-name>
<param-value>auto|native|commons</param-value>
</context-param>
```

You will have to configure three options, namely auto, native, and commons:

- auto: This is the default mode, and PrimeFaces tries to detect the best method by checking the runtime environment. If the JSF runtime is at least 2.2, the native uploader is selected; otherwise, commons is selected.
- native: The native mode uses servlet 3.x part API to upload the files, and if the JSF runtime is less than 2.2, then an exception is thrown.

- commons: This option chooses the commons file upload regardless of the environment. The advantage of this option is that it works even in a servlet 2.5 environment.

If you have decided to choose the commons file upload, you need the following filter configuration in your web deployment descriptor:

```
<filter>
<filter-name>PrimeFacesFileUpload Filter</filter-name>
<filter-class>
org.primefaces.webapp.filter.FileUploadFilter
</filter-class>
</filter>
<filter-mapping>
<filter-name>PrimeFacesFileUpload Filter</filter-name>
<servlet-name>Faces Servlet</servlet-name>
</filter-mapping>
```

Note that servlet-name should match the configured name of the JSF servlet, which is Faces Servlet in this case. Alternatively, you can configure based on the URL pattern as well.

The file upload component works in two modes, the simple mode and the advanced mode. In the simple mode, the component is bound to a file object in the backing bean. This works like a legacy system. The following is the code snippet used for the simple mode:

```
<h:form enctype="multipart/form-data">
  <p:fileUpload value="#{fileBean.file}" mode="simple" />
  <p:commandButton value="Submit" ajax="false"/>
</h:form>
```

In the backing bean, you need to add one property using org.primefaces.model.UploadedFile. Now you can perform the operation to save the file in the filesystem on a button submit itself.

The next type is the advanced mode in which you need to specify a handler method in the fileUploadListener attribute. The fileUploadListener is the way to access the uploaded files in this mode. When a file is uploaded, the defined fileUploadListener is processed with FileUploadEvent as the parameter. Now, let's see how we are performing this in this printing station application:

```
<h:form id="centerForm" enctype="multipart/form-data">
<h:inputHidden value="#{locationController.location}"/>
<p:fileUploadfileUploadListener="#{fileUploadController.
handleFileUpload}"
```

```
      mode="advanced" dragDropSupport="true"
   sizeLimit="100000"
   allowTypes="/(\.|\/)(gif|jpe?g|png)$/" />
</h:form>
```

When you look at the preceding code, you can see that the form tag is specified with multipart form-data, since we are handling file operations through the same form tag. Next, look at the fileUploadListener method that is bound to the handleFileUpload method in the controller. Let's see how the controller handles the file upload:

```
public void handleFileUpload(FileUploadEvent event) {
       //get uploaded file from the event
UploadedFileuploadedFile = (UploadedFile) event.getFile();
       //create an InputStream from the uploaded file
InputStreaminputStr = null;
try {
inputStr = uploadedFile.getInputstream();
       } catch (IOException e) {
          //log error
       }
ServletContextservletContext = (ServletContext)
FacesContext.getCurrentInstance().getExternalContext().getContext();
       String newFileName = servletContext.getRealPath("")
       + File.separator + "photocam" + File.separator
       + uploadedFile.getFileName();
       //create destination File
       File destFile = new File(newFileName);
       //use org.apache.commons.io.FileUtils to copy the File
try {
FileUtils.copyInputStreamToFile(inputStr, destFile);
       } catch (IOException e) {
          //log error
       }
    }
```

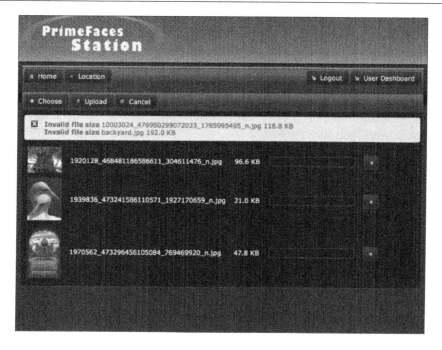

The file download component

PrimeFaces provides another useful component used to download a file. This component makes the file download easier. All we need to do is just bind a `fileUpload` object to the component as shown in the following code snippet:

```
<p:commandButton id="downloadLink" icon="ui-icon-arrowthichk-s"
value="Download" ajax="false"
onclick="PrimeFaces.monitorDownload(start, stop)">
<p:fileDownload value="#{fileUploadController.getFileforJobId
(fileUploadController.jobId)}" />
</p:commandButton>
```

In the preceding implementation, the `value` attribute is assigned a method with the `jobId` parameter.

Working with the sample code

If you wish to work on the sample code, all you need to do is just clone it from the GitHub repository at https://github.com/sudheerj/PrimeFaces-blueprints, where you can use your preferred IDE. From there, change the MySQL user ID and password and then you can start playing with the code. You can run the code for this chapter by using the mvn jetty:run command in the chapter08 folder in the Maven console, and then navigate to http://localhost:8080/web. You can use admin@admin.com/admin or ram@ram.com/ram as the customer credentials, or you can create your own profile and use the user ID and password as the credentials.

Summary

In this chapter, you learned how to develop your own online printing station application. This application may become a big hit in the coming days. You learned how to implement file upload and file download; you also learned about the dashboard components from PrimeFaces.

In the next chapter, you will learn how to build another real-time business web application. You will also learn about the simplified version of social networking. The highlight of the next chapter is to create a simple chat application and a blog with the help of the PrimeFaces Push technology.

Creating an Online Chat Application

In the previous chapter, you learned about an online printing station application—you must now be familiar with how to handle files with the help of PrimeFaces' advanced components. You also found many ways to limit the user from introducing errors using PrimeFaces' input components.

In this chapter, you will learn about another real-world example; social networking. You will also learn how to build a chat application easily. We all know how much social networking contributes to the real world nowadays. This chapter gives the basic functionalities of social networking and a basic multichannel chat application. This application is designed and developed using PrimeFaces 5.0 and the PrimePush technology. On top of that, you will learn about some of the advanced components from PrimeFaces, namely the inline edit component, sticky, focus, `defaultCommand`, `dataScroller`, `editor`, and `fieldset`. Here, some of the components are special-purpose components.

The application use case

The aim of this chapter is to design and develop an application that utilizes the PrimePush technology and some of the advanced components from PrimeFaces. In this application, you will have a user registration page as the landing page, and the user can provide their basic information to register their user profile. This page utilizes various input components and some special-purpose components. Once registered, the user can use the registered e-mail ID and password to log in to their blog page, which contains all the user's posts and comments. The page will load the content in an infinite fashion using the `dataScroll` component. The logged-in user can post their comments on any post. The logged-in user can also chat with other users who are available in the chat room. The user can also select a single user and send them a private message.

Requirement analysis

This online chat application is similar to the `www.tumblr.com` application. The landing page needs to have a user registration; once registered, the users can use their credentials to log in to the system and view all the comments. They can also post their comments and create their own posts. The content posts need to be seen in an infinite scroll fashion. You need to be able to navigate to all the pages.

The users are allowed to get into a chat room and chat with all the available users, and they can also send private messages to a specific user.

A flow diagram

The following flow diagram depicts the application flow. Any user can register to the application using the registration page. Only registered users are allowed to post an article or post comments. They are also allowed to chat in the chat room.

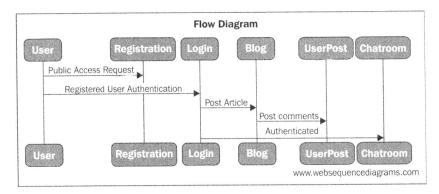

The architecture

This application uses the same architecture that you have seen in the previous chapters. On top of that, you will be using many advanced PrimeFaces components. Here, you will be using **MySQL** as the database. **Project Lombok** is used to reduce the effort to create boilerplate code. The PrimeFaces Push technology uses the Atmosphere framework to satisfy the chat application's requirements.

Implementing the requirements

In this section, you will learn more about how to implement the various components in order to satisfy the user requirements. Each component is carefully crafted in such a way that it meets the specific needs. Beginning with the ER diagram, you will see the detailed implementation phase one by one.

The ER diagram

By understanding the database design, you will be able to design the application faster. Once the DB design is done, you are pretty much done with the full business requirements.

The following diagram depicts the database design that includes the tables and their fields used in this project:

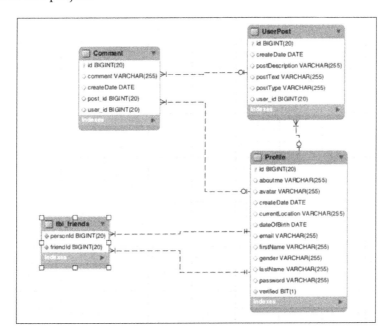

Creating an Online Chat Application

In this application, you will be using four different tables, namely `Profile`, `UserPost`, `Comment`, and `tbl_friends`. The `Profile` table is used to store all the user profiles. The `tbl_friends` table is used to store the relationship between two profiles, which tells us exactly who is whose friend. The `UserPost` table stores all the posts with relation to the user profile. The `Comment` table holds all the user comments, and it also holds the user profile ID and the post ID in order to maintain the relationship between all three tables.

Implementing, deploying, and running the application

Similar to other applications, this application is also developed with an embedded jetty and tomcat Maven plugin. You can run the application using the `mvn jetty:run` command or the `mvn tomcat:run` command. Once you execute the Maven command, the application will start running without any errors in the Maven console, and then you can navigate to the start-up page using `http://localhost:8080/web`. You will see the following screen, which provides you with an option to log in with the user credentials or you can register your own user profile. In this application, you will use the e-mail ID as the username.

In the preceding screenshot, you will be using various PrimeFaces input components such as the `textbox`, `calendar`, `selectOneButton`, and `editor` components. Each input component has a property called placeholder that tells the user exactly what the value should be. This is the newest way to put labels near input components. You can see the detailed description of each component used in this application in the following sections.

The editor component

The `editor` component is a very useful component, which is an input component with rich text-editing capabilities. This component has many advantages over the text area component. You can edit the content directly as you see in the screen; this concept is called WYSIWYG (what you see what you get). You can style the text content, embed images in text, and so on. This component has other advantages as well; we can limit the user input by customizing the toolbar that appears in the `editor` component. The following is the screenshot of the `editor` component that you used in this application:

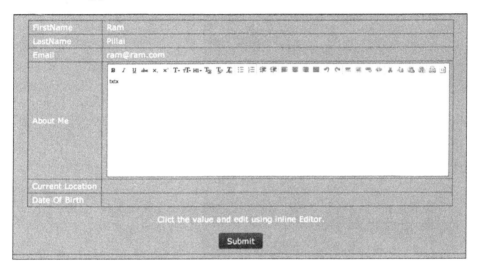

The `editor` component has been used in two pages of our application.

The selectOneButton component

The `selectOneButton` component is used as an input component. This component is used in the same way as a combobox. The only difference is that instead of a list of dropdowns, this component provides a list of buttons. The user can select only one button at a time. The **Gender** field, in the following screenshot, uses the `selectOneButton` component.

The password component

PrimeFaces provides an embedded password strength meter along with the `password` component, which evaluates the user password input and informs the user about the strategy of the password so that the user can change the password accordingly to increase the strength of the password. The following screenshot gives you a demonstration of the password strength meter. You can experience the functionality in the home page of the application.

The following code snippet will enable the password strength in PrimeFaces's `password` component:

```
<p:password value="#{userController.user.password}" size="49"
placeholder="Password " feedback="true" autocomplete="false"/>
```

When you enable the `feedback` attribute in the `password` component, PrimeFaces will automatically add the password strength meter to the `password` component.

Code walk-through – the landing page before login

On the landing page, you will have two sections of code; one section will only be displayed when the user is logged in, and the other section will be displayed if no user is logged in. In order to make the code readable, you can use the UI:Include tag and separate the code for the logged-in user on a different page.

You can find the following code in the `loggedin.xhtml` file. This code is included in the `welcome.xhtml` file when the user is not logged in.

The following is the code for the `welcome.xhtml` page:

```
<p:panel styleClass="base-color-panel no-margin-no-padding"
rendered="#{not userController.loggedIn}">
<h:inputHidden value="#{chatUsers.users}"/>
<ui:include src="loggedin.xhtml"/>
</p:panel>
```

Here is the code for the `loggedin.xhtml` page:

```
<h:form id="forFocus" prependId="false">
<p:focus />
<p:fieldset widgetVar="fieldsets" styleClass="center_align no-margin-
no-padding-no-border">
<p:panelGrid columns="1" style="float: right;" styleClass="no-margin-
no-padding-no-border">
<p:outputLabel value="Sign Up" style="font-size: 48px;"/>
<p:outputLabel value="It is always FREEEEE!..." style="text-align:
right; margin-left: 130px;"/>
<h:panelGrid columns="2" columnClasses="no-margin-no-padding-no-
border" cellpadding="0">
<p:inputText id="txtFname" value="#{userController.user.firstName}"
size="23"
    placeholder="First Name"/>
<p:inputText id="txtLname" value="#{userController.user.lastName}"
size="22"
    placeholder="Last Name"/>
</h:panelGrid>
<p:inputText value="#{userController.user.email}" size="49"
    placeholder="Email Id" autocomplete="false"/>
<p:inputText value="#{userController.re_email}"  size="49"
    placeholder="Re-Enter Email Id" autocomplete="false"/>
<p:password value="#{userController.user.password}" size="49"
    placeholder="Password " feedback="true" autocomplete="false"/>

<p:calendar value="#{userController.user.dateOfBirth}" size="49"
placeholder="Select your Date Of Birth"/>
<h:panelGrid columns="3">
<p:outputLabel value="Gender" style="padding-right: 90px;"/>
<p:separator/>
<p:selectOneButton value="#{userController.user.gender}" style="float:
right;">
<f:selectItem itemLabel="Male" itemValue="male" />
<f:selectItem itemLabel="Female" itemValue="female" />
</p:selectOneButton>
</h:panelGrid>
<p:outputLabel value="Tell about you"/>
<p:editor id="editor" value="#{userController.user.aboutme}"
width="500" height="150"/>
```

```
<p:scrollPanel mode="native" style="height:100px; width: 500px;">
<p style="padding-left: 10px;"><i>By clicking Sign Up, you agree to
our Terms and that you have read our Data Use Policy, including our
Cookie Use.
</i></p>
</p:scrollPanel>
<p:commandButton id="signup" value="Sign Up" style="height: 70px;
font-size: 32px;"/>
<p:commandButton resetValues="true" value="Reset" update="forFocus"
    action="#{userController.prepareAddNewUser}"/>
<p:defaultCommand target="signup"/></p:panelGrid>
</p:fieldset>
</h:form>
```

In this section, you will learn about some of the new special-purpose components—most of the components are already described in the previous chapters. There are many other utility components that are also used in this page. Some of the components don't show up on the screen, but they have their own meaning when used inside the pages. In the following sections, you will see some of the special-purpose tags.

The focus tag

The `focus` tag is one of the special-purpose tags; the main aim of the `focus` tag is to set focus on the page landing. This is similar to the old JavaScript way of setting the startup focus on the page load. By default, the focus will find the first enabled and visible input component on the page and apply focus. The input component can be any element such as input, text area, and select. On this application landing page, the e-mail ID field will be focused when this page initially opens up, as it is the first active input component. The input text with the `txtFname` ID will receive the focus when we set the `for` attribute, pointing to the `txtFname` field manually. Another useful feature of the `focus` component is when validations fail, the first invalid component will receive a focus. So on our page, if the `txtFName` field is valid but the `txtLName` field has no input, a validation error will be raised for `txtLName`. In this case, the focus will be on the `txtLName` field implicitly.

Note that for this feature to work on Ajax requests, you need to update the `p:focus` component as well.

The defaultCommand component

Similarly, another special-purpose tag is called the defaultCommand tag. This tag is used to inform the browser about which command button should be used to submit the form when the *Enter* key is pressed. This is a common problem in web apps, not just specific to JSF. Browsers tend to behave differently as there doesn't seem to be a standard, and even if a standard exists, IE probably will not care about it. There are some ugly workarounds, such as placing a hidden button and writing a JavaScript code for every form in your application. The defaultCommand component solves this problem by normalizing the command (for example, button or link) to submit the form tag and requires target option to reference to one of the clickable command, which may not be browsers default selection. Note that an input must have focus due to browser nature.

The landing page after login

Once the user has logged in to the portal, the landing page will be displayed with a list of the posts from various users. The user will have the option to post their comments and also to post their replies for some other user's post.

The dataScroller component

The dataScroller component displays a collection of data with on-demand loading using the scrolling feature; this component enables the page to use the scroll functionality infinitely in fewer lines of code. The following screenshot displays all the user posts using the dataScroller component:

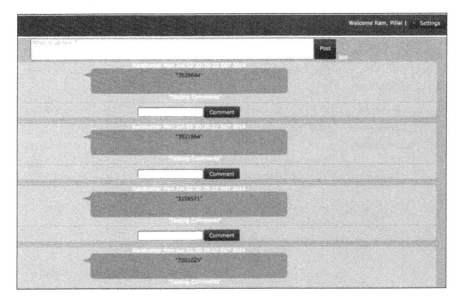

When the user submits their post, the information will immediately be populated in the `dataScroller` component.

Code walk-through

This code walkthrough will show you the implementation of the `dataScroller` component in the chat application:

```
<p:dataScroller value="#{userController.lazyModel}" var="post"
lazy="true" chunkSize="10" id="datascroll"
styleClass="no-border no-margin-no-padding-no-border">
<div class="panelpost">
"#{post.user.firstName} "#{post.createDate}"
<div class="bubble" style="color: #000;">"#{post.postText}"</div>
<ui:repeat value="#{userController.getAllCommentForPostId(post)}"
var="c">
<ul >
"#{c.comment}"
</ul>
<hr/>
</ui:repeat>
<p:inputText value="#{userController.userComment.comment}"/>
<p:commandButton value="Comment" update=":form:datascroll"
actionListener="#{userController.saveUserComment(post)}"/>
</div>
<hr/>
</p:dataScroller>
```

The dataScroller component and the LazyData loading

The `dataScroller` component needs to bind with a `LazyDataModel` class. In the following snippet, you can see how to populate the `LazyDataModel` class used for the `UserPost` collection:

```
public void lazyLoad() {
        lazyModel = new LazyDataModel<UserPost>() {
        @Override
        public List<UserPost> load(int first, int pageSize, String
           sortField, SortOrder sortOrder, Map<String, Object> filters)
             {
              String sortOrderValue = null;
              if (sortField == null) {
                  sortField = "prodname";
              }
```

```
            if (sortOrder.ASCENDING.equals("A")) {
                sortOrderValue = "ASC";
            } else if (sortOrder.DESCENDING.equals("D")) {
                sortOrderValue = "DSC";
            } else {
                sortOrderValue = "ASC";
            }
            myPosts = getAllMyPosts();
            //productsInfo = dao.getAllProducts(first, pageSize,
            //sortField, sortOrderValue, filters);
            // rowCount
            int dataSize = myPosts.size();
            this.setRowCount(dataSize);
            // paginate
            if (dataSize > pageSize) {
                try {
                    return myPosts.subList(first,first + pageSize);
                } catch (IndexOutOfBoundsException e) {
                return myPosts.subList(first,first
                + (dataSize % pageSize));
                }
            } else {
                return myPosts;
            }
        }
    };
}
```

You can find the preceding code snippet in the `welcome.xhtml` and `UserController.java` files. The `dataScroller` component is bound to the `LazyDataModel` class and this implementation enables lazy loading. Based on the required page size and current page number, you can populate records or you can also implement the same thing using a database query passing the current page number and fetch size. The filter object in the lazy data model class will hold all the parameters required for the pagination.

Supporting components

As in the other chapters, you will be using the more commonly used additional components such as the `panelGrid` and `growl` components in this chapter's example.

The `growl` component is one of the very frequently used components. This component is used as an information alert component. Using this component, you can inform the user about the status and updates. This will show an overlay at the top of the screen and inform the user in a very descriptive manner.

The User Profile page

In this application, we have a **User Profile** page. This page will allow the logged-in user to edit their information. In this page, you will see a variety of component called the inline edit component. This component looks nothing at first glance, but when the user clicks on the value, the inline editor component immediately allows the user to edit the appropriate information. The following screenshot shows you how the screen looks before the user clicks on the inline editor component:

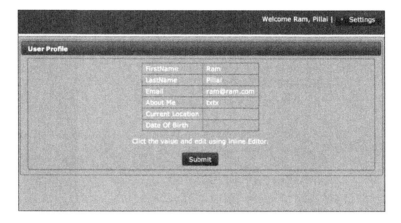

When you see this page, it looks simple—with no edit option enabled. When the user clicks on the value of any component, it immediately enables the edit option. The following screenshot shows the page after the edit option is enabled:

In the next session, you are going to learn about the chat module. This module is the highlight of this application. Before you get into the chat module, you will have to understand the Push technology.

The Push technology

The Push technology, or the server Push technology, can be described as a way of recent Internet-based communication. The communication requests are started and initiated by the publisher called the **central server**. This is contrasted with pull, where the same requests are received by a receiver or a **client system**. In our application, one user will initiate the chat and push the message to the server, and the server will update all the listeners. This concept is a commonly-used practice that is called **publish/subscribe**. The same concept already exists in the server-side technologies using Queue, Topic, and Messaging; that is, one publisher will publish the communication and the subscribers will listen to the incoming message and process the request. The same concept is now implemented as a client/server interaction medium using the Push technology.

There are various technologies that implement the same mechanisms to achieve the experience of a server push, namely:

- **Native Comet** (the web server has an API for Comet)
- **Native websockets** (the web server has an API for websockets)
- **Websockets**
- **Long-polling**
- **HTTP streaming**
- **JSONP**
- **Server-sent events**

Every method has its own disadvantages. Websockets is a one of the leading new frameworks and is gaining popularity in the web market. However, a lot of browsers do not natively support websocket yet. Atmosphere is one of those frameworks that provides a wide array of support options for the server and the client side of the server push mechanism. PrimeFaces 3.4 introduced this Push technology with the help of the **Atmosphere Framework**.

PrimeFaces Push (PFP) is a server push framework built on top of the **Atmosphere Framework**. Atmosphere Framework's creator, **AsyncIO**, is a partner company of PrimeTek and the developer of PFP. Atmosphere is highly scalable, supports several containers and browsers, utilizes various transports, such as websockets, long-polling, streaming, and JSONP. For more information, please visit `https://github.com/Atmosphere/atmosphere`. Based on Atmosphere, PrimeFaces provides easy push mechanisms to web applications. The uses of the push-enabled web applications include market data distribution (stock tickers), online chat/messaging systems (web chat), online auctions, online betting and gaming, sport results, monitoring consoles, and sensor network monitoring.

Implementing the chat module using PrimePush

PrimeFaces Push requires Atmosphere's runtime dependencies to add the dependency below the Maven dependency in your project's `pom.xml` file:

```xml
<dependency>
<groupId>org.atmosphere</groupId>
<artifactId>atmosphere-runtime</artifactId>
<version>2.1.3</version>
</dependency>
```

The PrimePush component needs to have its servlet channel registered. These channels play a major role in PrimeFaces Push. In order to register the servlet channels, you will have to add the following code snippet to your `web.xml` file. This is basically a servlet directing a special request to the Push servlet and enables the magic of server push:

```xml
<servlet>
  <servlet-name>Push Servlet</servlet-name>
  <servlet-class>org.primefaces.push.PushServlet</servlet-class>
  <async-supported>true</async-supported>
</servlet>
  <servlet-mapping>
    <servlet-name>Push Servlet</servlet-name>
<url-pattern>/primepush/*</url-pattern>
</servlet-mapping>
```

The following screenshot shows you how two different browsers interact with the use of the chat module:

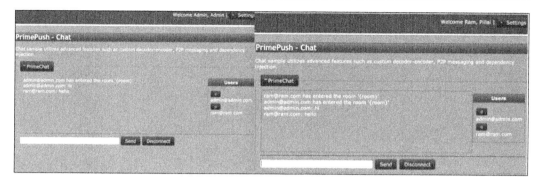

Code walk-through

In this section, you will see how to implement the concepts to develop a chat application using PrimePush.

The following code can be found in the `ChatResources.java` file. This is the main file that enables and controls the overall session of the chat application. First, you will have to specify the path as `@PushEndpoint("/{room}/{user}")`:

```
@PushEndpoint("/{room}/{user}")
@Singleton
public class ChatResource {

    private final Logger logger =
    LoggerFactory.getLogger(ChatResource.class);

    @PathParam("room")
    private String room;

    @PathParam("user")
    private String username;

    @Inject
    private ServletContext ctx;

    @OnOpen
    public void onOpen(RemoteEndpoint r, EventBus eventBus) {
        logger.info("OnOpen {}", r);
        eventBus.publish(room + "/*",
        new Message(String.format("%s has entered the room '%s'",
        username, room), true));
    }
```

```
    @OnClose
    public void onClose(RemoteEndpoint r, EventBus eventBus) {
        ChatUsers users= (ChatUsers) ctx.getAttribute("chatUsers");
        users.remove(username);

        eventBus.publish(room + "/*", new Message(String.format
            ("%s has left the room", username), true));
    }

    @OnMessage(decoders = {MessageDecoder.class},
    encoders = {MessageEncoder.class})
    public Message onMessage(Message message) {
        return message;
    }

}
```

@PushEndPoint is the the easiest way to create a PFP application by using the @PushEndPoint annotation. This annotation simplifies the process to build an application using PFP, avoiding the need to interact with Atmosphere's more sophisticated API. This annotation significantly reduces the amount of code required to build a powerful real-time application by transparently installing Atmosphere's components, such as heartbeat, idle connection detections, and disconnect state recovery. It also allows the use of an external dependency injection framework such as **CDI**, **Spring**, or **Guice**. This annotation provides one attribute called path to define the resource path, which is the path to the resource. The default is /; so, if you have mapped the Push servlet to /*, all the requests will be delivered to your annotated class. You can also customize the path. The path value will be used to map an incoming request's URL path to an annotated PushEndpoint class.

The @Singleton annotation is used to forcibly create a single, thread-safe instance of a PushEndpoint annotated class. For example, if your application has set the @PushEndpoint class's path attribute with a path, a new instance of the annotated class will be created by default. However, when it is annotated with @Singleton, a single class will be created. This annotation implements the singleton pattern.

Besides the preceding two annotations, there are some more annotations that support the chat application, namely onOpen, onMessage, and onClose; each of these annotations provides an option to perform a specific task on each event. The OnOpen() annotation will be invoked when the underlying connection is ready to be used.

Here, we perform the write operation:

```
@OnOpen
public void onOpen(RemoteEndpoint r, EventBus e);
```

The `RemoteEndpoint` attribute represents the physical connection and can be used to write some data back to the browser. The `EventBus` attribute can be used to fire messages to one or more `RemoteEndpoint` attribute using the regex expressions. `EventBus` publishes the message to all the channels. The `OnMessage()` annotation will be invoked when a message is ready to be delivered, for example, as a result of an `EventBus` publish operation or when a browser posts some bytes. The annotation's attribute encoders and decoders will interpret the message and secure the message before passing it to the transport layer. The encode and decode logic can be done as you wish by implementing the appropriate interface, `org.primefaces.push.Encoder` or `org.primefaces.push.Decoder`. The `@OnClose()` annotation will be invoked when the client disconnects, for example, when the connection is closed due to a network outage or when a proxy closes the connection.

The `PathParm` annotation is used to inject the parameters to the server-side implementation. The `@PathParam` annotation is used to automatically parse the path and assign path tokens to the class variables.

How does this work?

In the chat controller, when the `sendPrivate` and `sendGlobal` functions are called via a send button in the chat page, all the clients (the active browsers) receive asynchronous updates on the specified channel. This triggers the JavaScript method to update the messages table:

```
<p:socket onMessage="handleMessage" channel="/{room}"
autoConnect="false" widgetVar='subscriber'/>
```

The JSF page responds to a message on the channel/messages. It invokes the JavaScript function, `handleMessage`, when an asynchronous server push event is received:

```
<p:remoteCommand name="updateList" update="users" process="@this"/>
```

This makes a JavaScript function available, which calls the `chatController` function `loadMessages` after which it updates the chat transcripts. The JavaScript function, `handleMessage`, updates the chat transcript and in effect, the `chatController` function.

Similarly, you can also force the UI to update the contents from the server side by using the following snippet:

```
RequestContext requestContext = RequestContext.getCurrentInstance();
requestContext.execute("PF('subscriber').connect('/" + username + "')");
```

The private chat option

In this chat application, you will also have the private chat option enabled; this means that this chat application is a common chat room. If any user wishes to send a private message to a particular user, they can select them from the list and send the message privately. The following screenshot will pop up when you click on the user from the users list:

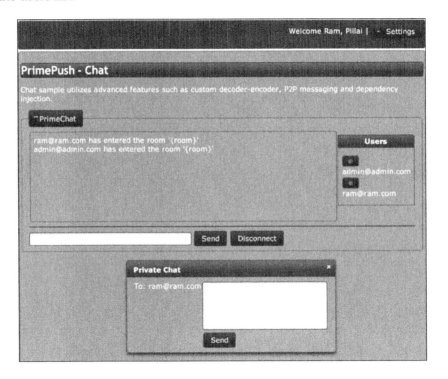

The following code snippet is used to send private and public messages:

```
eventBus.publish(CHANNEL + "*", username + ": " + globalMessage);
eventBus.publish(CHANNEL + privateUser, "[PM] " + username + ": " + privateMessage);
```

The first line of the code is issued to send the user to a public room where they are visible to all the users in the list. Likewise, in the second line, we also specify the private username as a parameter to the channel.

Here is a list of the important Java classes and their use in this application:

- `ChatController.java`: This class is used to track the chat session and to interconnect all the chat components.
- `ChatUsers.java`: This class is on the application scope. This class holds all the users when the user is logged in to the system. The users are registered in this class as a list of users.
- `ChatResource.java`: This class is the endpoint, which is responsible for the Atmosphere integration. You will be using the PrimePush API to integrate the Atmosphere Framework.
- `UserController.java`: This class acts as a controller, which is responsible for all the user transactions such as user registration, validation, and user login.
- `Message.java`: This class is a simple POJO used as a transfer object to hold the user messages.
- `MessageDecoder.java`: This class is used to implement the custom decoder logic.
- `MessageEncoder.java`: This class is used to implement the custom encoder logic.

Working with the sample code

If you wish to work on the sample code, all you need to do is just clone it from the GitHub repository at `https://github.com/sudheerj/PrimeFaces-blueprints` where you can use your preferred IDE. From there, change the MySQL user ID and password and then you can start playing with the code. You can run this chapter's code by using the `mvn jetty:run` command in the `chapter09` folder in the Maven console, and then navigate your browser to `http://localhost:8080/web`. You can use admin@admin.com/admin or ram@ram.com/ram as the user credentials, or you can create your own profile and use the user ID and password as the credentials.

Summary

In this chapter, you learned how to develop your own chat application. You also learned how to implement PrimePush and some special-purpose components from PrimeFaces 5.0. You have seen how easy it is to get an application up and running using PrimeFaces. Make sure to check out the PrimeFaces website for the latest and greatest components and classes that we explored throughout this walkthrough.

In the next chapter, you will learn how to develop another real-time business application. The application demonstrates how to showcase healthcare products using various advanced PrimeFaces components.

10
Creating a Healthcare Products Application

In this chapter, we will learn how to create a simple healthcare products application. To use menu navigations and display the huge amount of data, you can find `megaMenu`, `dataScroller`, `tree`, and `treeTable` components used in this application. Apart from these regular UI components, there are many utility components that are used to make the daily development tasks easier. The PrimeFaces library provides you with all the fancy UI widgets with customized skinning and theming styles that display an awesome theme design on the screen. PrimeFaces uses a powerful ThemeRoller CSS framework and popular theme converters that enable us to create our own theme designs within minutes. An important goal of this project is to demonstrate the data hierarchy and data display components that can be used to display the huge amount of related information and common utility components in regular development works as well as apply the ThemeRoller CSS framework when creating custom PrimeFaces themes. To explain all these components, we will develop an application in which the user logs in to this application to view and buy the required healthcare products. The specific topics that will be covered are as follows:

- A brief introduction to the healthcare products application, use cases, and the architectural design
- The project creation and application screens' implementation using data hierarchy, data display, and utility components
- Applying themes in your PrimeFaces applications
- Working with the project code of the healthcare products application

Introducing our healthcare products application

The healthcare products application (which we will call the HealthKart application) is used to list out all the various healthcare products for the diagnosis, treatment, and prevention of diseases and injuries, and to improve body fitness with attractive offers on various brands. The application needs to be designed so that users can view the list of all the products available and the list of products under a particular product category that is selected. Each product should be displayed with the user ratings, discount, and price value.

We will make use of the data hierarchy and data-display components to hold the huge data sets, and to display specific selected products and tree-formatted data in HealthKart and admin screens. The library provides MegaMenu, DataScroller, Tree, and TreeTable components to achieve these functionalities. Apart from these regular components, you can also find a few utility components in screens' development. Once all the screens are developed, we can create our own themes from scratch with the help of the powerful ThemeRoller CSS framework and Theme Converters.

Before you implement the application screens using the PrimeFaces library, we will take a brief look at the project's requirements and architectural designs in the following sections.

Application use cases

The purpose of this application is to list out all the healthcare products and provide the product feedback, discount, and price details. At first, the shopping cart user needs to log in to the application to view all the listed products. Based on the user demand, more products will be fetched from the database by scrolling down each time. The user also has the ability to view the products under a particular product category by selecting a particular menu item under the MegaMenu component.

The admin user also has access to view the products' hierarchy and sales details over a particular period.

The UML use case diagram

The following use case diagram is used to represent the various functionalities that occur in the entire application process. The functionalities, such as the login and reset functionalities, which display all the products' data and specific product category data, products hierarchy, and product sales use cases, will be adopted in this application.

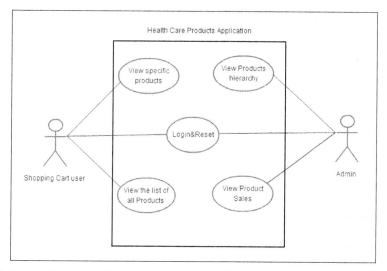

A diagram illustrating the responsibilities of the shopping cart user and admin in the healthcare products application

The two actors who perform all the functionalities in this application are **Shopping cart user** and **Admin**.

The architectural design

The architecture of this application can be presented as follows:

- The presentation layer will be composed of standard JSF and PrimeFaces components
- **XHTML** or **Facelets** are used as the view technology in order to render the UI components
- You will use the PrimeFaces built-in **home** theme to skin or style the web pages
- The managed beans will be used to hold the session tracking and event handling as well as execute the business logic
- The data access layer is used to interact with the MySQL database using the **hibernate** framework
- The Apache Maven build tool will be used to build the project and for dependency management

The following architecture diagram represents the three major layers of the web application and their interaction with the **MySQL** database. The flow from the presentation layer to the other layer components and database is represented by straight lines:

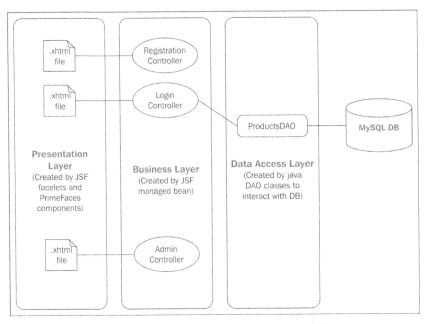

A diagram illustrating the connection between the three different layers

Here, the hibernate JPA implementation is used between the DAO layer and MySQL database.

Creating a project and implementing the application screens

This section will show you how to implement the healthcare products application using the PrimeFaces data display, data hierarchy, and utility components, and finally it will show you how to apply your own themes in PrimeFaces projects. The first step is to start the project by creating the template structure using standard JSF Facelets. Then, you need to create the HealthKart and admin screens using the MegaMenu, DataScroller, Tree, TreeTable, and utility components.

Laying out our application structure

The structure of the application should consist of the presentation, business, and data access layers in order to create a proper web application. After properly implementing these sections, the project structure in the navigator view should look as follows:

After that, you should make sure you have configured them all using the step-by-step configurations detailed in *Chapter 1, Creating a "Hello World" Application*.

Designing the application template

You are going to use a single main template formed by the combination of three smaller template files. The masterTemplate.xhtml file uses the Facelets' ui:insert and ui:include tags for the header, content, and footer sections, as shown in the following code snippet:

```
<div id="header">
    <ui:insert name="header">
      <ui:include src="/templates/common/header.xhtml" />
    </ui:insert>
</div>
<div id="content">
    <ui:insert name="content">
      <ui:include src="/templates/common/content.xhtml" />
    </ui:insert>
</div>
```

```
<div id="footer">
    <ui:insert name="footer">
      <ui:include src="/templates/common/footer.xhtml" />
    </ui:insert>
</div>
```

The `header` section deals with the website logo, advertisements, and logout functionalities. On the other hand, the `footer` section deals with the application information through the command links. Finally, the `content` section or template is provided for default content.

Database configurations

A JPA provider or implementation called **hibernate** is used to map between Java entities and RDBMS. The hibernate application can be created in the following two ways:

- XML configurations
- Annotations

We will use the configuration mechanism of annotations in this application. In this approach, we have to configure the hibernate MySQL dialect details in the hibernate configuration file, whereas the mapping information is applied on the entity itself using annotations. Please take a look at the hibernate configuration and entity mapping annotations code in the Blueprints GitHub repository for reference (https://github.com/sudheerj/primefaces-blueprints).

Implementing application screens using data hierarchy, data display, and utility components

Before we see the data hierarchy and data display components, we need to implement the login screen.

Implementing the login screen

The login screen is implemented by creating the `username` and `password` fields that accept the credentials of either the healthcare user or admin role. The page navigates to either the HealthKart or admin screens based on the user role. If the user is not authenticated, then the login screen throws an invalid login message. Apart from the login button, you can also find the reset button that clears the input fields in the login screen.

The login screen is created with the username, password, and reset input form components as follows:

```
<h:panelGrid columns="3" cellpadding="5">
  <h:outputLabel for="username" value="Username:" />
  <p:inputText value="#{loginController.username}" id="username"
      required="true" requiredMessage="Username cannot be empty"
      label="username">
  </p:inputText>
  <p:watermark for="username" value="Enter username" />

  <h:outputLabel for="password" value="Password:" />
  <p:password value="#{loginController.password}" id="password"
      required="true" requiredMessage="Password cannot be empty" />
  <p:watermark for="password" value="Enter password" />

  <h:outputText />
  <p:outputPanel style="margin-left:1%">
      <p:commandButton id="loginButton" value="Login" update="login"
          action="#{loginController.validateUser}" ajax="false" />
      <p:commandButton id="resetButton" value="Reset" update="panel"
          process="@this">
          <p:resetInput target="panel" />
      </p:commandButton>
  </p:outputPanel>
</h:panelGrid>
```

In the preceding code, the `resetInput` component uses the panel as the target element. It will clear all the input fields under this panel. After using the preceding code snippets, we also used the `defaultCommand` component that provides the default action to the login button as follows:

```
<p:defaultCommand target="loginButton" />
```

The managed bean of the login screen holds the `username` and `password` fields. It will also contain the method to authenticate either the shopping cart user or administrator based on the user role, and then navigates to the respective pages. If the user is not a valid user, then it throws an invalid login message. The following code snippet is used to validate either HealthKart customers or administrators:

```
public String validateUser() throws SQLException {
  FacesMessage msg = null;
  boolean isValidUser = false;
  if (username.equalsIgnoreCase("healthcare")
```

```
      && password.equalsIgnoreCase("healthcare")) {
        return "/views/HealthKart?faces-redirect=true";
    }
    else if (username.equalsIgnoreCase("admin")
      && password.equalsIgnoreCase("admin")) {
        return "/views/admin?faces-redirect=true";
    }
    else {
      msg = new FacesMessage(FacesMessage.SEVERITY_WARN, "Login Error",
            "Invalid credentials");
      FacesContext.getCurrentInstance().addMessage(null, msg);
      return null;
    }
  }
}
```

Before logging on to this application, the login screen will be as follows:

Incorrect or unauthorized credentials results in the display of an invalid login message at the top login header, which stops the navigation to other screens.

Login credentials

The application has been provided with two types of login credentials based on the user role. The credentials for different user roles are as follows:

- Healthcare user: healthcare/healthcare
- Administrator: admin/admin

Implementing the HealthKart screen

A huge amount of data in the HealthKart screen is displayed with the help of data components such as the `dataScroller` component. The `dataScroller` component loads a huge amount of data on demand using the backing lazy data model. We can also filter the displayed data based on the product category selection from the `MegaMenu` component.

The `dataScroller` component created with the lazy-loading feature to display the product details is as follows:

```
<p:dataScroller id="productsList"
  value="#{HealthKartController.lazyModel}" var="product"
  chunkSize="4" lazy="true">
<f:facet name="header">
        Products Summary  (Scroll Down to Load More Products)
</f:facet>
<h:panelGrid  style="width:100%" columnClasses="logo,detail">
  <p:graphicImage value="/resources/images/products/
  #{product.prodcat}/#{product.prodimage}.jpg" width="200"
  height="100" style="margin-left:300px" />
  <p:outputPanel style="margin-left:300px">
    <h:panelGrid columns="2">
    <h:outputText value="Product Name:" />
    <h:outputText value="#{product.prodname}"
    style="font-weight: bold" />

    <h:outputText value="Rating:" />
    <h:outputText value="#{product.rating}"
    style="font-weight: bold" />

    <h:outputText value="Discount:" />
    <h:outputText value="#{product.discount}"
    style="font-weight: bold" />

    <h:outputText value="Price:" />
    <h:outputText value="#{product.price}"
    style="font-weight: bold" />
      </h:panelGrid>
    </p:outputPanel>
  </h:panelGrid>
  <p:separator />
</p:dataScroller>
```

In the preceding code, the lazy-loading feature is enabled by setting `lazy=true` and `chunkSize` with an integer value to fetch the bulky data instantaneously.

To filter the bulky data of the products' information, the MegaMenu component is created with nested submenus and menu items. The shopping cart user can select a particular product category from the MegaMenu component. The following code snippet is used to display the different varieties of healthcare products in a categorized format:

```
<p:cache region="testcache" key="megaMenu">
  <p:megaMenu>
      <p:submenu label="Health Devices" icon="ui-icon-document">
    <p:column>
      <p:submenu label="Patient producte">
        <p:menuitem value="Mattress" actionListener=
        "#{HealthKartController.selectCategory('mattress')}"
        update="productsList" />
        <p:menuitem value="Wheel chairs" actionListener=
        "#{HealthKartController.selectCategory('wheelchair')}"
        update="productsList" />
        <p:menuitem value="Walking and Hearing aids" actionListener=
        "#{HealthKartController.selectCategory('walking-hearing')}"
        update="productsList" />
      </p:submenu>
              ...
            </p:column>
        </p:submenu>
        ....
    </p:megaMenu>
</p:cache>
```

In the preceding code, the MegaMenu component is surrounded with a cache component to reduce the page load time after initial page rendering.

The managed bean should be defined with the lazy data model that retrieves the data when the page loads or selects a particular product type from the MegaMenu component. The following code snippet is used to create a lazy model for the large set of healthcare products:

```
public void lazyLoad() {
    lazyModel = new LazyDataModel<Product>() {
                @Override
                public List<Product> load(int first,
                int pageSize,String sortField, SortOrder sortOrder,
                Map<String, Object> filters) {
```

```java
      String sortOrderValue = null;
      if (sortField == null) {
        sortField = "prodname";
      }
      if (sortOrder.ASCENDING.equals("A")) {
        sortOrderValue = "ASC";
      } else if (sortOrder.DESCENDING.equals("D")) {
        sortOrderValue = "DSC";
      } else {
        sortOrderValue = "ASC";
      }

      productsInfo = dao.getAllProducts(first,
      pageSize, sortField,sortOrderValue, filters);
      // rowCount
      int dataSize = productsInfo.size();
      this.setRowCount(dataSize);
      // paginate
      if (dataSize > pageSize) {
        try {
          return productsInfo.subList(first,first + pageSize);
        } catch (IndexOutOfBoundsException e) {
          return productsInfo.subList(first,first +
            (dataSize % pageSize));
        }
      } else {
        return productsInfo;
      }
    }
  };
}
```

After accessing the data access layer, the `dataScroller` component populates data of either all the products or of a specific selected product category, as shown in the following screenshot:

If there is still more data, then scrolling down the page fetches the next chunk of records from the database.

Implementing the admin screen

In the admin screen, you can find the hierarchy of the products and product sales in successive tabs of the `TabView` component. The products hierarchy is represented in the form of a horizontal tree, whereas the product sales hierarchy is represented in the tree table format. The PrimeFaces horizontal tree and TreeTable components will be used to create tree and tree table representations.

A horizontal tree is created to display the data in a linear format as follows:

```
<p:tree id="productsHierarchy" value="#{adminController.
productHierarchyRoot}" var="node"
   selectionMode="single" orientation="horizontal"
   selection="#{adminController.selectedNode}" dynamic="true">

   <p:treeNode>
     <h:outputText value="#{node}" />
   </p:treeNode>
</p:tree>
```

The backing managed bean holds the connected nodes from the root to the end nodes as follows:

```
public void  productTree() {
```

```
productHierarchyRoot = new DefaultTreeNode("HealthCare Products",
null);
TreeNode node0 = new DefaultTreeNode("Health Devices",
productHierarchyRoot);
TreeNode node1 = new DefaultTreeNode("Diabetes Care",
productHierarchyRoot);
TreeNode node2 = new DefaultTreeNode("Beauty Care",
productHierarchyRoot);
TreeNode node3 = new DefaultTreeNode("Vitamins and Supplements",
productHierarchyRoot);
TreeNode node4 = new DefaultTreeNode("Sports and Fitness",
productHierarchyRoot);

TreeNode node00 = new DefaultTreeNode("Patient Care", node0);
TreeNode node01 = new DefaultTreeNode("Monitoring Devices", node0);
       ....
}
```

In the preceding code, each node is instantiated using `DefaultTreeNode` and assigned to the `TreeNode` type. All the nodes are connected in a parent-child relationship.

Now, the horizontal tree displays the products hierarchy in a tree format as follows:

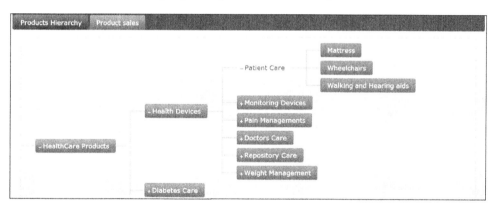

The TreeTable component is created to display the **Product sales** details in a parent-child table format. The `contextMenu` component is integrated with the TreeTable component to view the additional details of a particular product type as follows:

```
<p:contextMenu for="productSales">
   <p:menuitem value="View" update="productPanel"
    icon="ui-icon-search" oncomplete="PF('productDialog').show()" />
</p:contextMenu>
```

Creating a Healthcare Products Application

```
<p:treeTable value="#{adminController.productSalesRoot}"
  var="product" id="productSales" selectionMode="single"
  selection="#{adminController.selectedProductNode}">

 <f:facet name="header">
      Right-Click to See Options
 </f:facet>

 <p:column style="width:150px">
 <f:facet name="header">
         Product Type
     </f:facet>
 <h:outputText value="#{product.prodtype}" />
  </p:column>

  <p:column style="width:100px">
  <f:facet name="header">
         Gain/Loss Percentage
      </f:facet>
  <h:outputText value="#{product.gainloss}" />
    </p:column>
 </p:treeTable>
```

The backing managed bean holds the connected nodes from the root to the end nodes as follows:

```
public void productSales(){
   productSalesRoot = new DefaultTreeNode("root", null);

   TreeNode node0 = new DefaultTreeNode(new ProductSales
   ("Health Devices", "80k","90k","1billion","2billion","+40%"),
   productSalesRoot);
   TreeNode node1 = new DefaultTreeNode(new ProductSales
   ("Diabetes Care", "60k","80k","1.5billion","2.5billion","+30%"),
   productSalesRoot);
   TreeNode node2 = new DefaultTreeNode(new ProductSales
   ("Beauty Care", "80k","90k","2billion","3billion","+20%"),
   productSalesRoot);
   TreeNode node3 = new DefaultTreeNode(new ProductSales
   ("Vitamins and Supplements", "70k","80k","1billion",
   "3billion","+30%"), productSalesRoot);
   TreeNode node4 = new DefaultTreeNode(new ProductSales
   ("Sports and Fitness", "50k","80k","2billion","3billion","+40%"),
   productSalesRoot);
   TreeNode node00 = new DefaultTreeNode(new ProductSales
   ("Patient Care", "10k","10k","200million","400million","+30%"),
   node0);
```

```
    TreeNode node01 = new DefaultTreeNode(new ProductSales
    ("Monitoring Devices", "10k","10k","200billion",
    "400million","+50%"), node0);
    .....
}
```

Now, the `ProductSales` TreeTable displays the product category and the gain/loss details in table format as follows:

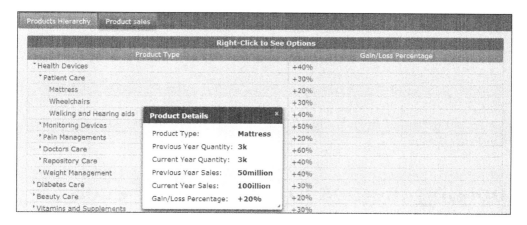

The preceding screenshot shows the additional product details such as the number of items sold in the previous and current years, the number of sales in the previous and current years displayed along with product category, and the gain/loss values using integrated `contextMenu`.

Implementing the view-expired message using idleMonitor

If there is no user activity on the application for quite some time, then the web application needs to notify the user about the inactivity. To make this process easier, PrimeFaces implemented `idleMonitor` with a default timeout setting value.

The `idleMonitor` component is implemented with a timeout value of 20 seconds to notify the shopping cart user/administrator as follows:

```
<p:idleMonitor timeout="20000"
onidle="PF('idleDialog').show()" onactive="PF('idleDialog').hide()" />
<p:dialog header="View is Expired!!!" resizable="false"
    widgetVar="idleDialog" modal="true" width="400">
  <h:outputText value="Hello user, are you there?" />
</p:dialog>
```

The healthcare application notifies the user with the view-expired message as follows:

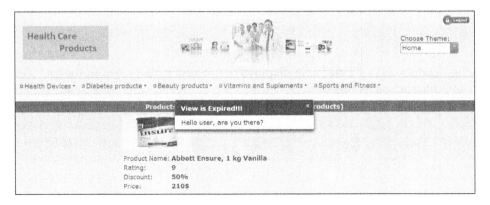

Once the user performs any activity on the web page, then the view-expired pop-up message disappears.

Applying themes in your PrimeFaces applications

PrimeFaces is well integrated with the powerful ThemeRoller CSS framework. You can use either the predefined themes from PrimeFaces or create new themes from scratch for the application design. Currently, there are more than 30 predesigned themes available in the PrimeFaces theme gallery (http://www.primefaces.org/themes.html).

Applying existing themes

Applying a theme to your PrimeFaces project is quite easy. Each theme is packaged in a JAR file. First, you have to download the JAR file from the PrimeFaces theme gallery and then add it to your classpath. After that, you need to define the primefaces.Theme context parameter in your deployment descriptor (web.xml) file with the theme name as its value.

You can download it either directly from the theme gallery or from the PrimeFaces repository.

For example, the **home** theme configured on the `primefaces.Theme` context in your deployment descriptor file is as follows:

```
<context-param>
  <param-name>primefaces.THEME</param-name>
  <param-value>home</param-value>
</context-param>
```

By default, the **aristro** theme will be applied in the PrimeFaces project.

Creating a new theme from scratch

If you would like to create your own new theme instead of using the predefined one, then there is a powerful online tool available named ThemeRoller from the jQueryUI site. The main advantage of this development tool is the speed with which you get the feedback to the changes made in the design. Any changes that are made in the theme design are instantaneously reflected in the widgets defined in the same page. The following figure represents how to create your own themes from the ThemeRoller framework:

Let's create our own theme in a step-by-step approach for the healthcare products application.

First, we have to navigate to the ThemeRoller online development screen, which is available under the jQueryUI site (http://jqueryui.com/themeroller/).

Font settings

This font section is used to set the properties of the font style for our custom theme. These font settings are applied to all widgets available in the application. Expanding the **Font Settings** section displays the three properties of the font style, such as font-family, weight, and size.

We will define the font properties for our healthcare products application as follows:

- In the font **Family** field, enter Tahoma, Geneva, sans-serif
- In the **Weight** field, select **bold**
- Increase the font size a little from 1.1em to 1.2em

After making these changes, we are able to see some sample widgets on the right-hand side of ThemeRoller as follows:

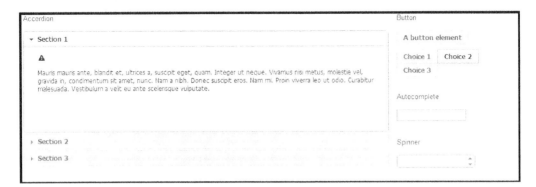

Corners

All the jQuery UI widgets have corners, and they are controlled by a single **corner radius** property setting. This property is used to define the roundness of the widget. Rounded corners are much better than straight lines. This property is based on the **CSS3 border-radius** property, and it is supported in all the major browsers except IE8 or earlier.

We will define the corner radius properties for the healthcare products application as follows:

1. Continuing our theme design, expand the **Corners** section.
2. Change the value of the **Corners** field to 10px.

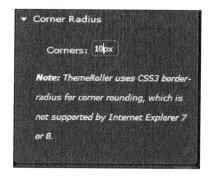

After making these changes, we are able to see some sample widgets on the right-hand side of ThemeRoller as follows:

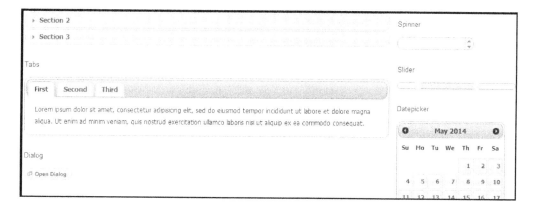

Header/Toolbar

Like any web page that has page headers, some of the jQuery widgets also have headers. These headers will stand out from the rest of the content to gain more user attention. This section contains two main categories of properties: first, the background color and texture; and secondly, the border, text, and icon.

We will define the header properties for the healthcare products application as follows:

1. Continuing our theme design, expand the **Header/Toolbar** section.
2. In the **Background color & texture** section, change the background color, texture, and opacity properties to `# e30f0f, dots_small` (the generated name that appears in the tooltip), and `65%` respectively.
3. In the border settings, change the **Border**, **Text**, and **Icon** colors to `#504646`, `#110505`, and `#130d0d` respectively.

After making these changes, we are able to see some sample widgets on the right-hand side of ThemeRoller as follows:

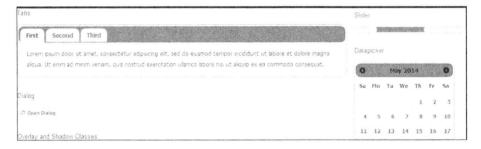

Content

The same properties of the **Header/Toolbar** section will be available in the **Content** section as well; that is, the settings of the **Header/Toolbar** section are the same as the **Content** settings. If the widget has a header, then the **Content** section is obvious and these settings are complimentary to each other.

We will define the **Content** properties for the healthcare products application as follows:

1. Continuing our theme design, expand the **Header/Toolbar** section.
2. In the **Background color & texture** section, change the background color, texture, and opacity properties to `#234378`, `fine_grain`, and `65%` respectively.
3. In the border settings, change the **Border**, **Text**, and **Icon** colors to `#151515`, `#f8f8f8`, and `#8f8787` respectively.

After making these changes, we are able to see some sample widgets on the right-hand side of ThemeRoller as follows:

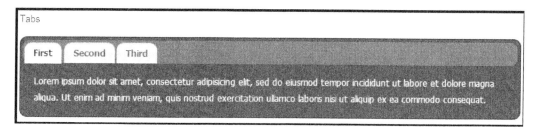

Clickable states – default, hover, and active state

The jQueryUI widgets are always in more than one state. These states play a very crucial role in the theme design. A widget in one state looks different than the widget in other states. These states will be changed based on mouse events. For example, any widget exist in the default state, when you place your mouse over the widget, it results to the hover state and then clicking on the widget changes to the active state.

We will define the state properties for the healthcare products application as follows:

1. In the **Background color & texture** section, change their respective background color, texture, and opacity properties. The default values are `#b0adad`, `inset_hard`, and `65%`. The hover values are `#fa9595`, `glass`, and `65%`. The active values are `#fcfafa`, `highlight_hard`, and `65%`.

2. In the border settings, change their respective **Border**, **Text**, and **Icon** colors. The default values are `#191616`, `#373636`, and `#636060`. The hover values are `#3c3636`, `#130e0e`, and `#2a2525`. The active values are `#151111`, `#130e0e`, and `#2b2323`.

After making these changes, we are able to see some sample widgets on the right-hand side of ThemeRoller as follows:

Cues – highlight and error

In web applications, it is important to have the ability to notify users about the events that have taken place. For example, when an order was processed successfully or when the registration field was entered incorrectly, users are notified of the events that occurred. Basically, we will categorize these events in two sections:

- **Highlight**: This is something informational that needs to be brought to the user's attention
- **Error**: This is something exceptional that should not have happened

We will define the state properties for the healthcare products application as follows:

1. Expand the **Highlight/Error** section, and change the background color, texture, and opacity as follows:
    - **Highlight**: #b8a958, inset_soft, and 50%
    - **Error**: #5ff97a, inset_hard, and 95%

2. In the border settings, change the **Border**, **Text**, and **Icon** colors as follows:
   - **Highlight**: `#4a4941`, `#151111`, and `#075ddb`
   - **Error**: `#3a2e2e`, `#bd1616`, and `#9d0808`

After making these changes, we are able to see some sample widgets on the right-hand side of ThemeRoller as follows:

Overlays and shadows

These are the special theme settings that allow us to specify how overlays that are used with the dialog widget look and how the widgets that are used with shadows look. The dialog overlays are defined with the opacity level when the model dialog is displayed, and shadows are defined when the CSS classes are specified explicitly.

We will define the state properties for the healthcare products application as follows:

- Expand both **Modal Screen for Overlays** and **Drop Shadows**, and then change the background color, texture, and opacity as follows:
    - **Overlays**: `#f55353`, `dots_small`, and `5%`
    - **Shadows**: `#fb5757`, `fine_grain`, and `5%`

- Expand both **Modal Screen for Overlays** and **Drop Shadows**, and then change the overlay and shadow opacities and shadow and thickness values as follows:
    - **Overlay Opacity**: `20%`
    - **Shadow Opacity**: `20%`
    - **Shadow**: `20px`
    - **Top offset**: `10px`
    - **Left offset**: `10px`
    - **Corners**: `10px`

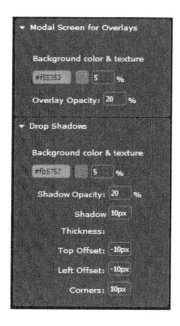

After making these changes, we are able to see some sample widgets on the right-hand side of ThemeRoller as follows:

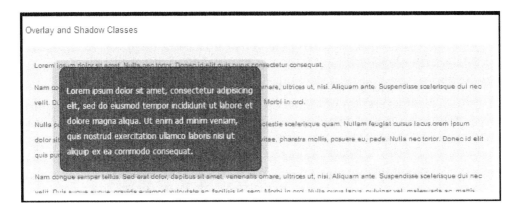

Now, we have created the custom jQueryUI theme entirely from the ThemeRoller. It will generate a long URL based on the theme settings added. You can add/edit the theme settings any time by saving the theme URL somewhere else, or you can download the theme by clicking on the download theme button.

However, we need to migrate the theme generated from ThemeRoller to the PrimeFaces infrastructure. You need to integrate the theme to the particular application by creating it as JAR and adding it to the classpath. The JAR file must have the following structure:

```
- jar
    - META-INF
        - resources
            -primefaces-yourtheme
                - theme.css
                - images
```

The downloaded theme will have an `Images` folder and a `css` file. Now, we have to do two conversions to make it available for the PrimeFaces project:

1. Extract the contents of the package and rename the `jquery-ui-{version}.custom.css` file to `theme.css`.

2. Image references in the `theme.css` file must be converted to an expression that the JSF resource loading can understand.

    For example, `url("images/ui-bg_highlight-hard_100_f9f9f9_1x100.png");` should be converted to `url("#{resource['primefaces-yourtheme:images/ui-bg_highlight-hard_100_f9f9f9_1x100.png']}");`.

Theme Converters

Currently, there are two types of theme converters available for converting ThemeRoller themes to PrimeFaces themes. They are as follows:

- PrimeFaces Theme Converter
- ThemeRoller to PrimeFaces Themes Converter

PrimeFaces Theme Converter

This is a third-party converter that converts jQuery ThemeRoller themes to PrimeFaces themes in a simpler way. First, you have to download the converter from the Softpedia tools website (http://www.softpedia.com/get/Programming/Other-Programming-Files/Primefaces-theme-converter.shtml). After that, browse the ThemeRoller zip distribution, add the theme name, and then add the additional CSS properties (if any) to convert it as a PrimeFaces theme JAR file.

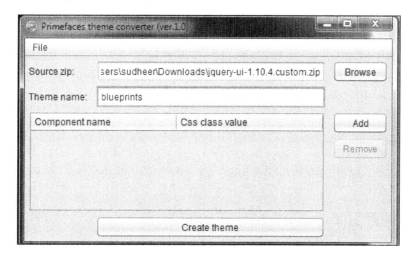

The drawbacks of using the PrimeFaces Theme Converter are as follows:

- Currently, this plugin supports older ThemeRoller versions
- We have to add the ui-inputfied and ui-selectonemenu CSS properties externally

ThemeRoller to PrimeFaces Themes Converter

Creating PrimeFaces themes using this converter is easier than ever. Once you have downloaded the ThemeRoller zip distribution, just upload the `zip` file with the theme name you want and you will get a PrimeFaces theme `jar` in return. It is created from **osnode** (`https://themeroller.osnode.com/`).

After downloading the `blueprints.jar` file, you have to configure it for the Maven local repository and then add the Maven coordinates to the `pom.xml` file. The following steps need to be performed to apply the customized user theme:

1. Install the downloaded theme `jar` file to the local Maven repository (usually, `~/.m2`) using the following command:

   ```
   mvn install:install-file -Dfile=blueprints.jar -DgroupId=com.
   packtpub -DartifactId=blueprints -Dversion=1.0-SNAPSHOT
   -Dpackaging=jar
   ```

   The theme is locally installed to `~/.m2/repository/com/packtpub/blueprints`

2. Add a dependency to the project's POM file (`pom.xml`):

   ```
   <dependency>
     <groupId>com.packtpub</groupId>
     <artifactId>blueprints</artifactId>
     <version>1.0-SNAPSHOT</version>
   </dependency>
   ```

Once you restart the application, the login screen's look and feel will have changed as follows:

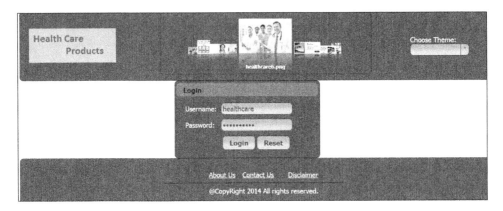

Chapter 10

After logging in to the application with the shopping cart user, the HealthKart screen's styles and skinning will have changed as follows:

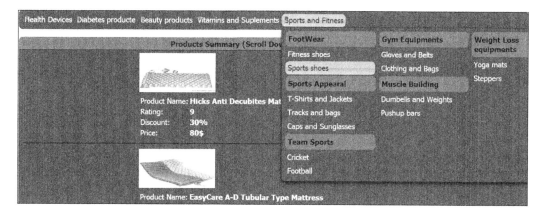

After logging in to the application using the admin role, the admin screen's theme will have changed as follows:

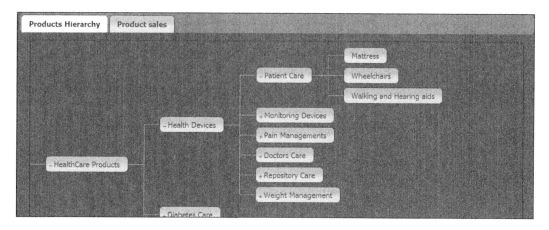

To apply the preceding custom theme design, make sure you add the **blueprints** theme dependency in your `pom.xml` file.

Changing themes on the fly using ThemeSwitcher

The PrimeFaces library introduced the ThemeSwitcher component to modify theme changes on the fly without refreshing the page. To notify the theme changes, you can use the stateful ThemeSwitcher component that uses Ajax behavior. The advanced ThemeSwitcher component enables custom content such as previewing themes during the selection of themes.

The ThemeSwitcher component is similar to the basic SelectOneMenu component, where you can select the themes dynamically. You can apply different themes on the healthcare products application using the ThemeSwitcher component that resides (as a dropdown) on the right side.

Working with the project code of the healthcare products application

If you wish to work on the sample code, all you need to do is download it from the Git repository at https://github.com/sudheerj/primefaces-blueprints, where you can use your preferred IDE. From there, you can start playing with the code. You can run it by using the mvn jetty:run command in the Maven console and then navigate your browser to http://localhost:8080/web, using the shopping cart and admin credentials to log in to the application.

Summary

In this chapter, you learned how to develop the healthcare products application. The topics covered in this chapter were: how to create HealthKart and admin screens using the data display and data hierarchy components such as DataScroller, MegaMenu, Tree, and TreeTable components; how to apply frequently-used utility components and create your own themes using the ThemeRoller CSS framework and Theme Converters; and so on.

After reading this book, you will now be equipped to create rich enterprise applications using the complete set of PrimeFaces components in a quick span of time. Based on the project requirements, you can start the project immediately by using these applications as blueprints.

The next major community release (5.1) is planned to improve the quality and provide responsive design capabilities to the core components along with fixing regular issues and developing new components.

We wish you all the best and a good time developing PrimeFaces projects!

Index

Symbols

@OnClose() annotation 247
@PushEndPoint annotation 246
@Singleton annotation 246

A

accordion component
  using 77
AccountsDAO 116
accountSummary managed bean 115
actors 89
Admin 253
administrator, employee
    registration application 31
admin screen, HealthKart application
  implementing 262-265
Advisor 88, 89
AdvisorController managed bean 112
Ajax behavior events 70
Ajaxified components
  Partial Page Rendering (PPR) 17
  Partial Processing 15, 16
  Partial submit 17
  poll component 18
  using 15
amazon.com 165
Apache Maven build tool 32
Apache MyFaces 9
application components
  implementation 202
  integration 202
  location page 202
  scheduling 199

application-level configuration,
    PrimeFaces 11-13
application persistence layer
  about 189
  errors, in hibernate DML 189
architecture, employee registration
    application 31, 32
architecture, global mutual funds
    tracking application 89, 90
architecture, HealthKart
    application 253, 254
architecture, investor information analysis
    and reporting application 124, 125
architecture, online chat application 233
architecture, online printing station
    application 209
architecture, online shopping
    application 167
architecture, Restaurant POS application
  about 60
  diagrammatic representation 61
aristro theme 267
AsyncIO 244
Atmosphere Framework
  about 243
  URL 244
autoComplete component 48
availableProducts component 179

B

blueprints theme 279
buy.com 165

C

captcha 186
Category table 168
CDI 246
central server 243
change password functionality
  using 53-55
chart component
  URL 214
  using 214
ChatController.java class 249
ChatResource.java class 249
ChatUsers.java class 249
checkout cart
  implementing, for online shopping application 180, 181
Chrome inspect element
  URL 81
Clickable states, ThemeRoller
  active 272, 273
  default 272, 273
  hover 272, 273
Client Side Validation. *See* CSV framework
CLIENT_SIDE_ VALIDATION context parameter 12
client system 243
close event 68
code generation tool
  CRUD application, generating 23
  entities, adding 23
  PrimeFaces pages, generating 23
  working with 22
Comment table 188
configuration option, fileUpload component
  auto 226
  commons 227
  native 226
configuration, PrimeFaces
  for Maven users 9, 10
  for non-Maven users 11
contentFlow component
  using 215
contextMenu component 102, 263
controllers
  MenuItemController.java 82
  UserController.java 82

corner radius property 269
Corners, ThemeRoller
  border-radius property 269
  corner radius property, defining 269
CRUD application
  about 7
  generating, in NetBeans 23
CSS
  using 84
CSS3 border-radius property 269
CSV framework
  enabling 44-53

D

dashboard component
  using 220
dashlets 220
Data Access Object (DAO) 189
database, global mutual funds tracking application
  configuring 92
database, HealthKart application
  configuring 256
Data Definition Language (DDL) 182
dataGrid component
  about 111, 179
  columns attribute 74, 75
  using 74
Data Manipulation Language (DML) 189
dataScroller component
  about 259
  binding, with LazyDataModel class 240, 241
  using 239
Datasource 32
dataTable component
  using 76
dataTable list, PrimeFaces pages
  creating, dialog component used 25
  updating, dialog component used 26
  viewing, dialog component used 26
Dealer 88, 89
DealerController managed bean 108
defaultCommand component
  using 239, 257

dialog component
    used, for creating dataTable list
        of PrimeFaces pages 25
    used, for updating dataTable list
        of PrimeFaces pages 26
    used, for viewing dataTable list
        of PrimeFaces pages 26
dialog tag 73
DIR context parameter 12
drag-and-drop component
    about 165
    implementing 178, 179
draggable component 178

E

ebay.com 165
Eclipse
    about 18, 187
    PrimeFaces code completion, performing
        with 19, 20
editor component
    using 235
employee registration application
    architecture 31, 32
    change password functionality 53-55
    creating 30
    CSV framework, enabling 44-53
    form, exploring 40-43
    implementing 32
    implementing, form components used 34
    job posts list, tracking 55, 56
    login screen, creating 35-39
    managing, through admin 56, 57
    project code, working with 57
    structure 33
    template design 34
    UML use case diagram 31
    URL, for downloading project code 57
    use cases 30
entities
    adding 23
entity diagram, Restaurant POS
        application 62
ER diagram, online printing
        station application
    Customer table 210

Location table 210
PrintJobs table 210
ER diagram, online shopping application
    Category table 168
    ORDERS table 168
    Product table 168
ER diagram, online video portal
        application 188
errors, in hibernate DML 189
events, layout component
    close 68
    resize 68
    toggle 68
exportAsImage() function 156
extender client-side function 156

F

Facelets 31, 89, 124, 253
favorite list 77
fileDownload component
    about 156
    using 229
fileUpload component
    implementing 226-228
    using 226
focus tag
    using 238
form components
    used, for application screen
        implementation 34

G

getAllInvestments() method 139
getAllTransactions() method 142
GitHub repository
    URL, for cloning sample code 206
global mutual funds tracking application
    about 88
    architecture 89, 90
    creating 88
    database, configuring 92
    login credentials 97
    login screen, implementing 93-97
    mutual funds screens 98
    sample code 119
    structure, creating 91

template design 92
UML use case diagram, sketching 89
use cases 88
gmap component, options
center 203
style 203
type 203
zoom 203
grouping components
about 70, 179
column tag 70
dataGrid component 70
panelGrid component 70-73
row tag 70
growl component
URL 216
using 216, 241
Guice 246

H

healthcare products application (HealthKart application)
about 252
admin screen, implementing 262-265
architecture 253, 254
creating, with PrimeFaces 251
database, configuring 256
HealthKart screen, implementing 259-262
login screen, implementing 256-258
sample code 280
structure, creating 254, 255
template, designing 255, 256
UML use case diagram 252, 253
use cases 252
ViewExpired message implementing, idleMonitor component used 265, 266
"Hello World" application, PrimeFaces
developing 14, 15
hibernate framework 90, 125, 253
HibernateUtil.java class 183
HibernateUtil.java file 170
home page, online video portal application
about 190, 191
code 192, 193
home theme 253, 266

HTTP streaming 243

I

idleMonitor component
used, for implementing ViewExpired message 265, 266
implementation phase
about 187
application components, scheduling 199
ER diagram 188
working, on application persistence layer 189
working, on presentation layer 190
inline edit component
using 242
input components
used, for creating login screen 35-39
inputMask component
about 219
URL 219
inputSecret component 219
Integrated Development Environment(IDE)
about 18
Eclipse 18
NetBeans 18
integration, application component
LatLng 205
MapModel 204
markers 205
Intellij 187
Investor 88, 89
investor information analysis and reporting application
about 121, 122
architecture 124, 125
database, configuring 127, 128
login credentials 131
login screen, implementing 128-131
overview 122
sample code 163
structure, creating 126, 127
summary screens 143
summary tables 131
template design, creating 127
UML use case diagram 124
use cases 123

J

JavaScript API, layout component
  show 68
  toggle 68
JavaServer Faces. *See* JSF
job posts list
  tracking 55, 56
jobseeker/applicant, employee registration application 31
jQplot options
  about 156
  URL 156
JSF 8
JSF 2.2 13
JSF library
  URL, for downloading 11
JSF runtime
  compatibility, checking 13
JSONP 243

K

key performance indicators (KPIs) 220

L

landing page, online chat application
  coding, after login 239, 240
  coding, before login 236-238
  dataScroller component, binding with LazyDataModel class 240, 241
  dataScroller component, using 239
  defaultCommand component, using 239
  focus tag, using 238
landing page, online printing station application
  chart component, using 214
  coding, with chart component 214, 215
  coding, with contentFlow component 216
  coding, with scrollPanel component 213
  coding, with TagCloud component 212
  contentFlow component, using 215
  growl component, using 216
  implementing 210
  panelGrid component, using 216
  scrollPanel component, using 213
  TagCloud component, using 211, 212

layout component
  about 66
  Ajax behavior events 70
  events 68, 69
  forms, working with 67
  implementation 67, 68
  JavaScript API 68
  possible error 68
LazyDataModel class
  dataScroller component, binding with 240, 241
leftPan component 177
Lineitem collection variable 84
Location table 188
login credentials, global mutual funds tracking application
  Advisor 98
  Dealer 97
  Investor 97
  Service center user 97
login page, online printing station application
  implementing 216, 217
login screen, employee registration application
  creating, with input components 35-39
login screen, global mutual funds tracking application
  implementing 93-97
login screen, HealthKart application
  implementing 256-258
  login credentials 258
login screen, investor information analysis and reporting application
  implementing 128-131
login screen, Restaurant POS application
  accordion component, using 77
  dataGrid component, using 74
  dataTable component, using 76
  implementing 73, 74
long-polling 243

M

mandatory dependencies
  using 10
MegaMenu component 259

menubar component
  used, for creating menu in online
      shopping application 173
menu component 165
MenuItemController.java 82
menuItems child component 102
menuItems variable 84
menu, online shopping application
  creating, menubar component used 173
  store management 173
MessageDecoder.java class 249
MessageEncoder.java class 249
Message.java class 249
MovieSchedule table 188
Movie table 188
MOVIE_TAGS table 188
mutual funds screens
  account summary information screen,
      implementing 113-118
  advisor information screen,
      implementing 110-113
  dealer information screen,
      implementing 105-110
  service center information screen,
      implementing 98-105
mvn jetty:run command 57, 119, 183, 234
mvn tomcat:run command 234
MySQL database 90, 125, 187, 233, 254
MySQL Workbench
  about 188
  URL 188

N

native Comet 243
native websockets 243
NetBeans
  about 18
  CRUD application, generating in 23
  PrimeFaces code completion,
      performing with 21
  PrimeFaces component suite 21
Next Generation Ordering System (NGOS)
  about 166
  administration 166
  storefront 166

O

online chat application
  architecture 233
  coding, PrimeFaces Push technology
      used 245-247
  deploying 234
  developing, PrimeFaces Push
      technology used 232
  developing, PrimeFaces used 232
  editor component, using 235
  ER diagram 233, 234
  executing 234
  flow diagram 232
  implementing 234
  implementing, PrimeFaces Push
      technology used 244
  landing page, coding after login 239, 240
  landing page, coding before login 236, 238
  password component, using 236
  private chat option, enabling 248, 249
  requisites 232
  requisites, implementing 233
  sample code 249
  selectOneButton component, using 235
  URL, for sample code 249
  User Profile page 242, 243
  working 247
online printing station application
  architecture 209
  ER diagram 209, 210
  functional requirements 208
  landing page, implementing 210
  login page, implementing 216, 217
  print job order, implementing 223, 224
  registration page, implementing 218, 219
  requirement analysis 208
  requirements implementing,
      PrimeFaces used 209
  sample code 230
  URL, for sample code 230
  usage 207, 208
  user dashboard page, implementing 220
online shopping application
  about 165
  architecture 167

creating menu, menubar component
    used 173
  ER diagram 168
  file structure 182, 183
  flow diagram 176
  functional requisites 166
  implementation 168
  persistence layer 169, 170
  sample code 183
  storefront 177
  URL, for sample code 183
  use case 166
online video portal application
  home page 190, 191
  login, enabling 193, 194
  overview 185
  registration, enabling 193, 194
  requisites 186, 187
  sample code 206
  system architecture 187
  user dashboard page 197, 198
OnMessage() annotation 247
optional dependencies
  using 10
Oracle Mojarra 9
ordering platform, Restaurant
    POS application
  component, updating 79
  controllers, using 82-84
  CSS, using 84
  implementing 80, 81
ORDERS table
  about 168
  orderDetails field 168
osnode
  about 278
  URL 278

P

panelGrid component
  about 70-72
  advantage 73
  using 216, 241
Partial Page Rendering (PPR) 17
Partial Processing 15, 16
Partial submit 17

password component
  using 236
PathParm annotation 247
p:clientValidator CSV component 44
persistence layer, online shopping
    application
  administration 171, 172
  back office module 171, 172
  implementing 169, 170
  presentation layer 171, 172
Plain Old Java Object (POJO) 187
p:message component 39
p:messages component 36, 39
poll component 18
populateCategory method 177
presentation layer 190
PrimeFaces
  about 7, 8, 173
  application-level configuration 11-13
  configuring, for Maven users 9, 10
  configuring, for non-Maven users 11
  features 8
  HealthKart application, creating 251
  "Hello World" application,
      developing 14, 15
  JSF runtime compatibility, checking 13
  URL 11
  used, for building Restaurant POS
      application 59, 60
  used, for developing online chat
      application 232
  used, for implementing online printing
      station application requirements 209
PrimeFaces applications
  existing themes, applying to 266, 267
  themes, applying to 266
PrimeFaces code completion
  code generation tool 22
  performing, with Eclipse 19, 20
  performing, with NetBeans 21
PrimeFaces CRUD generator 22
PrimeFaces library 29
PrimeFaces pages
  dataTable list, creating 25
  dataTable list, displaying 24
  dataTable list, updating 26
  dataTable list, viewing 26

generating 23
menu features, displaying 24
page layout, displaying 24
PrimeFaces Push technology
  used, for coding online chat
    application 245-247
  used, for developing online chat
    application 232
  used, for implementing online chat
    application 244
PrimeFaces Theme Converter
  about 277
  drawbacks 277
  URL, for downloading 277
PrimeFaces theme gallery
  URL 266
PrimeFaces toolbar component 191
print job order, online printing station
    application
  coding, with slider component used 225
  implementing 223, 224
  implementing, file download
    component used 229
  implementing, fileUpload component
    used 226
  implementing, slider component used 224
private void populateCategory() method 83
private void updateTotal() method 83
ProductController.java 182
ProductService.java class 182
Product table 168
Project Lombok
  about 187
  URL 187
  using 233
public void addLineItem()
    method 83
public void addToFavorite()
    method 83
public void findAllMenuItemsFor
    Category() method 83
public void init() method 83
public void loadFavorites() method 83
publish/subscribe 243
Push technology
  about 243, 244
  PrimeFaces Push technology, using 244

R

registration page, online printing station
    application
  coding 219
  implementing 218, 219
resetInput component 257
RESET_VALUES context parameter 12
resize event 68
Restaurant Point of Sale application
    (Restaurant POS application)
  about 59
  architecture 60
  building, PrimeFaces used 59, 60
  entity diagram 62
  implementing 62
  implementing, template tags used 63
  integrating, with ordering platform 78, 79
  login screen, implementing 73, 74
  sample code 85
  use cases 60
rowIndexVar attribute 76
RTL support 113

S

scheduler component
  code 200, 201
scrollPanel component
  URL 213
  using 213
SECRET context parameter 12
selectOneButton component
  using 235
server-sent events 243
ServiceCenterController managed bean 100
ServiceCenterDAO 100
Service center user 88, 89
Shopping cart user 253
slider component
  URL 224
  using 224
spinner component 48
Spring 246
start theme 89
StoreController.java 182

storefront, online shopping application
  about 177
  checkout cart, implementing 180, 181
  drag-and-drop component,
      implementing 178-180
  implementing 177
store management, online shopping
    application
  category page, adding 175, 176
  new products, adding 174, 175
SUBMIT context parameter 12
summary screens, investor information
    analysis and reporting application
  account summary data, analyzing with
      bar charts 153-159
  account summary data, analyzing with
      pie charts 153-159
  account summary data,
      exporting 144-149
  charts, implementing 153
  export functionality, implementing 143
  investment summary data, analyzing with
      line charts 160, 161
  investment summary data,
      exporting 149, 150
  tips and tricks, exporting 152
  transaction summary data, analyzing
      with donut charts 161-163
  transaction summary data,
      exporting 151, 152
summary tables, investor information
    analysis and reporting application
  account summary table,
      implementing 132-135
  investment summary table,
      implementing 136-139
  transaction summary table,
      implementing 140-143
sunny theme, PrimeFaces library 31
Support-Pac project 61

T

TabView component 262
TagCloud component
  using 211, 212
Tags table 188

template design, employee registration
    application 34
template tags
  grouping components 70
  layout component 66
  UI composition tag 63-65
  used, for implementing Restaurant
      POS application 63
templating 63
THEME context parameter 12
theme converters
  about 277
  PrimeFaces Theme Converter 277
  ThemeRoller to PrimeFaces Themes
      Converter 277
ThemeRoller
  Clickable states 272, 273
  Content 271
  Corners 269
  Drop Shadows 274-276
  Font settings 268
  Header/Toolbar 270
  Highlight/Error 273, 274
  Modal Screen for Overlays 274-276
  URL 268
  used, for creating themes 267, 268
ThemeRoller to PrimeFaces Themes
    Converter 277-279
themes
  applying, to PrimeFaces applications 266
  creating, ThemeRoller used 267, 268
  existing themes, applying to PrimeFaces
      applications 266
  modifying, ThemeSwitcher component
      used 280
ThemeSwitcher component
  used, for modifying themes 280
toggle event 68

U

ui:composition tag 65
ui:define tag 64
ui:include tag 66
ui:insert tag 64
UI composition tag 63-65
ui-lightness theme 125

UPLOADER context parameter 12
UserController.java 82, 182, 249
user dashboard page, online printing station
        application
    coding, with dashboard
            component 220-223
    implementing 220
    implementing, dashboard component
            used 220
user dashboard page, online video portal
        application 197, 198
user interface (UI) 8
User Profile page, online chat application
    creating 242, 243
user registration page, online video portal
        application
    code 195, 196
users, global mutual funds tracking
        application
    Advisor 88
    Dealer 88
    Investor 88
    Service center user 88
User table 188

V

validateUser() method 36, 94
ViewExpired message
    implementing, idleMonitor component
            used 265, 266

W

websockets 243
wizard component 181

X

XHTML 31, 60, 89, 124, 253

Thank you for buying
PrimeFaces Blueprints

About Packt Publishing

Packt, pronounced 'packed', published its first book "*Mastering phpMyAdmin for Effective MySQL Management*" in April 2004 and subsequently continued to specialize in publishing highly focused books on specific technologies and solutions.

Our books and publications share the experiences of your fellow IT professionals in adapting and customizing today's systems, applications, and frameworks. Our solution based books give you the knowledge and power to customize the software and technologies you're using to get the job done. Packt books are more specific and less general than the IT books you have seen in the past. Our unique business model allows us to bring you more focused information, giving you more of what you need to know, and less of what you don't.

Packt is a modern, yet unique publishing company, which focuses on producing quality, cutting-edge books for communities of developers, administrators, and newbies alike. For more information, please visit our website: www.packtpub.com.

About Packt Open Source

In 2010, Packt launched two new brands, Packt Open Source and Packt Enterprise, in order to continue its focus on specialization. This book is part of the Packt Open Source brand, home to books published on software built around Open Source licenses, and offering information to anybody from advanced developers to budding web designers. The Open Source brand also runs Packt's Open Source Royalty Scheme, by which Packt gives a royalty to each Open Source project about whose software a book is sold.

Writing for Packt

We welcome all inquiries from people who are interested in authoring. Book proposals should be sent to author@packtpub.com. If your book idea is still at an early stage and you would like to discuss it first before writing a formal book proposal, contact us; one of our commissioning editors will get in touch with you.

We're not just looking for published authors; if you have strong technical skills but no writing experience, our experienced editors can help you develop a writing career, or simply get some additional reward for your expertise.

PrimeFaces Cookbook

ISBN: 978-1-84951-928-1   Paperback: 328 pages

Over 90 practical recipes to learn PrimeFaces – the rapidly evolving, leading JSF component suite

1. The first PrimeFaces book that concentrates on practical approaches rather than the theoretical ones.

2. Readers will gain all the PrimeFaces insights required to complete their JSF projects successfully.

3. Written in a clear, comprehensible style and addresses a wide audience on modern, trend-setting Java/JEE web development.

Instant PrimeFaces Starter

ISBN: 978-1-84951-990-8   Paperback: 90 pages

Design and develop awesome web user interfaces for desktop and mobile devices with PrimeFaces and JSF2 using practical, hands-on examples

1. Learn something new in an Instant! A short, fast, focused guide delivering immediate results.

2. Integrate Google Maps in your web application to show search results with markers and overlays with the PrimeFaces gmap component.

3. Develop a customizable dashboard for your users that displays charts with live data, news feeds, and draggable widgets.

Please check **www.PacktPub.com** for information on our titles

PrimeFaces Beginner's Guide

ISBN: 978-1-78328-069-8   Paperback: 378 pages

Get your JSF-based projects up and running with this easy-to-implement guide on PrimeFaces

1. Detailed explanation on how to use basic PrimeFaces UI components such as form controls, panels, and layouts.
2. Delve into PrimeFaces advanced UI components such as dataTables, menus, charts, file uploading, and themes.
3. Easy to read and learn with its step-by-step instructions in Time for action and What just happened sections.

Learning PrimeFaces Extensions Development

ISBN: 978-1-78398-324-7   Paperback: 192 pages

Develop advanced frontend applications using PrimeFaces Extensions components and plugins

1. Learn how to utilize the enhanced Extensions' components in the existing or newly created PrimeFaces based applications.
2. Explore all the components major features with lots of example scenarios.
3. Features a systematic approach to teach a wide range of Extensions component features with the JobHub web application development.

Please check **www.PacktPub.com** for information on our titles

CPSIA information can be obtained at www.ICGtesting.com
Printed in the USA
LVOW03s0416291014

410993LV00009B/814/P

9 781783 983223